The Italian Urban System

Towards European Integration

Edited by
PIERO BONAVERO
The Catholic University of Milan, Italy

GIUSEPPE DEMATTEIS
Polytechnic and University of Turin, Italy

FABIO SFORZI
Polytechnic and University of Turin, Italy

Routledge
Taylor & Francis Group
LONDON AND NEW YORK

First published 1999 by Ashgate Publishing

Reissued 2018 by Routledge
2 Park Square, Milton Park, Abingdon, Oxon, OX14 4RN
711 Third Avenue, New York, NY 10017, USA

Routledge is an imprint of the Taylor & Francis Group, an informa business

A Library of Congress record exists under LC control number: 99072845

ISBN 13: 978-1-138-34447-1 (hbk)
ISBN 13: 978-1-138-34448-8 (pbk)
ISBN 13: 978-0-429-43849-3 (ebk)

THE ITALIAN URBAN SYSTEM

Contents

List of figures

List of tables

List of contributors

Piero Bonavero, Institute of Geography,
The Catholic University of Milan

Giuseppe Dematteis, Dipartimento Interateneo Territorio,
Polytechnic and University of Turin

Cesare Emanuel, Dipartimento Impresa e Territorio,
University of Eastern Piedmont, Novara

Francesca Governa, Dipartimento Interateneo Territorio,
Polytechnic and University of Turin

Carlo Salone, Dipartimento Interateneo Territorio,
Polytechnic and University of Turin

Fabio Sforzi, Dipartimento Interateneo Territorio,
Polytechnic and University of Turin

Preface

This book is a product of research carried out on the subject of 'the Italian urban system towards European integration' since 1996 at the Dipartimento Interateneo Territorio of Turin.

The relations between urban development, territorial cohesion and the European urban system have already been clearly identified in the document *Europe 2000*, published by the EC Commission in 1991. In later Commission documents, cities have been seen as one of the main instruments for achieving the goals of social and economic cohesion and competitiveness sanctioned by the Treaty of Maastricht and specified in the White Paper *Growth, competitiveness, employment* (1993). Although the problem of the cities is not mentioned explicitly in these two documents, it still appears evident that the goals indicated imply an integrated European urban system. Thus, the more recent document *Europe 2000+* (EC DG XVI 1995) paid special attention to the role of the urban structure in the future spatial organisation of the Union, and many of the studies promoted in it have concerned systems of cities. More recently, the European Commission has promoted studies for the *European Spatial Development Perspective* (ESDP). The latest edition of this document, approved by ministers of the member states (June 1998, Glasgow meeting), sees in the achievement of a 'multi-centred and balanced' urban system and in the networking of infrastructures instruments for accomplishing the future integrated organisation of European space.

In working out these strategies, some member countries such as France, Germany and the Netherlands have played a particularly active role over the years. Other countries, including Italy, have only recently begun to draw up a systematic vision of the city-space relationship as a strategic factor in European integration.

Among those who have worked on this, alongside Italy's Department for the Co-ordination of Community Policies at the Presidency of the Council of Ministers (Camagni 1996a), we should note the particularly incisive initiatives taken on the technical level in recent years by the Directorate for Territorial Co-ordination (Dicoter) of the Ministry of Public Works with the *Itaten* research program on the transformation of Italian settlement patterns (Clementi, Dematteis and Palermo 1996). Thanks to these new activities, in the last three years the Italian representatives have been able to play a pro-active role in Community meetings, capable of introducing original points of view into European scenarios and territorial plans, some of them in common with other countries, such as those of the Mediterranean and the Alpine area.

Although the research illustrated in this book is autonomous from these initiatives, it has always kept them in mind. Its publication aims to broaden reflection and debate on these issues. At the same time, it intends to confirm the utility of an integrated multidisciplinary approach to urban and territorial problems, as already authoritatively proposed and practised by other groups and scholars (Fuà 1991; Palermo 1992; Camagni and De Blasio 1993; Bagnasco 1994).

This study is the work of different authors, whose research and writings have been closely co-ordinated. Chapter 1 offers a general introduction to the research topic, its hypotheses and methodological approach. Chapters 2, 3 and 4 examine the Italian urban structure starting from aggregate data for the 748 local urban systems. In Chapter 2, the local urban systems are analysed from the point of view of the changes in their economic base from 1981 to 1991, with particular attention paid to the relations between manufacturing industry and business services and to firms' size. Chapter 3 analyses the demographic change in the last twenty years as an indicator of the evolution of the Italian urban system and the spatial dynamics of the individual urban systems, according to their position in demographic and urban transition. Chapter 4 examines the international openness of the Italian urban system in the European context through an analysis of the endowment of international functions. Chapter 5 is dedicated to in-depth examination (for some major cities) of the relationship between milieu endowments, local and global networks as the driving force of urban development.

The last two chapters give a synthesis of the study. Chapter 6 looks at the classifications provided in the previous chapters and, for the 148 largest local urban systems, synthesises them in terms of relation between *network interaction* (long distance) and *territorial interaction* (through physical proximity). Typologies that derive from it allow us to outline a picture of the Italian urban network that highlights some weaknesses, but also great potential, which can be exploited by urban and regional integration policies at the Italian and European levels. Chapter 7 deals with these issues, focusing on weak and strong points of the Italian urban system in the European context.

The core of the research presented in this book was proposed by the Department for the Co-ordination of Community Policies of Rome to Directorate XVI of the European Commission, which entrusted the study to the Polytechnic of Turin, providing valuable financial support. Part of the research (specifically the work illustrated in Chapter 4) was funded by Dicoter (Ministry of Public Works). The research was carried out at the Dipartimento Interateneo Territorio of the Polytechnic and University of Turin, with Giuseppe Dematteis directing. Piero Bonavero (as co-ordinator), Cesare Emanuel, Francesca Governa, Carlo Salone and Fabio Sforzi took part in the research. A valuable contribution during the collection of statistical data was given by Cristiana Rossignolo and Francesco Fiermonte. Data processing and automatic mapping were implemented at the Laboratory of Territorial and Urban Research (LARTU) by Antonio Cittadino and Paola Guerreschi, supervised by Giovanna Di Meglio, while Biagio Santaniello prepared the camera-ready copy. The translation of the Italian manuscript is by David Henderson.

Other people whose help we wish to acknowledge include Claudia Azzini and Alex Fubini of Dipartimento Interateneo Territorio, Eric Dufeil and Nicola De Michelis of DG XVI in Brussels, Clara Collarile of the Department for the Co-ordination of Community Policies in Rome, Michele Talia of the 'La Sapienza' University of Rome and Aldo Orasi of ISTAT (the Italian National Institute of Statistics).

1 Introduction. Cities as nodes of urban networks

Giuseppe Dematteis

Cities in crisis in the global society

UN statistics (UN Centre for Human Settlements 1996) say that in the European Union 79% of the population lives in settlements classified as cities. Even in countries like Italy, where the percentage is lower, the dependence on cities for employment and services is so great that, nowadays, it can be stated that all components of society and the economy, and all parts of the territory, are highly dependent on cities.

But are the cities up to this task? When this research was begun, the EU Commission, through 12 of its Directorate Generals, supported about thirty initiatives on the European scale concerning in some way the problems of the cities. Today, these programmes are even more numerous. As the Brussels experts underlined:

> The cities are the main sites and sources of economic development, technical innovation and collective services. At the same time, they offer the worst examples of congestion, pollution, industrial decline and social exclusion (CEC DG XVI 1993, p. 1).

The urban problem is not only a technical and organisational problem. As is well known, modern Europe began to be formed with the great urban recovery of the early Middle Ages. Now that a thousand years have passed, Europe finds itself having to come to terms with its cities, and thus in a certain way with its origins and with its very cultural identity.

Paraphrasing what Blaise Pascal attributed to the relationship between human beings and the universe, it could be said that the cities have this peculiarity: that they are materially included within much vaster political and territorial entities, yet are capable of incorporating and dominating them. The urban élites have always, by controlling the key places for the collection, elaboration and transmission of knowledge, regulated the dialectic between conservation and innovation, between stability and change, and have thus dictated the rules of the game to the rest of the world.

Today, these processes have become so evident and have accelerated so rapidly that our technological society of the end of the century is characterised as the information society. In terms of 'intangible' economic activity, it has been calculated that in the industrialised countries the activities concerning the pure treatment of information (covering, among other things, most office work), have prevailed since the eighties over the others, even in sectors such as manufacturing industry, traditionally thought of as a place of material work (Hepworth 1989). At the higher levels (financial and management services, research and development etc.) these activities are closely related to those of management and control. With them, they form indivisible complexes of functions known as the 'advanced tertiary' and 'quaternary' sectors, which are the new engines of urban development. In successful cities, these new sectors tend to replace manufacturing industry as the prime sources of employment and income. The corresponding new professional classes become socially central, while manufacturing workers lose visibility.

The problems of the cities become clear in this transition. Firstly, because not all cities participate in it in the same way. The rise of the information economy goes hand in hand with the globalisation of the production processes and with the growth in the trans-national mobility of capital, services, information and innovation. Up until about mid-century, many production and trade circuits were circumscribed to the regional or national scale, and were based on a fairly complex and articulated pattern of cities. Now that the same circuits operate on the continental and global scale, most of the service and management activities necessary for them to function tend to be concentrated in a few major cities.

The competition to join this select club has so far seen few winners and many losers. In particular, the cities with an important past in heavy industry (steel, petro-chemicals, shipyards etc.) or of a 'Fordist' type (production of mass consumer goods) have had problems of employment and urban and environmental renewal that have penalised them. Also disadvantaged are the cities located in peripheral positions compared to national and continental core regions, even if they are major cities such as Naples, Palermo, Marseilles, Athens and Seville.

Yet paradoxically, the urban crisis also appears in the most decidedly successful cities, i.e. the 'global' cities such as London or Paris or in the 'Eurocities' such as Brussels, Amsterdam, Milan, Lyon, Frankfurt, and others. This derives both from the excessive growth (congestion, property and infrastructure prices, pollution, difficulty of waste disposal etc.) and from social imbalances and tensions. The successful cities do in fact attract both the richest and the poorest classes. They are characterised by social and ethnic fragmentation, by the simultaneous presence of great well-being and great deprivation, by high levels of marginalisation, crime, and unmediated conflicts.

From the nuclear cities to extended cities and network-cities

Talking of successful and unsuccessful cities, we tend to think of them as unitary and autonomous collective actors, capable of adjusting their own behaviour at will just as individuals or companies normally do.

This can happen. In fact, urban government and planning set this objective. But it is a goal to be reached, not something taken for granted. In reality, what we call a city is not in itself either a clearly defined territorial unit, nor a unitary social organisation, but simply a complex node of relations: a place in which 'bundles' of social, economic, cultural and political relations converge, concentrate and interconnect through the local action of individual and collective, public and private actors (Bagnasco and Le Galès 1997). The geometry, the identity, indeed the fortunes of a city, vary with the variations in these interconnections. When internal cohesion is strong, the city's identity and borders are particularly clear. If, instead, the networks of local relations are poorly linked, it is difficult to distinguish the inside from the outside and to understand whether the city has its own behaviour or whether each component goes its own way.

Cities are, therefore, voluntary constructions which must be continually renewed. However, each of them conserves over time a unitary image, which is exactly what induces us to personify them. Over the course of history, cities, precisely because they are the nodes of relations, create successive layers on their territory not only of buildings and material infrastructure, but also a milieu, made of artistic and environmental qualities, memories, cultural traditions and institutions (Chapter 5). All of this can be thought of as a sort of collective heritage, at the disposal of each generation. It forms a substratum which, rooted in the site of the city, ensures it extraordinary temporal continuity. It is enough to remember that few European cities were founded in the modern or contemporary era: most of them existed already in the Middle Ages and many were founded in Roman times or earlier.

The presence of bequests from the past does not, however, guarantee the vitality of the city. For a city to be alive, the local actors must capture and connect supra-local flows of goods, people, capital and information; the values of the local milieu must be transformed into cultural and economic values capable of circulating in the global exchange circuits. But this external openness of the city presumes a network of relations (even ones of conflict) between the internal actors, so that they can make the most of the urban heritage accumulated in the course of history in the form of 'relational assets' capable of producing 'sociality' as an autonomous value (Bonomi 1996).

The networks of relations between the various urban actors once remained within a nuclear municipal space, often enclosed by walls, and in any case circumscribed by the town boundaries. Today, a major city is an extensive territorial entity. It is normally made up of a central municipality and by one or more rings of peripheral municipalities, where many of the elements which were previously in the core have been distributed over recent decades: production plants, infrastructure, services, offices, housing. In smaller towns, the radius of this decentralisation is much smaller; however, in the industrialised countries, even these towns have expanded because, providing employment and services to the surrounding area, they have formed a single functional entity with it.

The size of a city today corresponds to the range of its most direct influence over the surrounding territory. Among the various ways of defining these 'urban fields' - all in some way partial and arbitrary - the easiest and most common is based on commuter movements converging on one or more main centres, thus obtaining what is called the 'daily urban system'. From the functional point of view, this is today's equivalent of the old municipalities. Like the latter, the 'daily urban systems' cover the entire territory. This is the equivalent of considering the whole space as urbanised, even if with varying intensity and in differing ways: a representation that in the industrialised countries is now close to reality and will soon be exact.

For these reasons, the urban entities normally considered in this research will not be the nuclear cities (individual municipalities), but the 'extended cities' corresponding to the concept of the 'daily urban system'. In Italy there are today 784 *local urban systems* of this type (Chapter 2).

These urban systems are known as *local* ones to distinguish them from larger urban systems: regional, national, European and global. While local urban systems are compact areas, the higher level systems appear instead in the geographically discontinuous form of 'urban networks'. They are formed by sets of cities that maintain stable relations of an economic, cultural, political and institutional type and which constitute nodes in the network (Gottmann 1991, Dupuy 1991, Conti, Dematteis and Emanuel 1995). There are *regional* networks of cities, based essentially on relations of physical proximity, but there are also ones of continental or world-wide scope, where the reciprocal distance between nodes counts little. For example, in the networks of European university co-operation, the intensity of exchanges depends on the specialisation and importance of the universities and not on the size of the cities nor on the distance between them (Cabodi 1998).

The actors that establish relations within a local urban system (families, enterprises or other public and private institutions) each belong to one or more networks of supra-local networks, which also operate simultaneously in other urban systems. What happens to each urban node thus depends increasingly on interactions and decisions that occur in others. Rapid transport and telecommunications make these interdependencies more and more close-knit. As a consequence of the processes of globalisation, this happens even when the cities have no explicit strategy of internationalisation, and thus have to submit to external decisions. Cities can however also govern these spontaneous processes, creating their own voluntary networks of co-operation (Pyrgiotis 1991 and 1992, Rossignolo, 1998).

Our image of the city is backward with respect to the great changes underway. While we continue to think of the cities as individuals, they are becoming networks; when we look for local solutions to our problems, they demand a national, European and global vision. While we think of space as if it were divided once and forever into production regions or urban fields and we try to fashion political and administrative divisions onto them, the variable geometry of flows and networks modifies regional configurations continuously. To understand regional development and its imbalances, we can no longer refer to regions as entities taken for granted; we must start from the network connections that structure territorial spaces, activating and dis-activating the potential of places. In the mobile space of flows, only the cities appear as relatively stable attractors, nodes of networks and generators of spatial orders.

Geographical images of European and Italian urbanisation

In 1822, the geographer Karl Ritter wrote:

> Africa appears like a limbless torso, Asia seems ramified on three sides, but with the torso prevalent, while Europe is split in all directions, with the limbs predominant over the torso (*Erdkunde*, quoted in Rossi 1970, p. 25).

This interpenetration of land and sea is the geographical metaphor that best reveals the identity of our continent: the maritime and coastal origins of its civilisation and its constant openness to the rest of the world. The cities which were its breeding ground are also distributed 'in all directions' and, at least originally, 'with the limbs predominant over the torso', concentrated in other words along the shores of the Mediterranean, the North Sea and the Baltic and along the 'isthmus' through which the Rhine flows, uniting the southern and northern coastal branches (Levy 1997).

The figure that emerges is that of a slender body with two legs and two open arms or, more schematically, that of an X, as proposed by DATAR in a recent European scenario (De Roo 1994). Still today, more than half of the cities of European importance lie along this X, with a particular concentration in the segment that runs from the Italian peninsula to the British Isles (Figure 1.1).

This very simplified picture hides, however, greater complexity, the fruit of a lengthy and still developing history (Figure 1.2). In ancient times, European urbanisation was still arranged mainly along the northern arc of a Mediterranean ring, in which the Asian and North African components were significant.

The Roman Empire grafted onto this ring the first transcontinental branch of an urban structure that prefigured today's Rhône-Rhine corridor and the north-western British branch. The X was complete and was later reinforced by the 'urban blossoming' of the Middle Ages. This was organised on the European level as a complete network of cities (Hohenberg and Lees 1985), which joined the great Mediterranean cradles of economic and cultural development to those around the shores of the North Sea and with the Hanseatic-Baltic system. At the same time, the conflict with Islam led to the breaking of the Mediterranean ring. Its northern arc then became more and more integrated with the European system and then began to decline as the great transcontinental traffic shifted from the Mediterranean to the Atlantic.

Starting in the 16th century, the formation of the great continental states (Spain, France, Austria, Russia and then Germany) set up a centralised and hierarchical model of urbanisation in contrast with the maritime-networked medieval model. Its pivots were in the inland heart, where the great political capitals are still situated: Madrid, Paris, Vienna, Moscow and Berlin. Only Britain, and for a short period Holland, escaped this trend successfully. As has been underlined by Carl Schmitt (1974), the new order was not only territorial, but also political, military and judicial. It tended to give stability to the great territorial systems and to root cities in them. They were to become the central places of a highly articulated regional hierarchy, including up to seven distinct levels in each country. In this model, the external relations of each city depend on its position in the urban hierarchy and on its distance from the central places of an equal level.

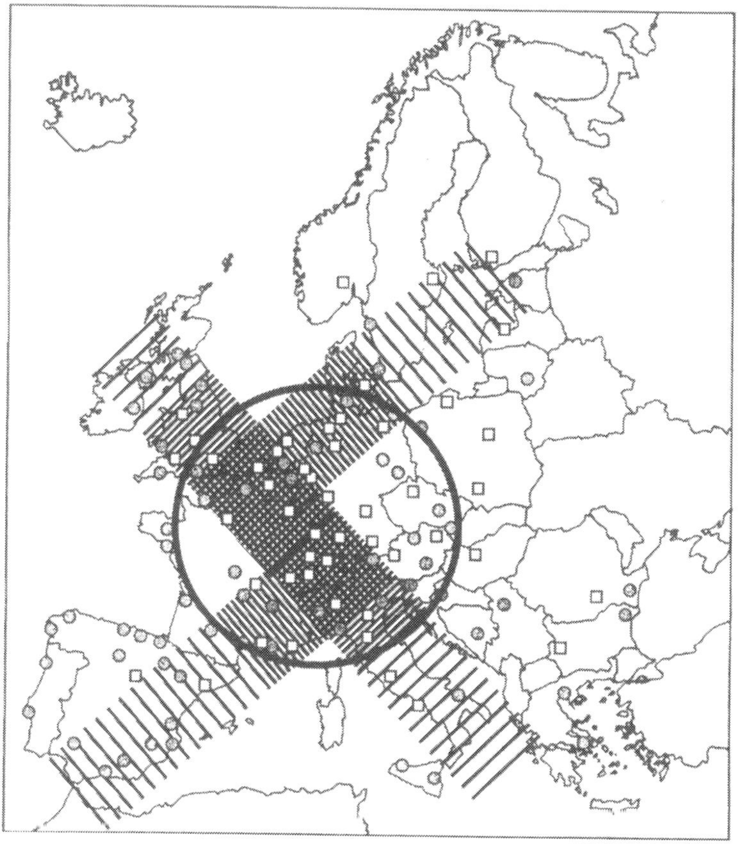

Figure 1.1 The geographical distribution of the main European cities

Small squares indicate the cities of international importance, small circles the cities of mainly national importance (according to the classifications of Cattan *et al.* 1994 and BfLR 1994). The shaded areas represent the original X shape of European urbanisation. The circle of 600 km around the centre of the 'Rhine megalopolis' indicates the area of greatest concentration today.

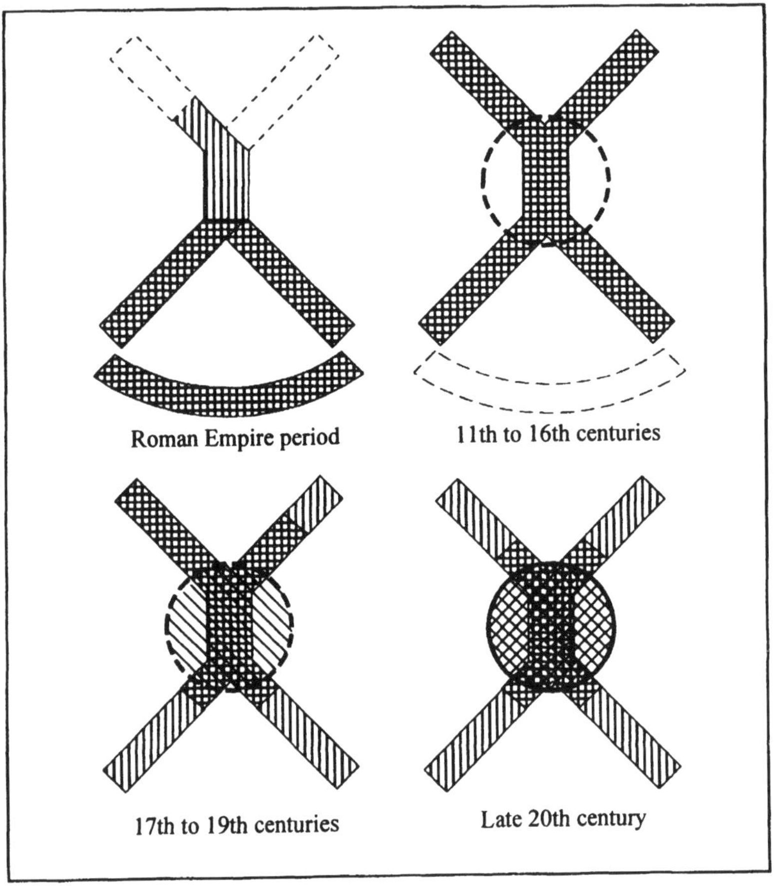

Figure 1.2 Schematic representations of European urbanisation through the centuries

The historical X configuration of European urbanisation has evolved from the original concentration around the Mediterranean Sea, to full development during the Middle Ages, and the strengthening of the continental core with respect to the extremities during the modern and contemporary eras.

Between the end of the 18th and the beginning of the 20th centuries, the industrial revolution and trade with the colonies once again strengthened, for a certain period, the systems of coastal cities corresponding to the great ports, but with a clear advantage for those on the Atlantic. But already in the 19th century, the development of industry was offering advantages to some of the continent's inland systems: those best connected to the ports by canals, navigable rivers and then railways and motorways; those close to coal and mining areas; those which, with a vast flat area, offered the space for the great agglomerations of the 'Fordist' city of the early 20th century.

The result of this evolution of the European urban system was the strengthening of the continental torso (the central part of the X) over the 'limbs'. In different ways, this trend has continued up to now. In the second half of our century, the decline of the British colonial Empire, the further weakening of the Mediterranean periphery and the geopolitical division of the Baltic have favoured the reinforcement of the central urban system. Along it has been formed what is called the *European megalopolis*. Within a radius of 600 kilometres from its centre are today concentrated more than half the cities of European significance (Figure 1.1). The original situation has thus been turned upside down: the torso has grown to the detriment of its limbs. Between the central part of the X and its extremities, a negative core-periphery gradient has occurred that was unknown in the 16th century: then, in fact, the great cities of the North, the Centre and the South, such as Seville and Bruges, Naples and Antwerp, Danzig and Frankfurt, Florence and London occupied positions of equal functional importance in the European urban network.

The great historical cities of the Mediterranean periphery have not disappeared. Many of them are still, at least from the demographic point of view, important cities, with considerable human resources and a rich cultural milieu. But this potential is blocked not only by the peripheral position, but also by poor social, institutional, urban and environmental conditions: an effect of the lack of development, which is now becoming its principal cause.

Italy feels this imbalance between the European core and periphery particularly dramatically. From Greco-Roman times to the Baroque period, its cities were centres of the conception and dissemination of European civilisation, and many of them were also important nodes in the network of Mediterranean and continental traffic. The pattern of Italian cities is thus exceptionally dense and the cultural and civil legacy sedimented in the local milieu is particularly deep and diversified.

However, from the Middle Ages on, a split was produced between the Centre-North, a protagonist on the European scale of the economic, political and institutional flowering of the 'free communes', and the Mezzogiorno, where an early urban flowering (Amalfi, Gaeta, Naples) was soon suffocated by the rise and permanence up to the modern era of feudal structures. Authoritative historians such as Giuseppe Galasso have upheld the thesis that the origins of the Mezzogiorno's problems (including recent ones) lie in what Carlo Cattaneo called the 'early strangling' of the independence of the southern cities and their resorting to an economy founded on agricultural estate income (Compagna 1967).

In the modern age, the relations of the central-northern cities became increasingly circumscribed to the rural areas around them. The new unitary state that was formed in the 19th century thus inherited a fragmented urban system, which was to form a single network only in the second half of our century. It was to be very unbalanced, because added to the centuries-old weakness of the southern part were the selective effects of modern industrialisation, polarised by the so-called 'industrial triangle' of Milan-Turin-Genoa and, in the 1950s and 1960s, the great migration from the countryside to the cities. This migration headed to the industrial cities of Northern Italy, but also fed the 'growth without development' of the major southern cities and the capital itself.

The 1950s and 1960s, a period of tumultuous growth of the Italian economy and the accelerated modernisation of society, saw a phase of great urban concentration which penalised the pattern of small and medium-sized cities. At the beginning of the 1970s, about 30% of the Italian population was concentrated in the ten major urban systems: Milan, Naples, Rome, Turin, Genoa, Florence, Palermo, Bologna, Catania and Bari. In the period of the greatest urban polarisation (1958-64), migrations towards the large cities and along the main communication axes, above all the coasts, meant that only 23% of municipalities saw demographic growth (Ministero del Bilancio e della Programmazione Economica 1969, Cafiero and Busca 1970, Dematteis 1983 and 1992, Martinotti 1993).

Between the 1970s and the 1980s, there was instead a partial reversal in the trend: like elsewhere, Italy saw processes of counter-urbanisation, sub-urbanisation and dis-urbanisation, typical of industrial Western countries in the same period. The number of municipalities with demographic growth more than doubled. Firstly in the North, then also in the Centre and South, the central cities in the major urban systems began to lose inhabitants, while the demographic growth extended in increasing external rings and forming the network patterns of the '*città diffusa*' (dispersed city) along certain lines (see Clementi, Dematteis and Palermo 1996).

In conclusion, the evolution of the Italian urban system reflects very well the processes that have characterised the whole European system: from its expansion in the Middle Ages along the continent's maritime branches, to its turning inwards to the continent in the modern age. This last phase in Italy was very problematic for three main reasons: because of the late unification of the country, its peripheral position compared to the continental heart of Europe and because of its nature as a peninsular and island country. In fact, the Italian urban system, structurally coastal, has adapted to a logic of continental organisation but without possessing the vast, flat spaces that countries like France and Germany have. It is not by chance that its most active and developed part is today the Po valley, i.e. the most continental part both for its position and for its size, allowing the development of a very well-connected network of centres.

Current trends and prospects

The last twenty years have seen such technological, organisational, institutional and geopolitical changes in Europe as to question the entire urban organisation of its territory and that of its relations with the other great continental spaces (Pumain and Saint-Julien 1996).

Firstly, possible alternatives - or at least variants - have asserted themselves over the classical model of continental centrality and urban concentration. The traditional hierarchical relations, based on the gravitation of minor cities around major ones, have been joined and in part replaced by network connections of a horizontal type (between cities of the same level, but belonging to different regional systems). This process is further forward in the central part of the European urban system, thanks to the greater density of urban nodes, especially of a higher level, and to the high degree of interconnection of the transport and communications networks. This central network is now tending to spread because of its excessive density, which provokes congestion and growing ecological, economic and social costs. One response is decentralisation towards the cities of the semi-peripheral zones. The range of this expansion, thanks to high-speed transport, now affects an area that goes from the Midlands of England and from southern Sweden to the Po valley, from north-west France to the frontier regions along the eastern borders of Germany.

Recent studies (Masser, Svidén and Wegener 1992, BfLR 1994) have shown, however, that this mere expansion of the central urban network not only fails to solve, but aggravates the problems of the more peripheral cities excluded from it. In a *closed* European system, the latter see their competitive advantages drop in favour of intermediate ones. In the Italian case, this means a relative advantage for the northern Italian system, but also a further deterioration of the human resources and the environmental and cultural assets of the cities of the South, with growing social and economic costs.

A real recovery of the peripheral cities demands either a strong cross-border aperture outside the European Union, or the return to the extended multi-centred network that characterised the medieval 'X'. The best solution would be a combination of the two.

As far as external cross-border aperture is concerned, the best prospects, even if not immediate, exist with continental and Baltic Eastern

Europe. The geopolitical situation of the Balkans, the Near and Middle East and some North African Islamic countries makes the trans-Mediterranean aperture of Europe rather complicated. To unblock this unfavourable situation, the European Union should develop effective economic integration policies towards the South of the world closest to it, in the same way that the United States and Japan have shown that this is possible (although not always in an exemplary or effective way) for the great regions bordering them to the South under their direct influence. Decisions in this direction include the economic association agreements for the Euro-Mediterranean regional co-operation programme decided at the 1995 intergovernmental conference in Barcelona, where the objective was also set of creating by 2010 a free trade and economic and technological co-operation zone with other Mediterranean countries.

For the Italian urban system and the Mezzogiorno in particular, the fall of the geopolitical barriers would mean moving from a marginal position to a bridgehead towards the urban systems of the southern and eastern Mediterranean. These include numerous cities, ten or so of which have more than a million inhabitants. The first steps in this direction are the planned strengthening of links with Greece across the Adriatic and the recently opened container terminal of Gioia Tauro.

In addition, the cross-border links should be seen as the pre-conditions for the development of some of the potential already present in the cultural and economic base of the cities of the Mezzogiorno: technology transfer and co-operation, the management of primary water and agricultural resources, tourism services, training at various levels etc.

Furthermore, for the time being, the achievement of a new model of well-distributed multi-centrality is not something that will occur spontaneously, although this is envisaged by the European Spatial Development Perspective (ESDP). It goes in the direction of certain technological innovations (telecommunications, teleworking etc.) and enterprise's trend towards 'flexible' multi-location, i.e. capable of exploiting all the possible local advantages. This must be launched, however, by policies co-ordinated at the Community, national and local levels. These policies, to be realistic, must use certain pre-conditions that already exist in the peripheral cities as a lever to attract specific inward investment and also to spark off endogenous development processes so as to enable today's disadvantaged cities to enter the competitive European arena. It is necessary, however, to strengthen the infrastructures that guarantee the access of the cities furthest from the European networks: above all 'information highways' and airports.

Hypotheses and limits of the study

This study intends to provide a basis for understanding of urban network policies at the regional, national and European levels, and thus mainly addresses the description of the ongoing transformations. It can not, however, neglect the influence still exercised by historical structures and legacies, not only as factors of inertia and as constraints, but also as reservoirs of potential for future development. The fundamental question which it tries to answer is 'Where are Italian cities going (or where could they go) *as they are*?'. In particular, we shall attempt to illustrate the specific pathways of the Italian local urban systems in the process of urban transition common to the whole of Europe, in relation to the potential and the limits intrinsic to their structures: geographical position and distribution, the legacy of the past, the position in the continent's political, economic and territorial hierarchy.

To avoid a banal description, urban transition will be considered in the theoretical and more general framework of what goes under the name of *post-Fordism*. While, in the Taylor-Fordist model, the great industrial enterprise with its vertically integrated and hierarchical structure held a dominant position in the relations between the economy, society and territory, post-Fordism is characterised by the loss of centrality of the mass production systems and by less rigid and hierarchical forms of entrepreneurial and institutional organisation, with consequences on the change in the forms of the regulation of society and space.

From a territorial perspective, the pushes towards change come today above all from the two extremes of the global and the local levels. The globalisation of the economy and of information flows accentuates network interdependence and makes capital and information very mobile and flexible, re-locatable on the planetary scale. These characteristics allow enterprises to fragment and subdivide their operations, placing them in the most favourable locations, to the point of becoming embedded there and depending in part on them (Vaccà 1993). What derives from this is a new territorial organisation with a reduced importance of areal control and of the relations of physical proximity on which the intermediate levels of government (regional and national) are based, to the advantage of the extreme levels: that of the global (or at least continental) levels and that of the local systems (Veltz 1996). This gives rise to the growing protagonism of the cities as the nodes of global networks, manifested in various forms of competition and co-operation.

One of the fundamental hypotheses of this research is that the cities, as nodes of global and continental networks, are one of the fundamental factors for concrete achievement of the economic and social cohesion of the European Union. The interdependence between the two levels, that of the supra-local networks (European, national, regional) and that of the local urban system, means that the principle of cohesion assumes two specific meanings: that of the interdependence between the nodes of the European urban network and of the internal cohesion between the local network of actors and the social components of the individual cities.

In this perspective, a good part of the problems of economic disparity, core-periphery territorial imbalances, social exclusion and environmental imbalances can be treated as problems of internal *cohesion* and *interconnection* of nodes and urban networks.

At the European level, core-periphery regional imbalances can be seen as imbalances between the higher level nodes of the urban network (Figure 1.3). In today's conditions of great capital and information mobility, the remedies cannot be reduced to the improvement in the infrastructure connectivity between the 'nodes' of the peripheral regions and the 'nodes' of the core. This is a condition necessary for network interaction, but it is not enough. Real cohesion of the European network demands first of all internal cohesion between the actors operating in each 'node'.

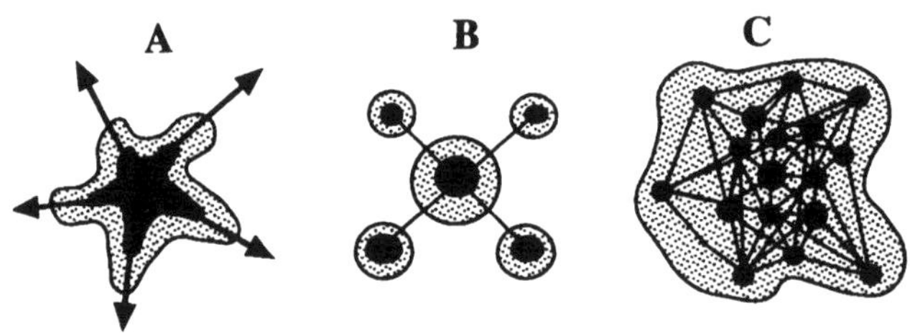

Areas of regional development driven by the extension of urban centrality
Central areas

A = extension of the central core along axes
B = hierarchical decentralisation through the development of rebalancing peripheral sub-poles
C = uniform distribution of urban centrality among the core and peripheral cities

Figure 1.3 Three different models of the expansion of urban centrality in the European context

Source: Dematteis (1996).

Our hypothesis is that this cohesion can be achieved when local actors organise themselves around city development projects that mobilise their milieu's specific resources (Chapter 5), transforming them from potential 'competitive advantages' into values (economic, social, cultural) capable of circulating in the global networks. It follows that, to move from an urban centrality that tends to be concentrated in the European core to a more distributed centrality (Figure 1.3C), it is necessary above all to promote forms of self-organised local development in the peripheral urban 'nodes' and, through them, their access to the networks of global exchanges.

This hypothesis of interactive local/global development is closely connected to that of the competitiveness of the local systems as the condition for the global competitiveness of the EU (EC Commission DG XVI 1995). This also concerns the issue of *sustainable development* which, although not being the specific subject of our research, underlies it implicitly. In particular, it is assumed that development is sustainable when two conditions are satisfied together: 1) the organisation is based on widespread social cohesion (i.e. non-exclusion of human resources); 2) the valorisation of milieu endowments (cultural and natural) is reproductive rather than destructive. The social and environmental dimensions (local level) are therefore essential components of development on a par with the economic dimension (global level). To consider only the latter would in fact mean reproducing the current urban pathologies (social marginalisation, pollution etc.). These appear inevitable, in fact, if the social and environmental problem is reduced to its passive-negative side, i.e. to curing the ills that could largely be prevented through a positive vision of the problem: that of seeing the local society and environment as potentially active resources in development processes.

One last hypothesis that lies at the base of our research concerns urban and territorial planning. In the post-Fordist transition, the true subject of planning can no longer be the territory, understood as a passive physical support, while sustainable local development (in the sense specified above) could be. In this case, the plan is no longer the drawing of the transformed city or territory, but the 'invisible map' of local identities and potential, already active or that can be activated in the processes of local development and network interconnections. Territorial policy, and urban policy especially, thus becomes a policy of nodes and networks (Gambino 1994), understood as complex and interactive aggregations of actors operating at different territorial scales. It is not merely a question of distributing given quantities of investment, employment, flows etc., but the creation of network conditions and synergies at the various territorial scales to trigger development processes capable of generating them internally. Not only should there be a shift from the logic of comparative advantages to competitive advantages, but also from the logic of zero sum games to positive sum games.

While our research fits into the theoretical framework outlined, it is far from embracing it completely. First of all, it has some intrinsic limits in its purpose: the urban problem is seen here above all as a problem of the spatial organisation of the networks or systems of cities on scales that go from the macro-regional to that of the European continent. At the local scale, our analyses are limited to two case studies aimed essentially at providing examples of the relations that are established between global networks and local milieu and to illustrate the composition of the latter in the major Italian local metropolitan systems (Chapter 5). Other major issues such as that of the internal urban structure of the cities and related socio-economic problems (including that of non-European immigration) falls outside the scope of this study.

Other limits derive from the difficulties in analysing directly the flows and interactions that link cities together, because of the scarcity of data available and comparable at the various territorial scales. Recourse has thus largely been made to stock data (local endowments). Starting from their size, qualitative composition and geographical localisation, we have attempted to extract information on the probable networks of flows and interactions that connect the local urban systems. As will be seen, the picture that emerges has a fair wealth of indications, but is far from complete and must be verified better and looked into in depth with field research or by adopting other indicators that become available.

2 Economic change

Fabio Sforzi

Introduction

This chapter analyses the economic change in the Italian urban system between 1981 and 1991. Its aim is to provide elements for the interpretation of the contribution given by the local urban systems, individually or through their geographical patterns, to the construction of the nation's urban network in the perspective of European integration.

The processes of globalisation of the economy and society have highlighted the active role played by the urban systems in achieving competitive advantages for individual nations, as the conditions that lie at the base of competitive advantage are geographically located, identified in the local urban systems and in the networks of supra-local relations that they are capable of constructing. This capability depends largely on the conditions of internal cohesion within the local urban systems that facilitate exchanges with other urban systems and with the external environment in general. These conditions are expressed through the different capacity to valorise knowledge and professional skills, and to stimulate innovative attitudes that find concrete application in the continual improvement of local human resources and the redefinition of organisational practices.

The acknowledgement that the competitive advantage of nations depends on the competitiveness of their constituent local urban systems goes with the rediscovery of the *local system* as an integrated production unit, and the analytical re-composition, through the conceptualisation of the *complete production process*, of the indissoluble bond between the production of commodities and the reproduction of the human and environmental factors that are its prerequisites and conditions of development.

This re-found awareness draws attention once again to the sustainability of growth and economic change both from the point of view of social cohesion (in other terms, the non-exclusion of human resources) and of the valorisation of the milieu endowments (cultural and natural) through which they are achieved. While an assessment of environmental sustainability lies outside the range of this analysis, an evaluation of social cohesion is *de facto* internal to the analysis, to the extent to which it may be made evident and assumed for the purposes of this study, as one of the keys to understanding of the overall state of development of the Italian urban system.

For the Italian urban system, the 1980s marked a break with the past, at least in the post-World War II period. After decades of uninterrupted growth, in fact, employment in manufacturing dropped and was overtaken by jobs in services. This was a process of structural transformation that had already begun in the 1970s, but which became more rapid in the 1980s and assumed more marked traits, and driven more by the shift towards services than by phenomena of de-industrialisation.

The ways in which change occurred reflect the characteristic features of the industrial structure of the Italian urban system, which distinguish it in particular from the other urban systems of the rest of Europe. It is well known that Italian manufacturing industry is largely dominated by small and medium-sized firms, which represent a higher share of employment than in other European urban systems (Sengenberger, Loveman and Piore 1990). This circumstance has always attracted the attention of Italian and foreign scholars. Much less attention has been paid, however, to the fact that small and medium-sized firms are organised above all around territorial agglomerations that are identified with the *industrial* local urban systems (Bagnasco 1977, Pyke, Becattini and Sengenberger 1991).

Drawing attention to this particular aspect is especially important for the explanation of the nature of the process of change, as it represents the convergence of different growth paths within the Italian urban system. On the one hand, we have the post-Fordist transition of individual urban economies dominated by major corporate structures, located typically in North-western Italy; on the other, we have the evolution of the model of light industrialisation that characterises the economy of North-eastern and Central Italy, also known as the Third Italy. Both processes of change move in the same direction, stimulating the externalisation of services and the formation of autonomous or semi-autonomous firms that are integrated locally with stages in the manufacturing process or that replace it, favouring initiatives of industrial relocation or the internationalisation of production.

The explanation of the growth in services, together with their geographical location, is important in helping to establish when the shift towards services should be interpreted as compensating for the reduction in industrial employment and when, vice versa, as an evolution of the industrial organisation towards activities with a higher information content. In addition, it is important to try to understand when manufacturing activities and the services connected to them tend to replace one another and when, vice versa, their features and connections tend to become increasingly integrated. They may reach the point of becoming functionally embedded, generating supra-local networks of interaction between the urban systems where they are concentrated, and locally, in the same urban systems, reshaping their network of connections and the internal cohesion of the local networks that structure their economic base.

The basic units of the Italian urban system

The cities as local urban systems

In the past, the researchers who have tackled the problem of economic change from a territorial perspective were hampered by the lack of adequate information to establish a definition of the basic units of the Italian urban system (the cities) that went beyond the mere administrative boundaries. Different solutions have been given to the problem, but none of these have been able to benefit from the availability of appropriate statistical data nor from tried and tested quantitative analytical methods (Hall and Hay 1980, van den Berg *et al.* 1982, Costa and Canestrelli 1983, Becchi Collidà 1984).

Between 1971 and 1981, ISTAT (the Italian National Institute of Statistics) introduced into the population Census a question on the daily journey-to-work. Initially, in 1971, the national analysis of the data on this question was conducted on a sample basis, but regions that applied were allowed to go ahead with full analysis on their own behalf. The availability of this information managed to bridge the considerable backwardness accumulated in Italy in the studies of urban regionalisation, favouring the exploration of different families of quantitative methods and the identification of urban systems responding to the different working definitions in vogue (Sforzi *et al.* 1982, Sforzi 1991).

When, in 1981, ISTAT processed the data on daily journey-to-work completely, all the conditions existed for testing a regionalisation of the entire country, and this study was effectively completed some years later (ISTAT-IRPET 1986). The results obtained revealed themselves to be satisfactory from many points of view and allowed the adoption of the geographical pattern of the urban systems for a multitude of research purposes and policy applications, as the interpretative importance of a unit of analysis that allowed researchers to go beyond administrative definitions, but also beyond a-territorial definitions such as the firm or the sector, traditionally used in the field of economics (Sforzi 1989a and 1989b, Costa, Martellato and van der Borg 1990, Goglio and Sforzi 1992, Ministero dell'Industria 1993). The premises were thus laid for overcoming definitively the analytical conceptions that interpret urban development as a mere territorial projection of economic facts.

Recently, the geographical pattern of the urban systems has been updated on the basis of the figures from the Census of 1991 (ISTAT 1997), and so we now have two patterns relating to 1981 and 1991. These are comparable, as they were both obtained through the application of the same methodology to information collected following the same criteria.

The definition of the local urban systems

The local urban systems have been defined within the logic of the daily urban systems (Hägerstrand 1970). From this theoretical framework, an urban system emerges as a time-space local concentration of population and economic activities that together form a relatively self-contained organisation of daily relations of interdependence.

For our purposes, the urban system can be defined as a territorial socio-economic entity that brings together employment, purchases, recreation and social opportunities as activities limited in time and space, accessible according to their location and the available transport technologies, given an individual residential base and the need to return there at the end of the working day.

As the dominant daily activity is labour, the urban system that satisfies the criterion of daily self-containment is considered in practice as being constituted by the system of localities where economic activities are found and where the people who work there live. In this sense, the boundaries that identify the daily urban system coincide with those of the local labour market area, and for this reason the latter aspect is often emphasised in the name it is given.

This defined, the urban systems represent the local level of the national urban system and may constitute nodes in a multitude of networks of supra-local connections.

The geographical pattern of the local urban systems

The local urban systems identified in 1981 and 1991 represent the territorial basis for the later analysis of economic change in the Italian urban system during the decade in question. The number of local urban systems in 1981 and 1991 is different: in 1981 there were 955 local urban systems, while there were 784 in 1991 (Figure 2.1). This means that there were processes of relocation of places of work and residence that reshaped the local networks of interdependence and, as a consequence, the boundaries of the local urban systems, with effects on their number.

The formation and transformation of the geographical pattern of the local urban systems, as we have defined them, and its stability over time, depends on the location processes of economic activity and of the population, in relation to job opportunities and the availability of housing. There is a constraint in the willingness of the working population, or those in search of work, to make recurrent journeys (commuting) requiring considerable time, or to make definitive moves (migration), together with their families, from their own residential base. These interdependent processes of location are influenced both by the local dynamics that occur within each urban system and by the stimuli that it receives, directly or indirectly, from the dynamics of other urban systems or from the dynamics that develop at the various scales of the urban network.

In this sense the pathways of change that distinguish each local urban system, and which differentiate it from others, are the result of original responses to internal and external stimuli, and derive from the capability of the local milieu to interpret the possibilities of evolution of its own economic base dynamically.

The localisation of industry and services

The localisation of manufacturing industry

Employment in the manufacturing industry decreased between 1981 and 1991 (-10.2%), and its contribution to national employment dropped (from 34.5% to 29.3%). However, it remained the main economic activity (Table 2.1).

The industrial urban systems, i.e. those dominated by employment in manufacturing industry, are located mainly in Northern and Central Italy, as occurred in the past (Figure 2.2). Nevertheless, the shift in industrial growth continues from the urban systems of the North-west to those of the North-east and Central Italy, above all to the urban systems situated along the Adriatic coast. A similar trend is also underway in the Mezzogiorno, i.e. the movement of industrial growth from west to east, as new industrial urban systems are established along the Adriatic coast while those on the Tyrrhenian coast show signs of de-industrialisation.

Figure 2.1 Local urban systems, 1991

Table 2.1
Employment change in industry and services in Italy between 1981 and 1991

	INDUSTRY				SERVICES			
	Agriculture	Construction	Mining	Manufacturing	Business	Consumer	Social	Traditional
Percentage change (1981-91)	-7.1	11.8	-15.6	-10.2	44.3	15.2	14.6	4.6
Percentage share (1981 - Italia = 100)	0.6	7.1	0.3	34.5	9.1	6.7	14.3	27.4
Percentage share (1991 - Italia = 100)	0.6	7.5	0.3	29.3	12.4	7.3	15.5	27.1

Source: calculated by the author from ISTAT data.

Note: agriculture includes agriculture, forestry and fishing. Business services include commission agents, road haulage contractors, accounting and legal services, R&D etc.; social services include education, compulsory social security etc.; consumer services include hotels and catering, recreational and other cultural services etc.; traditional services include retail distribution, transport and communication, public administration etc. (Esping-Andersen 1991, Sforzi 1995).

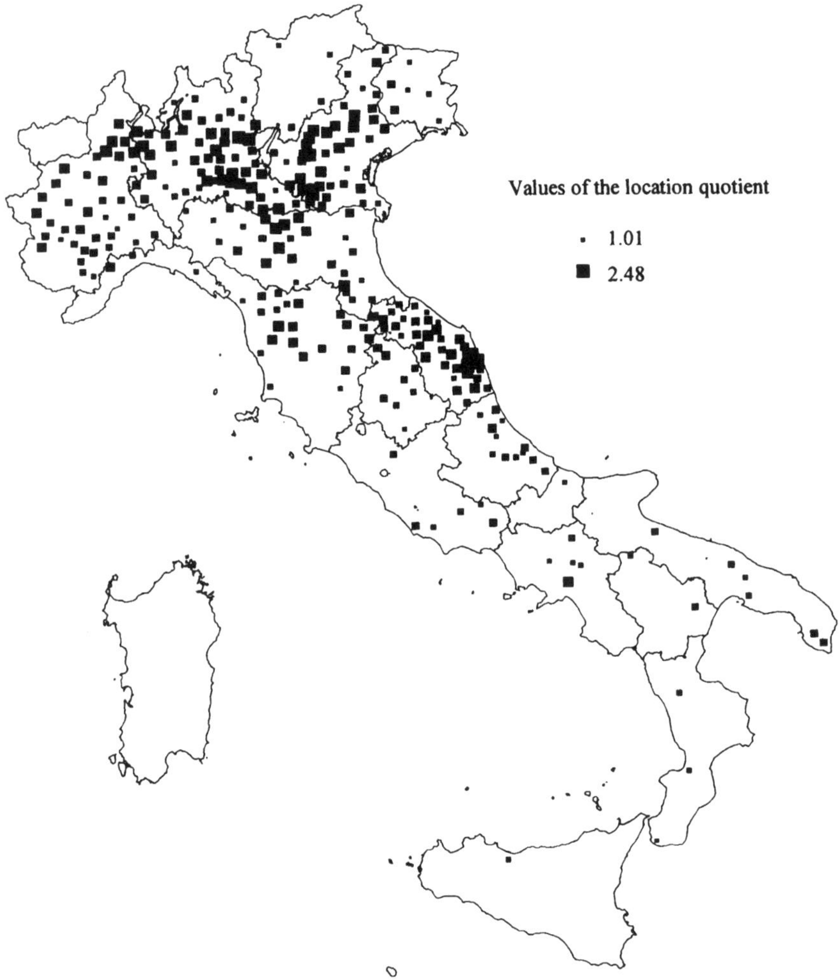

Figure 2.2 Industrial urban systems, 1991

Regional localisation indicates a greater relative presence of industrial urban systems in Piedmont, Lombardy, Veneto and Marche. These are followed by Friuli-Venezia Giulia, Emilia-Romagna, Tuscany, Umbria and Abruzzo, completing the list of 'industrial' regions (Figure 2.3 and Table 2.2). This is a geographical pattern which reshapes the traditional one of the 'Three Italies' (Bagnasco 1977). Firstly, because some regions of Northern Italy appear to be non-industrial: Valle d'Aosta and Liguria in the North-west, Trentino-Alto Adige in the North-east; then, because one region has split off from the South: Abruzzo; and finally because a differentiation in the number of industrial urban systems among the industrial regions has occurred.

Looking back, this geographical pattern of urban systems distinguishes itself from that of 1981 above all for the change that occurred among the industrial regions, quite apart from the fact that they are more numerous, as Friuli-Venezia Giulia and Abruzzo have joined this group.

At the beginning of the 1980s, the greatest relative presence of industrial urban systems was to be found in Piedmont and Lombardy, the regions of the earliest Italian industrialisation, followed at a certain distance by Veneto and Marche, then by Emilia-Romagna, Umbria and Tuscany. This was the classic distinction between the North-west on the one hand and the Centre and North-east on the other, with the well-known differentiations in the latter two due to the different weight of manufacturing compared to agriculture and tourism (Landini and Salvatori 1989).

The change that came about between 1981 and 1991 is attributed to the transformations in the models of local development that marked the urban systems of the industrial regions, linked above all to the spread of the model of light industrialisation.

In order to analyse this phenomenon in greater detail, the industrial urban systems have been characterised according to the relative degree of employment in small, small to medium-sized and large manufacturing firms. In this way, the industrial urban systems have been divided into three categories of firm, both for 1981 and 1991 (Figure 2.4).

While over the decade in Italy as a whole, as has already been said, manufacturing employment decreased by 10.2%, in the urban systems of small firms the growth rate was positive (+17.6%), much higher than in urban systems of small to medium-sized firms (+1.2%). In contrast, in the urban systems of large firms there was a negative growth rate (-29.5%), three times more than the average for the whole Italian urban system (Table 2.3).

Figure 2.3 Administrative regions and main cities

Table 2.2
Industrial urban systems by region, 1981 and 1991

Regions	1981		1991	
	Industrial urban systems as percentage of all urban systems	Location quotient	Industrial urban systems as percentage of all urban systems	Location quotient
Centre-North				
• Industrial regions				
Piedmont	77.0	2.00	76.0	2.14
Lombardy	81.2	2.11	78.6	2.21
Veneto	73.9	1.92	85.4	2.40
Friuli-Venezia Giulia	31.8	0.83	50.0	1.41
Emilia-Romagna	66.0	1.71	58.3	1.64
Marche	74.1	1.92	88.1	2.48
Tuscany	46.3	1.20	43.1	1.21
Umbria	50.0	1.30	50.0	1.41
• Non-industrial regions				
Valle d'Aosta	20.0	0.52	–	–
Liguria	26.3	0.68	18.8	0.53
Trentino-Alto Adige	9.1	0.24	14.3	0.40
South				
Lazio	23.5	0.61	22.2	0.62
Campania	10.8	0.28	7.7	0.22
Abruzzo	28.6	0.74	50.0	1.41
Molise	–		10.0	0.28
Puglia	2.2	0.06	15.4	0.43
Basilicata	–	–	8.0	0.22
Calabria	–	–	4.1	0.11
Sicily	3.7	0.09	1.2	0.03
Sardinia	4.3	0.11	–	–
Italy	38.5	1.00	35.6	1.00

Source: calculated by the author from ISTAT data.

Note: industrial regions are defined as those where the number of industrial urban systems - calculated as a percentage of the region's urban systems - is higher than the national average. In 1981, Friuli-Venezia Giulia was not one of the industrial regions, while it was in 1991. Lazio is attributed to the South according to the model of the Three Italies (Bagnasco 1977). Values higher than the national average (equal to 1.00) are highlighted to allow immediate visualisation of the phenomenon.

Figure 2.4 Industrial urban systems according to the firm's size, 1991

Table 2.3

Employment change in industry and services in the industrial urban systems by category of firm between 1981 and 1991

Urban systems	INDUSTRY				SERVICES			
	Agriculture	Construction	Mining	Manufacturing	Business	Consumer	Social	Traditional
Small firms	18.5	34.3	16.3	17.6	80.4	50.5	45.1	31.6
Medium-small firms	-6.0	16.0	-13.8	1.2	51.0	24.3	19.4	6.0
Large firms	23.4	5.2	10.4	-29.5	32.0	10.6	3.3	-5.3
Other urban systems	-17.1	7.9	-26.4	-10.6	42.4	9.2	13.2	3.9
Italy	-7.1	11.8	-15.6	-10.2	44.3	15.2	14.6	4.6

Source: calculated by the author from ISTAT data.

Note: see Table 2.1. The industrial urban systems of small firm are the ones where the share of employment concentrated in units up to 50 employees is higher than the national average; the industrial urban systems of medium-small firm are the ones where the share of employment concentrated in units from 51 up to 250 employees is higher than the national average; the industrial urban systems of large firm are the ones where the share of employment concentrated in units over 250 employees is higher than the national average. The definition of small and medium-sized firm takes into account the criteria adopted by the European Union (Ciampi 1994). The 'other urban systems' are non-industrial systems, i.e. local urban systems characterised by a share of manufacturing employment lower than the national average.

The regional location of industrial urban systems, divided into the different categories of firm, offers an effective picture of the change that occurred between 1981 and 1991 (Table 2.4). The industrial urban systems dominated by large firms are localised principally in Piedmont, Friuli-Venezia Giulia and Abruzzo. The urban systems with small-medium firms are found in Lombardy, Emilia-Romagna and Umbria. The urban systems with small firms are in Veneto, Marche and Tuscany. In greater detail, more complex situations are found in Friuli-Venezia Giulia because of the presence of urban systems with large and medium-small firms, and in Emilia-Romagna with the presence of medium-small and small firms.

If we consider small-medium and small firms together, a picture emerges of a geographical pattern that is very similar to that of the Third Italy, but that is marked by the presence of Lombardy and the absence of Trentino-Alto Adige and Friuli-Venezia Giulia. On the other hand, the urban systems with large firms remain typically localised in North-western Italy, in the industrial belt stretching from Turin to Milan.

Situations of change are also to be found in Southern Italy, as the number of the industrial urban systems localised in the various regions increases, despite the fact that, between 1981 and 1991, only Abruzzo joined the group of industrial regions. In 1991, the Mezzogiorno was still largely dominated by the large firm industrial urban systems, as new industrial urban systems of large firms are relatively more numerous than ones of small or medium-small firms. However, from the virtual absence in 1981 of industrial urban systems of small firms, with the exception of Sardinia, by 1991 their presence had become fairly widespread. In the cases of Puglia and Campania this was higher than the national average, while there was a decline in the industrial urban systems in Sardinia. In Campania in particular, the industrial urban systems of medium-small and small firms had become more numerous than those of large firms. This is an effect that stemmed from the processes of de-industrialisation set in motion in the 1980s above all by state-owned companies and which reshaped the structure of regional manufacturing. Nevertheless, the emergence of industrial urban systems of small and medium-sized firms should be interpreted also as the independent manifestation of phenomena of local development as well as the result of re-industrialisation initiatives.

The localisation of business services

Employment in business services increased at a higher speed than any other economic activity between 1981 and 1991. They grew by 44.3%, and by 1991 represented 12.4% of national employment (Table 2.1).

Table 2.4
Industrial urban systems by category of firm and region, 1981 and 1991 (location quotients)

Regions	Industrial urban systems as percentage of all urban systems (1981)	1981 Small firms	1981 Medium-small firms	1981 Large firms	1981 Small and medium-small firms	Industrial urban systems as percentage of all urban systems (1991)	1991 Small firms	1991 Medium-small firms	1991 Large firms	1991 Small and medium-small firms
Centre-North										
• Industrial regions										
Piedmont	77.0	0.48	1.07	1.46	0.81	76.0	0.27	1.04	2.07	0.64
Lombardy	81.2	0.91	1.08	1.00	1.00	78.6	1.02	1.28	0.57	1.15
Veneto	73.9	1.19	1.40	0.26	1.31	85.4	1.37	0.82	0.67	1.11
Friuli-Venezia Giulia	31.8	0.91	1.10	0.96	1.01	50.0	—	1.41	1.96	0.67
Emilia Romagna	66.0	1.10	1.17	0.68	1.14	58.3	1.10	1.21	0.56	1.15
Marche	74.1	1.92	0.83	0.25	1.31	88.1	1.66	0.76	0.32	1.23
Tuscany	46.3	1.79	0.41	0.95	1.02	43.1	1.51	0.77	0.54	1.16
Umbria	50.0	0.71	1.42	0.75	1.11	50.0	0.64	1.41	0.98	1.01
• Non-industrial regions										
Valle d'Aosta	20.0	—	—	3.38	—	—	—	—	—	—
Liguria	26.3	0.64	—	2.70	0.28	18.8	—	0.94	2.62	0.45
Trentino-Alto Adige	9.1	2.13	—	1.13	0.95	14.3	—	2.25	0.79	1.07
South										
Lazio	23.5	—	0.64	2.53	0.36	22.2	0.43	0.47	2.62	0.45
Campania	10.8	0.40	0.32	2.53	0.36	7.7	1.02	1.13	0.79	1.07
Abruzzo	28.6	—	0.96	2.11	0.53	50.0	0.64	0.94	1.64	0.78
Molise	—	—	—	—	—	10.0	—	—	3.93	—
Puglia	2.2	—	—	3.38	—	15.4	1.28	—	1.96	0.67
Basilicata	—	—	—	—	—	8.0	—	—	3.93	—
Calabria	—	—	—	—	—	4.1	0.85	0.94	1.31	0.89
Sicily	3.7	—	0.85	2.25	0.47	1.2	—	—	3.93	—
Sardinia	4.3	1.60	—	1.69	0.71	—	—	—	—	—
Italy	38.5	1.00	1.00	1.00	1.00	35.6	1.00	1.00	1.00	1.00

Source: calculated by the author from ISTAT data.

Note: see Tables 2.2 and 2.3.

Although locally widespread, the growth of employment in business services affected the Italian urban system in different ways. The main urban systems where business services were localised in 1991 were largely the same as in 1981 (Figure 2.5). In general, the changes that occurred were the outcome of a different intensity of the growth of employment in business services in the individual urban systems; in particular, it was the result of changes in the level of the services offered, which reflect the urban hierarchy and the pattern of both regional and national supra-local networks. On the other hand, the phenomenon fits into the changes in the Fordist model of production (in the urban systems of large firms) and the tertiary evolution of the model of light industrialisation (in the urban systems of medium-small and small firms).

Most of the urban systems where business services were concentrated in 1991 were located in Central-northern Italy, while there are only a few isolated ones in the South.

The regional location indicates a greater relative presence in Friuli-Venezia Giulia, Emilia-Romagna and Tuscany (of the industrial regions) and Liguria (of the non-industrial regions) (Table 2.5). This reflects the degree of polarisation that the various urban systems exercise over their respective regional space, in inverse proportion to their number. In fact, a great regional number of urban systems indicates that the supply of business services is more diffuse territorially. Vice versa, a lower number indicates that there are relatively few urban systems that supply services - even if, in all likelihood, of a higher level, and at the regional or national supra-local level. This is the interpretation suggested by the differences found between Piedmont, Lombardy, Veneto and Marche, on the one hand, and Friuli-Venezia Giulia, Emilia-Romagna and Tuscany on the other, given their individual urban systems and their level of economic functions.

Looking back, this geographical pattern of urban systems differs from that of 1981 mainly because of the changes that occurred in the industrial regions, quite apart from the changeover in the Mezzogiorno, where the relative importance of the urban systems of Lazio and Sardinia declined, while those in Abruzzo rose.

In the course of the decade, therefore, there was a widespread increase in the relatively high number of urban systems of business services in all the industrial regions; in particular, the urban systems of Tuscany stood out for their great dynamism. Among the non-industrial regions, a similar phenomenon characterised the urban systems of Liguria.

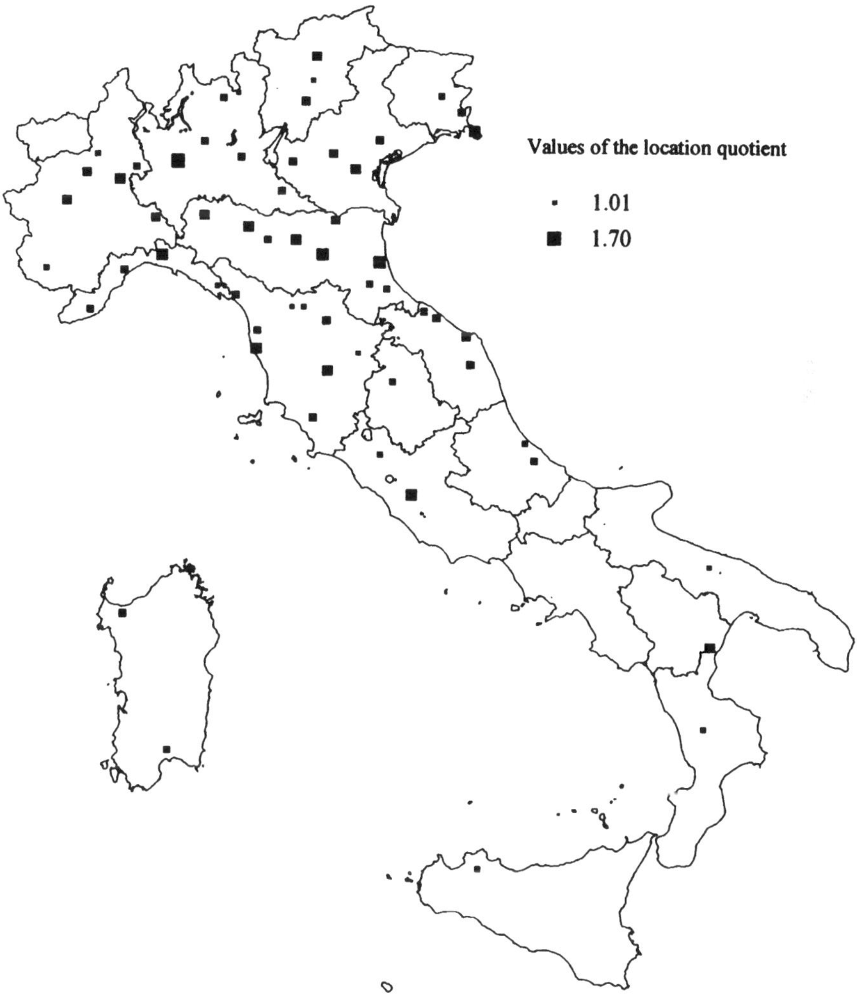

Figure 2.5 Urban systems of business services, 1991

Table 2.5
Urban systems of business services by region, 1981 and 1991

Regions	1981		1991	
	Urban systems of business services as percentage of all urban systems	Location quotient	Urban systems of business services as percentage of all urban systems	Location quotient
Centre-North				
• Industrial regions				
Piedmont	13.8	1.71	14.0	1.83
Lombardy	6.0	0.74	8.6	1.12
Veneto	7.2	0.90	8.3	1.09
Friuli-Venezia Giulia	18.2	2.26	25.0	3.27
Emilia-Romagna	20.8	2.57	18.8	2.45
Marche	14.8	1.84	9.5	1.24
Tuscany	13.0	1.61	17.6	2.31
Umbria	–	–	6.3	0.82
• Non-industrial regions				
Valle d'Aosta	–	–	–	–
Liguria	15.8	1.96	25.0	3.27
Trentino-Alto Adige	6.1	0.75	8.6	1.12
South				
Lazio	11.8	1.46	7.4	0.97
Campania	–	–	–	–
Abruzzo	3.6	0.44	8.3	1.09
Molise	–	–	–	–
Puglia	4.3	0.54	2.6	0.34
Basilicata	6.9	0.86	4.0	0.52
Calabria	–	–	1.4	0.18
Sicily	6.1	0.76	1.2	0.16
Sardinia	8.7	1.08	4.3	0.57
Italy	8.1	1.00	7.7	1.00

Source: calculated by the author from ISTAT data.

Note: see Tables 2.1 and 2.2.

Particular attention for this group of services is justified by the fact that after business services this is the set of activities that increased more than any other between 1981 and 1991. They rose by 15.2%, representing 7.3% of national employment in 1991 (Table 2.1).

Their development is connected to the valorisation of urban systems particularly endowed with environmental resources related to both the historical-artistic and natural heritage, and represents an alternative development pathway to one based on manufacturing industrialisation.

Figure 2.6 shows the urban systems of consumer services. Their regional localisation indicates a greater relative presence in Valle d'Aosta, Trentino-Alto Adige and Liguria, and then in Tuscany and Friuli-Venezia Giulia, followed by Lazio, Abruzzo, Calabria and Sardinia. This pattern reflects the territorial differentiations of Italian development and the varying dynamism of the urban systems in the 1980s (Table 2.6).

The comparison with the situation in 1981 highlights this geographical pattern's substantial stability over time, if we exclude the relative drop in the urban systems in Sicily and the increase of those in Abruzzo. However, attention should be drawn to the fact that there was an increase in the localisation of the urban systems in question that concerned above all the local situation in the Centre-North, including northern regions of the Mezzogiorno. This corresponds to an expansion of the urban systems of consumer services deriving both from the entry of new localities into the circuits of national and international tourism, also thanks to the improvement of their accessibility, and by the alternative that these activities represent in employment opportunities for the local population.

This last circumstance regards the urban systems that share an endowment of natural environmental resources together with the presence of manufacturing industry. For a long time, both have represented alternative pathways for local development that have co-existed in a state of latent conflict until a crisis in environmental compatibility arose.

The rise of new cultural models that are more aware of the reproducibility of natural resources, together with the increase in available income, has ended up by creating a conflict between the two pathways of development.

And this conflict has almost always been resolved in favour of the economic valorisation of natural resources, also favoured by the simultaneous beginning of de-industrialisation processes that have reduced the local role of industry or have caused it to disappear.

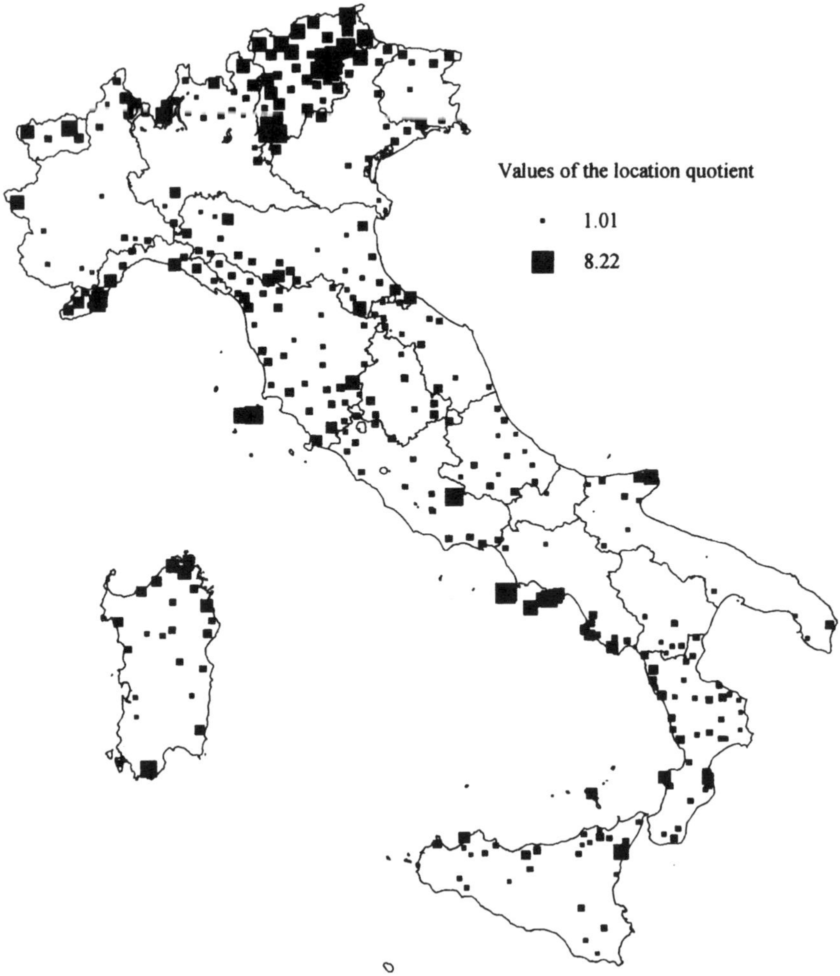

Figure 2.6 Urban systems of consumer services, 1991

Table 2.6
Urban systems of consumer services by region, 1981 and 1991

Regions	1981		1991	
	Urban systems of consumer services as percentage of all urban systems	**Location quotient**	**Urban systems of consumer services as percentage of all urban systems**	**Location quotient**
Centre-North				
• Industrial regions				
Piedmont	26.4	0.64	30.0	0.68
Lombardy	25.6	0.62	34.3	0.77
Veneto	31.9	0.77	29.2	0.66
Friuli-Venezia Giulia	59.1	1.43	66.7	1.50
Emilia-Romagna	45.3	1.09	56.3	1.27
Marche	33.3	0.81	26.2	0.59
Tuscany	53.7	1.30	70.6	1.59
Umbria	38.9	0.94	43.8	0.99
• Non-industrial regions				
Valle d'Aosta	100.0	2.42	100.0	2.25
Liguria	78.9	1.91	87.5	1.97
Trentino-Alto Adige	100.0	2.42	88.6	2.00
South				
Lazio	55.9	1.35	66.7	1.50
Campania	39.2	0.95	29.2	0.66
Abruzzo	35.7	0.86	54.2	1.22
Molise	20.0	0.48	10.0	0.23
Puglia	26.1	0.63	30.8	0.69
Basilicata	10.3	0.25	24.0	0.54
Calabria	52.0	1.26	50.0	1.13
Sicily	41.5	1.00	34.1	0.77
Sardinia	60.9	1.47	50.0	1.13
Italy	41.4	1.00	44.4	1.00

Source: calculated by the author from ISTAT data.

Note: see Tables 2.1 and 2.2.

Consequently, the activities represented by consumer services, above all the share aimed at non-local clients, have turned out to be a valid alternative for local development and maintenance of the population's living conditions.

The changeover in the 1980s

The complementarity between industrial and business services urban systems

The geographical patterns of the urban systems where manufacturing industry, business services and consumer services are localised outline complementarities and contrasts in the models of local development and bring out processes of transition.

The industrial and business services urban systems show, in 1991, close correspondence shared by almost all the industrial regions, the only exception being Umbria. From this point of view, a general process of convergence in the various regional models is found compared to the diversified situation present in 1981 (Table 2.7).

The regional diffusion of urban systems of services is the expression of the transition from a Fordist model of industrialisation - which internalises both production phases and services - to a model of flexible production that favours the externalisation and the proliferation in the local socio-economic environment of autonomous or semi-autonomous firms specialised in supplying services.

Traditionally, the local integration between manufacturing and services has represented the essential feature of the model of light industrialisation typical of the industrial urban systems of some regions of the Third Italy (most importantly, Tuscany and Emilia-Romagna). This has now spread to both North-western (Lombardy) and North-eastern Italy (Veneto), even though there are significant differences between the individual regions in the relative presence of urban systems of services. This is due to the fact that the diffusion of the urban systems considered here is also linked to the evolution in the model of light industrialisation that occurred in the 1980s.

More in general, these differences depend on the fact that the post-Fordist transition occurs in regional contexts already endowed with business services structures, as they have urban systems that have nurtured these activities in their economic base.

This is a phenomenon that should be considered in reference to the model of Fordist industrialisation that characterised North-western Italy.

Table 2.7
Industrial urban systems, urban systems of business and consumer services by region, 1981 and 1991 (location quotients)

Regions	1981			1991		
	Industrial	Business services	Consumer services	Industrial	Business services	Consumer services
Centre-North						
• Industrial regions						
Piedmont	2.00	1.71	0.64	2.14	1.83	0.68
Lombardy	2.11	0.74	0.62	2.21	1.12	0.77
Veneto	1.92	0.90	0.77	2.40	1.09	0.66
Friuli-Venezia Giulia	0.83	2.26	1.43	1.41	3.27	1.50
Emilia-Romagna	1.71	2.57	1.09	1.64	2.45	1.27
Marche	1.92	1.84	0.81	2.48	1.24	0.59
Tuscany	1.20	1.61	1.30	1.21	2.31	1.59
Umbria	1.30	—	0.94	1.41	0.82	0.99
• Non-industrial regions						
Valle d'Aosta	0.52	—	2.42	—	—	2.25
Liguria	0.68	1.96	1.91	0.53	3.27	1.97
Trentino-Alto Adige	0.24	0.75	2.42	0.40	1.12	2.00
South						
Lazio	0.61	1.46	1.35	0.62	0.97	1.50
Campania	0.28	—	0.95	0.22	—	0.66
Abruzzo	0.74	0.44	0.86	1.41	1.09	1.22
Molise		—	0.48	0.28	—	0.23
Puglia	0.06	0.54	0.63	0.43	0.34	0.69
Basilicata	—	0.86	0.25	0.22	0.52	0.54
Calabria	—	—	1.26	0.11	0.18	1.13
Sicily	0.09	0.76	1.00	0,03	0.16	0.77
Sardinia	0.11	1.08	1.47	—	0.57	1.13
Italy	1.00	1.00	1.00	1.00	1.00	1.00

Source: calculated by the author from ISTAT data.

Note: see Tables 2.1 and 2.2.

The services that developed in this part of the country (and in the other industrial urban systems of large firms, including the traditional port-towns like Genoa, La Spezia, Leghorn etc.) did not respond to the logic of the local integration of services that were not self-produced by manufacturing firms, in contrast with what happened in most of the urban systems in the regions of the Third Italy. They were more oriented towards supra-local than local markets, and also aimed at the firms from industrial urban systems in other regions, including those where the model of light industrialisation prospered, coming into competition with the urban systems that acted as service suppliers at the regional scale.

In the end, the pre-existing conditions of industrial development (the Fordist model of production and the light industrialisation model) and the time gap in the shift towards services manifested by manufacturing firms, as belonging to different models of industrialisation, represent the original and current causes of the characteristic features that in 1991 distinguished the different integration between industrial and services urban systems in the industrial regions. The alternation in their diffusion that was found also has the same origin, as the domination of the former corresponds to a relatively lower presence of the latter and vice versa. This confirms that they are different development pathways, however much they converge towards a similar model of 'flexible' industrialisation, at least to a large degree; however, specific local features are maintained, as is highlighted by the analysis of the industrial urban systems according to the different size categories of firm.

The local embeddedness of manufacturing industry and business services

The complementarity between industrial urban systems and urban systems of services suggests a need for further analysis of the local embeddedness of the two economic activities so as to be able to assess to what extent the phenomenon is widespread in the Italian urban system and where it is located.

The identification of the urban systems where manufacturing industry and business services are localised was conducted through the analysis of the harmonic mean of their respective location quotients, both for 1981 and 1991. The pattern of the industrial-tertiary urban systems thus obtained is given in Figure 2.7.

The regional localisation of the industrial-tertiary urban systems, separated according to the different firm categories, indicates in 1981 a greater relative presence in Emilia-Romagna and Tuscany, in line with the model of light industrialisation that characterises their regional development (Table 2.8).

The essential nature of the embeddedness of manufacturing industry and business services is confirmed in the Emilian and Tuscan models (Becattini 1986, Brusco 1989, Sforzi 1994).

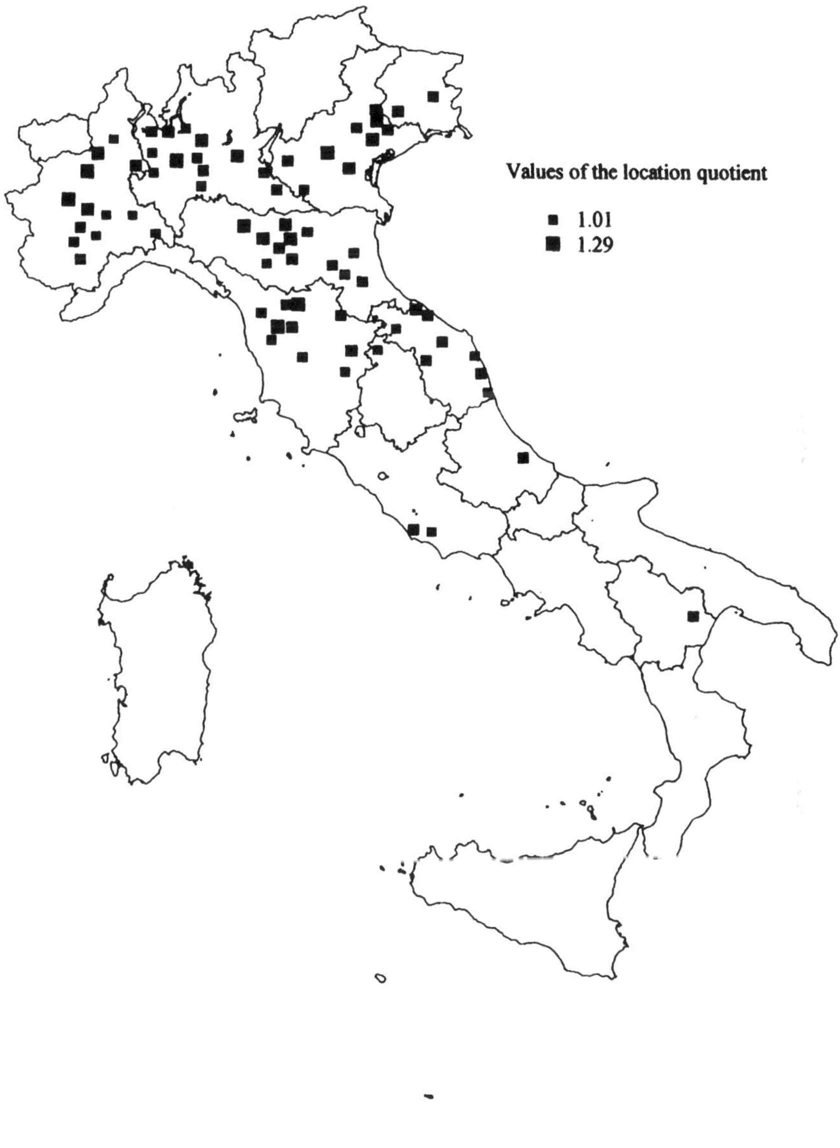

Figure 2.7 Industrial-tertiary urban systems, 1991

Table 2.8
Industrial-tertiary urban systems by category of firm and region, 1981 and 1991 (location quotients)

Regions	Industrial-tertiary urban systems as percentage of all urban systems	1981				Industrial-tertiary urban systems as percentage of all urban systems	1991			
		Small firms	Medium-small firms	Large firms	Small and medium-small firms		Small firms	Medium-small firms	Large firms	Small and medium-small firms
Centre-North										
• Industrial regions										
Piedmont	17.9	0.52	0.81	1.83	0.69	34.2	—	0.41	3.21	0.21
Lombardy	15.8	0.42	1.30	1.22	0.92	23.6	0.43	1.85	0.58	1.15
Veneto	17.6	0.70	1.36	0.81	1.07	22.0	1.54	0.89	0.42	1.21
Friuli-Venezia Giulia	14.3	—	—	3.67	—	33.3	—	2.67	—	1.36
Emilia-Romagna	42.9	1.05	1.30	0.49	1.19	42.9	1.15	1.56	—	1.36
Marche	12.5	1.89	0.98	—	1.38	21.6	1.38	1.00	0.47	1.19
Tuscany	32.0	2.75	—	0.46	1.20	45.5	2.49	—	0.38	1.22
Umbria	—	—	—	—	—	12.5	—	2.67	—	1.36
• Non-industrial regions										
Valle d'Aosta	—	—	—	—	—	—	—	—	—	—
Liguria	20.0	—	—	3.67	—	—	—	—	—	—
Trentino-Alto Adige	—	—	—	—	—	—	—	—	—	—
South										
Lazio	—	—	—	—	—	33.3	—	—	3.79	—
Campania	—	—	—	—	—	—	—	—	—	—
Abruzzo	—	—	—	—	—	8.3	2.77	—	—	1.36
Molise	—	—	—	—	—	—	—	—	—	—
Puglia	—	—	—	—	—	—	—	—	—	—
Basilicata	—	—	—	—	—	50.0	—	—	3.79	—
Calabria	—	—	—	—	—	—	—	—	—	—
Sicily	—	—	—	—	—	—	—	—	—	—
Sardinia	—	—	—	—	—	—	—	—	—	—
Italy	18.1	1.00	1.00	1.00	1.00	25.8	1.00	1.00	1.00	1.00

Source: calculated by the author from ISTAT data.

Note: see Tables 2.1, 2.2 and 2.3.

The differences found compared to the other regions marked by the light industrialisation model (Veneto, Marche and Umbria) are representative of the different development pathways followed by the industrial urban systems and by the time lapse after which industrialisation began there.

The change in the 1980s highlights the transition and evolution in the models of industrialisation, and the convergence between industrial urban systems characterised by different categories of firm (Table 2.8). The urban systems localised in Tuscany and Emilia-Romagna (with their respective firm sizes: the first, small firm, and mainly medium-small in the second) are joined by the urban systems situated in Friuli-Venezia Giulia and in Piedmont. The latter are of large firms, and the key to interpretation that they suggest is that of the post-Fordist transition: of industry, through the externalisation of service activities; of the local economic base, through the gradual substitution of services to industry. Although no direct information is available, the hypothesis that these are services above all for a non-local market is in line with the nature of the change and with the interpretations of the phenomenon put forward in the previous sections. The urban systems (of medium-small firms) localised in Friuli-Venezia Giulia should be considered in relation to the regional industrial structure, which in 1991 was dominated by industrial urban systems of large firms (Table 2.4). This means that the embeddedness of industry and services is achieved in the framework of the evolution of the model of light industrialisation, but does not refer, at least not obviously, to processes that can be traced to post-Fordist transition.

The urban systems localised in the other industrial regions also show evident signs of change, as the number of industrial-tertiary systems increased between 1981 and 1991, but at a lower speed than the national average. Despite this, it can be said that there are widespread processes of local integration between industry and services in the urban systems of small and medium-sized firms, i.e. the dominant ones in the model of light industrialisation, while similar phenomena are not found in urban systems of large firms (Table 2.8).

In conclusion, the processes of embeddedness of industry and services that occurred during the decade have underlined the post-Fordist dynamism of the industrial urban systems of large firms localised in North-western Italy (Piedmont) and the evolutive dynamism of the industrial urban systems of small and medium-sized firms in North-eastern (Friuli-Venezia Giulia) and Central Italy (Emilia-Romagna and Tuscany).

The contrast between industrial and consumer services urban systems

The urban systems where manufacturing industry and consumer services are localised show overlapping locations. The latter dominate the regions defined here as non-industrial (Valle d'Aosta, Liguria and Trentino-Alto Adige), and are widespread in the Mezzogiorno, although not to the same degree or as intensely as expected if one considers their lower level of industrialisation compared to the rest of the country (Table 2.7). This is an evident sign of the negative influence that the continuing general state of socio-economic depression in the South together with the criminal economy exercise on the processes of local valorisation. The only phenomenon of positive transition found there concerns the urban systems of Abruzzo. During the decade, these increased in consumer services, but at the same time, as said earlier, above all in manufacturing industry (as well as in business services). It is clear that these are pervasive processes of local development that have involved all of the region's urban systems and all of the economic activities, integrating through embeddedness (industry and business services) and complementarity (industry and tourism). It is not a trivial question to wonder to what extent the urban systems of Abruzzo were changed in comparison with the decline of the socio-economic environment of the South and to what extent they were influenced by the socio-economic context of the industrial development of the Third Italy and the development of tourism along the Adriatic. These are environmental conditions that have stimulated autonomous initiatives of local development, but have together attracted both public and private inward investment, and have enabled EU grants to be put to good use. A judgement of the local embeddedness of these development processes and their duration in time is, naturally, premature.

Other urban systems where consumer services are concentrated are found in industrial regional contexts (Friuli-Venezia Giulia, Emilia-Romagna and Tuscany). They are complementary to the industrial urban systems and in some cases existed before the development of the latter (Friuli-Venezia Giulia) or are predominant (Tuscany). In general, between 1981 and 1991, a trend towards growth identifies a dualism in the models of local development in these regions between activities oriented towards the production of commodities (the manufacturing industries) and leisure activities (consumer services).

A summary interpretation

The 1980s transformed the economic base of the Italian urban system. The expansion of services, and especially business services, characterised the changeover more than the downsizing of manufacturing industry, even if the two phenomena should be considered together.

The shift towards services is the joint result of a dual process of change: the post-Fordist transition of the urban systems of large firms and the tertiary evolution of the model of light industrialisation in the urban systems of small and medium-sized firms.

As far as the urban systems of large firms are concerned, the externalisation of service activities initially run inside the company, according to criteria of vertical integration with manufacturing production, or the replacement of the production of goods by activities oriented towards the supply of services, and the consequent relocation of services outside the local urban system, has been added to the 'normal' development of services that had existed in their economic base up until then and contributed to raising still further the level of the functions that they exercise. Over time, a socio-cultural and economic environment has been created and consolidated that is favourable to the formation of new activities in the field of services, which have gradually joined other activities of the same nature that flow in from the outside.

Although the phenomenon does not occur in the same way in all the urban systems of large firms, the economic change in the urban systems of North-western Italy does, however, reflect this dynamic, found both in the fall in manufacturing employment and the corresponding rise in business services (the post-Fordist transition of industry) and in the increase in employment in the latter as a consequence of the progressive diversification and specialisation in the local labour supply (post-Fordist transition of society). This is a sort of 'dual socio-economic circuit' which was previously distinct but now converges following the crisis of the Fordist model of production. This whole set of causes explains the high position occupied by the urban systems of large firms where business services were localised in 1981 and continued to be so in 1991.

The shift towards services experienced by the industrial urban systems of small and medium-sized firms is different from those of the post-Fordist transition, although there are some common causes, which can be identified in the growing search for economic competitiveness on the international markets. This assigns a strategic role to services in the stages both before and after the process of manufacturing production and helps to reinforce them.

The model of light industrialisation represents a production formula without vertical integration that does not limit itself to favouring the proliferation of manufacturing firms specialised in the various phases of the production process, but also extends to business services. The rapid growth of employment in these services that occurred between 1981 and 1991 represents a tendency for an increase in the relative importance of these functions in the production process. However, it occurred in an uneven manner in the industrial urban systems that share the same model of light industrialisation, highlighting different regional development paths and transition processes that were expressed in the form of an acceleration in the growth of business services.

Thus, in a framework of general growth, situations exist where the manufacturing component continues to prevail over business services, and situations where the opposite occurs; i.e. there continue to be more urban systems where one of the two activities is localised than those where, instead, both are found. This distinction corresponds to the geographical pattern of the urban systems where manufacturing growth shifted in the 1980s (North-eastern Italy and the Adriatic coast), and to the pattern of the urban systems where, instead, the model of light industrialisation has been embedded locally for longer (Emilia-Romagna and Tuscany).

In the urban systems of these last two regions, processes of diffusion of consumer services also occurred. These derive in part from the post-Fordist transition of local society following phenomena of de-industrialisation in the industrial urban systems of the tourist-industrial areas (Sforzi 1994). In part, and the cases here are more numerous, they represent the positive outcome of growth paths alternative to manufacturing industry, whether of large or small firms, derived from the enhancement of local socio-economic conditions. And the latter reason is the primary origin of the spread of urban systems of consumer services recorded in Southern Italy.

The shift towards services is a phenomenon that has a strong influence over the structuring of local and supra-local networks, and should be assessed as such.

Services, by their very nature, contribute to the construction of local networks by strengthening the external economies of agglomeration, but at the same time help the formation of supra-local networks, whether of regional, national or international scale. When the local concentration of services reaches high levels, for example over the national average, one can reasonably state that these are activities that are produced locally, but which are also, and sometimes above all, aimed at individual or company clients situated outside the urban system. This occurs to the extent that the services contain a high information content and can be used from a distance, through codified knowledge shared by the users. In other terms, they must be used locally, when the services require direct personal contact or are aimed at consumers, which presupposes the movement of users to the places of supply. The flows that develop along the networks are more numerous and more frequent the more that the individual urban systems where services are localised are accessible, both in virtual and physical terms, but also in relation to their belonging effectively to supra-local networks, i.e. to their possibility and capability of being part of them. In these conditions, in both cases, supra-local networks of urban systems can form and develop to varying degrees of intensity and stability, and be of a material or immaterial nature, to structure the Italian urban system internally and in relation to the European (and global) urban network.

3 The demographic transition

Cesare Emanuel

Introduction

This chapter describes how the recent demographic changes interact with the physical environment and the consolidated organisation of the Italian urban system, giving rise to new territorial patterns of the human settlements.

The analysis is carried out on three levels. First of all, the consolidated urban system will be examined in relation to the morphological and the environmental framework. We shall then go on to examine, at the *municipality scale*, the demographic changes between the 1970s and the 1990s. After this, the same changes will be examined for the *local urban systems* (see Chapter 2), focusing on the core-ring dynamics. This last analysis will allow the identification of the trajectories of demographic transition and the definition of a classification of the urban systems according to their stages of development. Finally, the geographical localisation of these typologies, related to those of the settlement patterns, will highlight the elements of permanence and novelty in the contemporary urban phenomenon in Italy.

Structure and organisation of the Italian urban system

By the expression 'urban system', we mean those sets of physical infrastructures and environmental conditions generated by historical processes of urbanisation that define the structure and material organisation of cities and settlements. In Italy, where urban development is a phenomenon rooted in the fabric of medieval towns, these structures have been quite widespread throughout the nation for a long time.

One first rough indication of their diffusion can be given by the presence of 8,100 municipalities and the network of more than 300,000 km of roads that link them. Over time, this fabric of settlements and connecting networks, although functioning as a whole as the frame for new urban and infrastructure construction, has gradually seen its functional and demographic hierarchies reshaped in relation to the different trends in local and regional development and the consequent flows of trade.

The nation-wide distribution of the population enables the identification of some major settlement patterns. The areas that correspond to the decidedly Alpine areas, the foothills, the coasts and the plains appear quite distinct. On the one hand, this general pattern is the expression of the relations that link the development of towns to the local characteristics of the places; on the other hand, it is the outcome of a geographically selective process of demographic and economic development that has occurred mainly in the last hundred years (and most intensely between the 1950s and the 1970s), related to industrial growth and provision of local infrastructure (Carozzi and Mioni, 1970, Insolera 1973, Mercandino and Mercandino 1976).

In particular, the progressive de-structuring of old rural systems, the loosening of ecological constraints which tied some manufacturing activities to specific mountain areas and the draw of urban development were all responsible for the decline and depopulation of the mountain areas (Saraceno 1991, De Vecchis 1992). In contrast with this, there were great concentrations in the zones around the major Alpine and Apennine valley corridors, in the foothills around the Po valley and along much of the coast. In the remaining areas of the plains, in particular in the low-lying plains along the Po river, the modernisation of agriculture acted above all in the direction of slowing down settlement and of freeing the workforce, with a consequent fall in population: the overall urban structure has thus remained more stable and regular over time, and still today has a relatively wider mesh than the piedmont and coastal settlement patterns, where the main structures of the Italian urban system are located (Gambi 1972, Dematteis 1988). Different dynamics and forms of development have affected these structures.

In the piedmont settlements belts around the Po valley, close-knit urban networks have taken shape, overlapping with the major urbanised areas: those of North-western Italy are focused on the cities of Milan, Turin and Genoa, while those of North-eastern are multi-centred, being regionally spread (Veneto, Friuli-Venezia Giulia and Emilia-Romagna).

In Central Italy, the coastal and piedmont urban network is in part influenced by the presence of large urbanised areas: the first one is dominated by Rome, while the second one is a multi-centred structure located in Northern Tuscany. Outside of these, it has a rather less compact structure and hinges, above all, around a well-distributed network of inland and coastal cities of medieval origin.

In Southern Italy, the coastal system dominates the whole settlement pattern. Of the eighteen municipalities with more than 100,000 inhabitants, only three (Sassari, Foggia and Cosenza) are not along the coast. Along the Apennines of Campania, Molise and Basilicata the inland urban network is more discontinuous and made up of small and medium-sized towns.

A national mosaic of fairly varied urban patterns is thus revealed, fashioned around the physical and environmental conditions of the territory, but above all on the local development processes that have occurred over time. Minor urban networks usually surround the dense, compact single- and multi-centred great urbanised areas of the North and this gives the urban network significant continuity at the regional scale. The multi-centred urban alignments constitute the main settlement structure of the regions of the Centre. Here, they are distributed fairly widely although, with the exception of the lower Arno valley and the area around Rome, they lack the compact network structures of the North. In the South, the compact settlement patterns are generally seen surrounding the main cities, while broad-meshed network structures characterise the outskirts of plains and hills.

From urban concentration to counter-urbanisation

Since the early decades after the World War II, the events that led Italy to a new economic and social development also determined a profound transformation in the urban structure. From when the circuits of national and international trade came to dominate regional and local ones, the cities have increasingly become the nodes of a system of relations that extend beyond their immediate outskirts. The urban networks and even industrial agglomerations which were still surrounded by vast agricultural areas not only changed their size but also their diffusion and their forms of spatial organisation.

In this process of urban development, two distinct periods or phases can be identified (Cori 1983, Muscarà 1992, Campos Venuti 1993, Dematteis 1995). The first one, between the 1950s and the early 1970s, was characterised by the concentration and polarisation of settlement as a consequence of the attraction to the cities of a vast workforce from the countryside. The second phase began in the early 1970s: a contrasting slowdown in the growth of the main cities and a recovery of the more peripheral areas and the minor urban centres. This phase of development and change is known as *counter-urbanisation* (Appendix 1). This is a rather emphatic term, but it expresses well the transformations that have occurred in the Italian urban system and the its internal relations. The demographic changes in the municipalities between 1958 and 1980 can be used as synthetic indicators of urban transformations. For this purpose, they have been calculated for three periods: 1958-64, 1968-73, 1974-79[1] and collected in three types that represent respectively *continuous*, or consolidated urban growth, the *urban decline of the first period and recovery in the later ones* and *persistent urban decline* (Appendix 2).

Figure 3.1 illustrates the geographical localisation of this typology. The black areas, which groups the municipalities that were already growing in the 1950s, outline the pattern of a highly polarised urban development. In this period, in fact, even though the natural demographic dynamic (the difference between births and deaths) was positive almost everywhere in Italy, the great migrations from the countryside to the cities and from inland areas to the coasts means that there was an increase in the population in only 1,915 municipalities (23% of the national territory) (Dematteis 1983). These includes (almost all) the main cities and their surroundings. Compared to the pre-World War II situation, the rural/urban pattern was therefore reshaped, driven mainly by spatial relations of proximity and polarisation. This process was also favoured by the construction of a motorway network to link the main centres, which then became the principal regional and national nodes of the traffic system.

Behind these changes there was an economic structure driven by the growth of large companies and the state intervention aimed at encouraging this type of development and regulating the most glaring distorting effects (Muscarà 1967, Goglio 1986).

Against all expectations, these trends were already reversed in the course of the 1970s. The negative effects of urban congestion and the crisis of the major cities became increasingly evident: in the large urban agglomerations, where the population and the employment base were being reduced, processes of selective restructuring began, based on the development of services and highly capital-intensive manufacturing activities (Indovina 1990, Fubini and Corsico 1994).

In the remaining urban agglomerations, instead, counter-urbanisation rose in the form of diffusion to peripheral areas of population and economic activities, not necessarily influenced by the major cities (Dematteis and Emanuel 1992, Misiti and Gesano 1994).

The welfare state too helped this process of decentralisation.

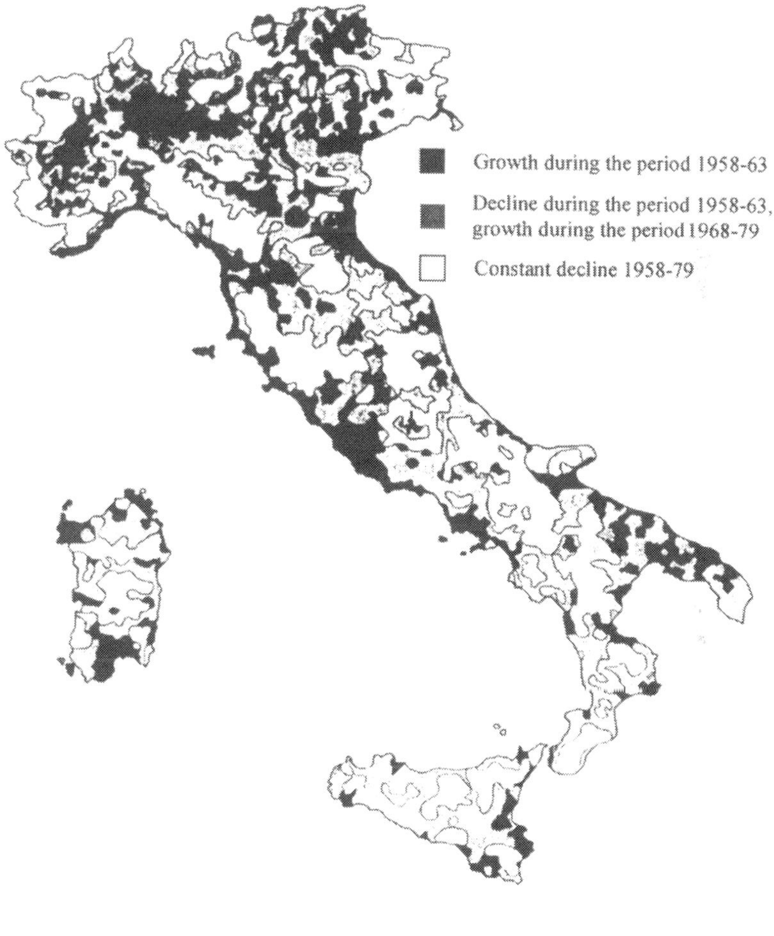

Figure 3.1 Demographic change between 1958 and 1979 by municipality

Source: Dematteis (1983)

It helped to create a full-scale network of elementary physical and social infrastructures capable of generating the preconditions for development on the local scale that had still been the exclusive prerogative of the main urban agglomerations in previous decades. The grey areas of Figure 3.1 correspond to the municipalities that between the late 1960s and late 1970s went from demographic decline to growth.

It should be said straightaway that these changes concern a small amount of population, a few hundred thousand people, while the exodus in the previous period towards urban agglomerations had involved millions of people. But it is the extension of the phenomenon that stands out above all: demographic recovery of the peripheral areas during the 1970s affected 59% of Italian municipalities, located in all regions. It concerned the still densely populated areas of the South, where the remaining population was supported by welfare state intervention, and the return of emigrants gave the opportunity to set up new activities, especially in services (Becchi Collidà 1979, Pugliese and Schettino 1988, Conti S. 1982). Above all, it concerned the areas of the North and the Centre, which by then also included in a single compact urbanised area municipalities that had already grown in earlier decades.

While the counter-urbanisation in Central and North-eastern Italy was driven by a considerable growth in clusters of small and medium-sized firms, localised in local systems which they dominated (Garofoli 1991, Sforzi 1990), in the surroundings of the major urban agglomerations it was based above all on the decentralisation of production and business services through de-localisation of factories, and on the residential re-location of households.

The changes in the 1980s

The municipality scale

Since the beginning of the 1980s, the unremitting fall in births, the contraction in the size of households, the steady increase of the aged population and the overall fall in employment are symptoms of a forthcoming reversal of the trend in Italy's demographic dynamics. Two aspects in particular appear to have a wealth of territorial effects. On the one hand, the above mentioned demographic behaviour extended from the 'mature' regions of the Northern and Central Italy to the Mezzogiorno (Conti 1991, SVIMEZ 1993). On the other hand, there was a notable accentuation in the shift of the population from the cities to the more external outskirts, which thus expanded and grew in population (Bonifazi and Cantalini 1988, De Santis 1991).

One first indication of the changeover that occurred can be seen from the demographic change by municipality in the two periods 1979-85 and 1985-91.

The spatial localisation of the phenomenon reveals, in fact, the substantial differences between the 1970s and the 1980s. Figure 3.2, which represents the demographic changes in the two periods, shows rather well the demographic fall in almost all municipalities of over 50,000 inhabitants, usually accompanied by the growth of smaller, contiguous ones.

This last aspect is highlighted well by the vast urbanised areas produced by the frequent 'merging' between the surroundings of the major cities, and which in many cases reach supra-regional dimensions, such as along the piedmont axis, in coastal areas and in the inland valleys of Central Italy.

Figure 3.2 allows a direct comparison with Figure 3.1. It reveals how in many cases the more dynamic areas fall back (especially in Southern Italy), while being consolidated as a whole along the main axes of Italy's settlement structure. These characteristics allow us to assume a recovery of urban polarisation after the relative weakening of the 1970s. As can be seen from the comparison, however, this phenomenon is now accompanied by the formation of numerous 'craters' of dis-urbanisation that coincide with the administrative perimeters of the main centres and with a more pronounced fringing of the external borders of the growing areas.

While both these aspects were present in Central and Northern Italy, because of the simultaneous extension of decline to the medium-sized cities and the growth of smaller localities included in their urban fields, in the Southern Italy the second feature prevails, above all in inland areas, through the effect of the contraction of peripheral growth along the main transport axes.

Fairly extensive areas of growth still remain, however, especially along the coasts of the Tyrrhenian Sea and Puglia. These are particularly evident around the main urbanised areas, where they push inland and include even the most peripheral urban localities. From the comparison of Figures 3.1 and 3.2, it can be seen how in the 1980s there were still situations of growth that did not depend on effects of urban overflow or polarisation, even though these did contract close to the main centres and localities. This is especially clear along the Adriatic, the piedmont settlement and along the main Alpine and Apennine valleys.

These aspects are illustrated in more detail in Table 3.1.

The table shows how demographic growth which had involved up to 55% of municipalities in the 1970s then fell to 47% in the late 1980s.

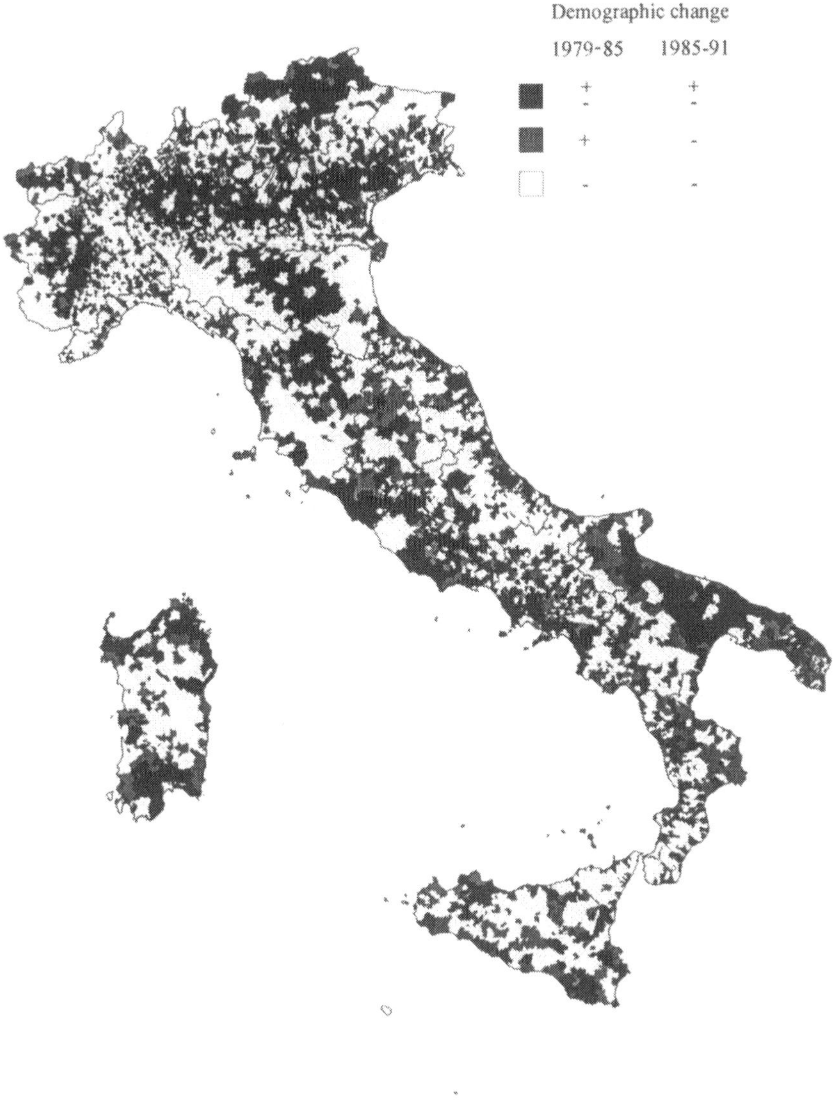

Figure 3.2 Demographic change by municipality between 1979 and 1991

Table 3.1
Number of municipalities in demographic decline (-) and growth (+) from 1973 to 1991

		1973-79		1979-85		1985-91	
		-	+	-	+	-	+
North	no.	2,109	2,436	2,375	2,170	2,196	2,349
	%	*46.4*	*53.6*	*52.3*	*47.7*	*48.3*	*51.7*
Centre	no.	434	567	483	518	509	492
	%	*43.4*	*56.6*	*48.3*	*51.7*	*50.8*	*49.2*
South	no.	1,096	1,458	1,349	1,205	1,576	978
	%	*42.9*	*57.1*	*52.8*	*47.2*	*61.7*	*38.3*
Italy	no.	3,639	4,461	4,207	3,893	4,281	3,819
	%	*44.9*	*55.1*	*51.9*	*48.1*	*52.9*	*47.1*

Source: calculated by the author from ISTAT data.

Table 3.2
Population of municipalities in demographic decline (-) and growth (+) from 1973 to 1991

		1973-79		1979-85		1985-91	
		-	+	-	+	-	+
North	no.	370,074	837,584	808,428	507,959	715,411	462,290
	%	*67.8*	*35.5*	*58.5*	*32*	*44.3*	*39.5*
Centre	no.	46,196	430,842	198,787	236,510	191,763	179,655
	%	*8.5*	*18.2*	*14.4*	*14.9*	*11.9*	*15.3*
South	no,	129,421	1,093,967	375,060	843,803	708,770	528,890
	%	*23.7*	*46.3*	*27.1*	*53.1*	*43.9*	*45.2*
Italy	no,	545,691	2,362,393	1,382,275	1,588,272	1,615,944	1,170,835
	%	*100*	*100*	*100*	*100*	*100*	*100*

Source: calculated by the author from ISTAT data.

The North, however, goes against this overall trend, with the number of expanding municipalities rising from 48% to 52%; in contrast, the percentage of municipalities growing in the South fell considerably from 57% to 38%, due above all to the fall in the birth rate.

Fairly similar trends can also be traced in Table 3.2, which illustrates the quantity of the population gained by the growing municipalities and the number lost by declining ones. Read together, the two tables demonstrate that although the overall population fell in the North, the growing municipalities (51.7% of the total) gradually increased to the point of occupying almost half the territory, thus completing the extensive process of urban decentralisation illustrated in Figure 3.2.

In the Centre, and above all in the South, instead, the growing population was gradually redistributed over an increasingly limited number of municipalities, leading to a rise in declining areas and a contraction in the growing ones.

The local urban systems

The overall picture offered by the analysis at the municipality scale can be improved by using spatial units that correspond better to the current dimensions of the individual urban systems. These allow a more realistic assessment of the settlement changes deriving from the decentralisation and the restructuring of production processes, and by the increased propensity for inter-city mobility and home-work commuting. Thus, the analysis that follows will refer to the *local urban systems* already illustrated in Chapter 1 and 2.

The local urban systems can be divided internally into a *core* (or central city), which has the main concentration of population and jobs, and a *ring* (or peripheral localities) within which housing and decentralised activities are re-located. This distinction is very useful for our analysis in that it enables the examination of the dynamic of settlement concentration/de-concentration, which is in turn an indicator of development.

In Central and Northern Italy, the local urban systems are distributed fairly uniformly among the various classes of demographic size, while in the South they seem more concentrated in the extremes of large and small. These characteristics are also reflected in their territorial size: this is more uniform in the Centre-North and more varied in the South. In this case, the reason for the differences is the centres' (especially the medium and medium-large ones) different capabilities to offer themselves as polarising localities for the surroundings, so that in the South there is a great extension of the areas around the larger cities and a relative fragmentation around the smaller ones.

In order to obtain an initial picture of the changes, the relations between the demographic growth rates and the size classes of the local urban systems were examined. These provide a statistical measurement of counter-urbanisation (Appendix 1).

The three curves in Figure 3.3 describe this relationship for the periods 1973-79, 1979-85 and 1985-91, previously examined at the municipality scale. In all three periods, it can be observed that the peaks of growth characterise medium or medium-large urban systems, while the negative variations concern the small ones, with fewer than 30,000 inhabitants. It should be noted that in Italy the reduction in overall demographic growth between the 1970s and the 1990s, despite lowering the curves, did not substantially modify the overall trend. Only in the last period does the slowing of the decline of the urban systems with more than 1,000,000 inhabitants (the major Italian cities) become evident. Figure 3.3 also shows how counter-urbanisation and the reduction of demographic growth in the medium-sized urban systems is a general phenomenon, which has proceeded over time from North to South.

The same analysis carried out by core-ring shows how since the 1980s the demographic changes of the cores of Northern Italy were negative everywhere, more accentuated as their size increases, and is compensated for by a positive change in the rings. In Southern Italy, this type of dynamic can be identified only for the urban systems of more than 100,000 inhabitants; in smaller ones, instead, it is generally the positive change of the cores to compensate for, or cushion, the negative trend in the rings.

Structures and dynamics of the local urban systems

The comparison between the demographic behaviour of the cores and the rings is able to offer a more detailed picture of the settlement dynamics. On the basis of the positive or negative values of demographic change of the core and ring of each local urban system, six different typologies are defined for each of the three periods:

A - *extensive urbanisation*, when both the core and the ring show positive demographic change;

B - *extensive decline*, when, in contrast, both show a negative change and thus a loss of population;

C - *urbanisation*, when the positive variation in the population of the centre compensates the loss of the ring and the urban system maintains a positive overall demographic position;

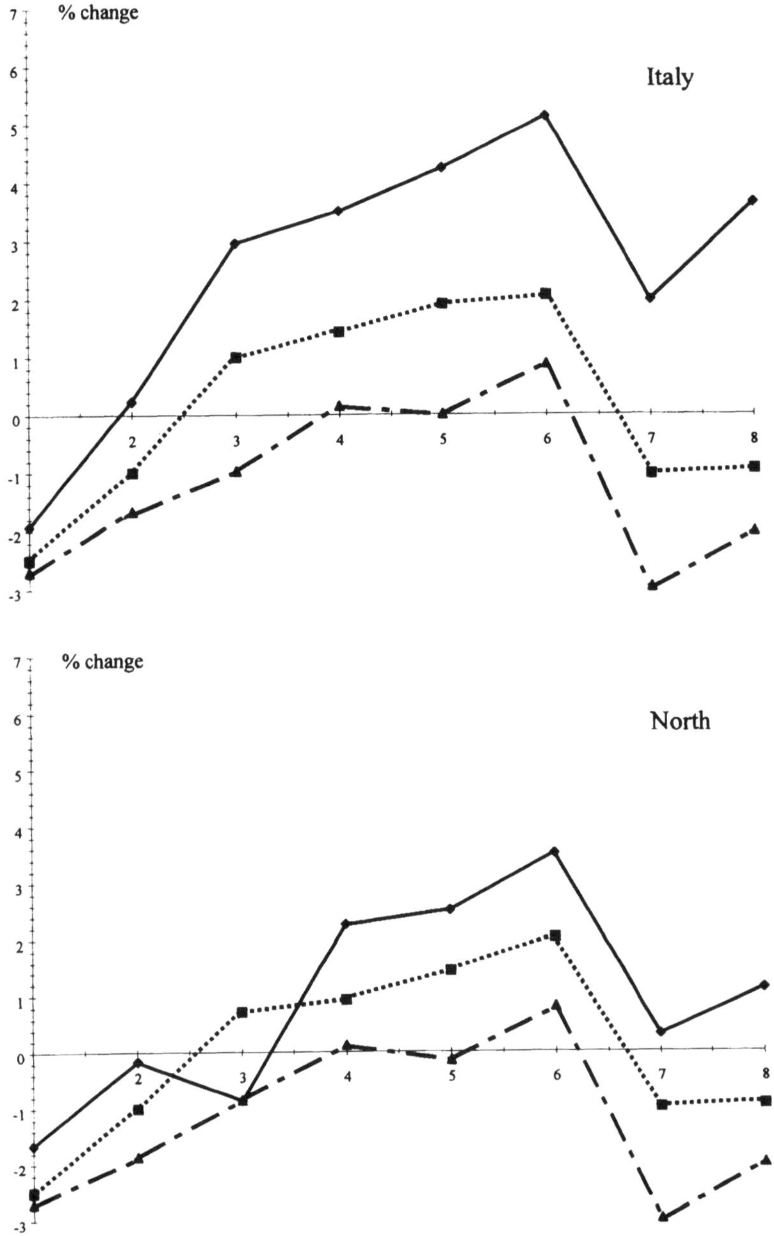

Figure 3.3 Demographic change between 1973 and 1991 by size of local urban systems

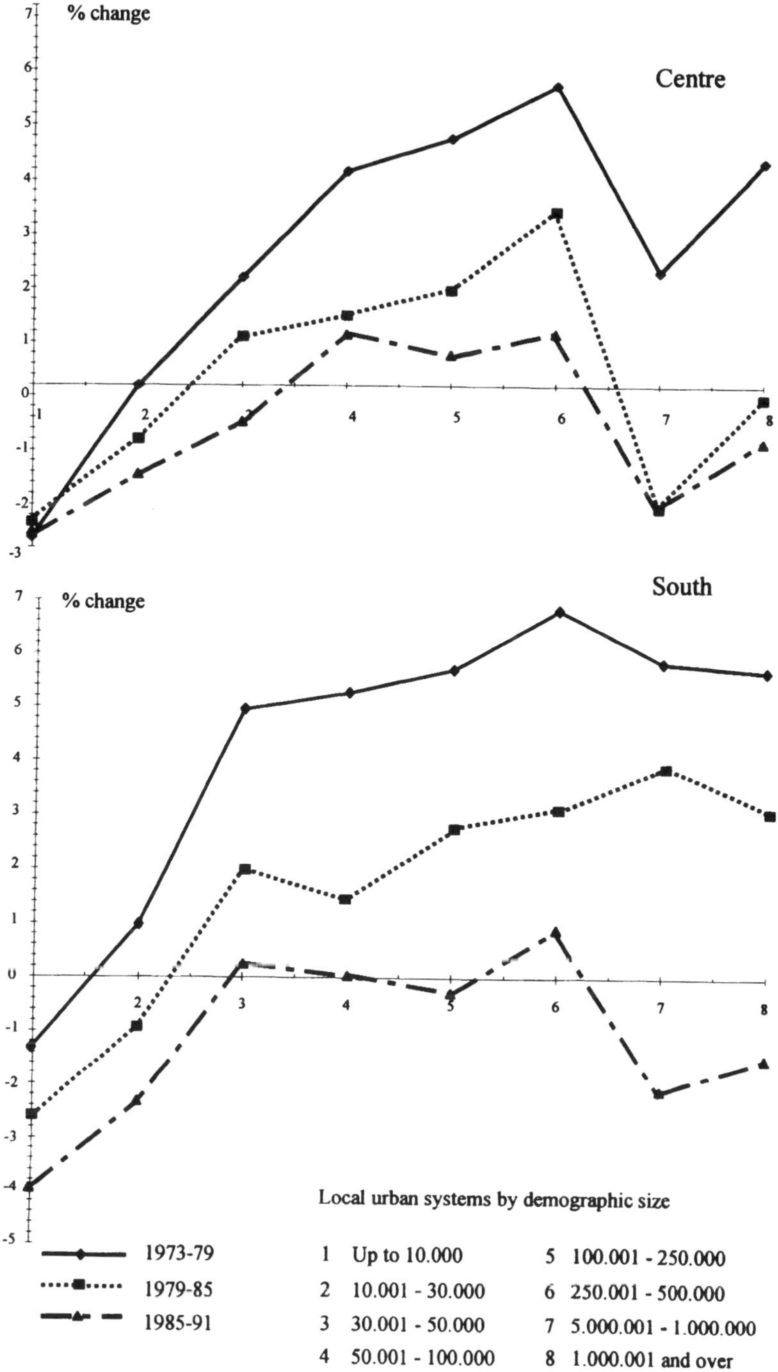
% change
Centre
% change
South
Local urban systems by demographic size
1973-79
1979-85
1985-91
1 Up to 10.000
2 10.001 - 30.000
3 30.001 - 50.000
4 50.001 - 100.000
5 100.001 - 250.000
6 250.001 - 500.000
7 5.000.001 - 1.000.000
8 1.000.001 and over

D - *relative urbanisation*, when the positive change in the core does not compensate the loss of population in the ring, but does lessen overall decline;

E - *sub-urbanisation*, when the positive change in the ring compensates the negative trend in the population of the core and the urban system maintains demographic growth;

F - *relative sub-urbanisation*, when the positive change in the population of the ring does not compensate for the negative change in the population of the core, but does attenuate the overall decline of the urban system (Appendix 3).

The joint analysis of evolution in the three periods 1973-79, 1979-85 and 1985-91 reveals the extensive transition between the above types in the urban systems in the last 15 years. While, in fact, in 1973-79, 64% of the urban systems show positive demographic dynamics (and 45% came under the heading of extensive urbanisation), in the period 1985-91 they were reduced to around 35%, while situations of absolute decline (43%) and of relative urbanisation and sub-urbanisation (22%) grew.

The urban systems characterised by positive dynamics (extensive urbanisation, urbanisation and sub-urbanisation) outline a more geographically meaningful pattern of recent settlement development than the one calculated at municipality scale in Figure 3.2. In Northern Italy, there are evident phenomena of growth around Turin and in Southern Piedmont, and above all along the urbanised area that runs from the western edge of Milan to beyond Venice and from Verona branching up to Trentino-Alto Adige. A vast area of growth also takes shape around Bologna and Florence: the two urban systems tend to merge, despite the Apennines between them. Along the Adriatic coast, the line of growth remains quite clear between Rimini and Pescara.

In Umbria, the positive dynamics of the Perugia urban system can be seen, interrupted towards Rome by the decline of Terni. Most of the growth in Southern Italy is concentrated around the main urban system, along the Tyrrhenian coast, in Puglia and along the coasts of Sardinia.

Outside these urbanised areas, the demographic dynamics are negative almost everywhere, although in many cases the decline is lessened by the positive dynamic of either the rings or the cores.

Vast areas of decline in Northern Italy mark all the lower plains, the Alps and the Apennines between Piedmont and Lombardy, the Apennines and the coast of Liguria and also the eastern tips of the country including the Alps of Veneto and Friuli-Venezia Giulia. In Central and Southern Italy, decline hits marginal urban systems, located above all in inland areas.

The urban demographic 'crisis' appears, therefore, both in structurally weak situations and in urban systems where there are processes of industrial restructuring which, although being negative on the demographic plane, could be positive from the economic point of view.

It also emerges that, in the areas of growth, there are extensive forms of decentralisation or diffusion of settlement both because of the effects of the sub-urbanisation that characterises the major urban systems and through the extensive urbanisation that marks the smaller ones. Thus, what appeared simply as decentralisation on the municipality scale, appears largely as wide-ranging sub-urbanisation when seen on the scale of the urban systems. This phenomenon, combining with the extensive urbanisation of many minor urban systems, gives rise to regional patterns characterised by a relative demographic agglomeration around the largest urban systems, where the population of the central cities falls in favour of the growth of the outer rings and more peripheral areas.

These forms of urban development are not present everywhere. In the inner Apennines and in most of the South, there are fairly frequent cases of traditional urbanisation, i.e. growth of the central cities to the detriment of the rings, still in decline, or certainly not very dynamic.

Demographic and settlement transitions

The comparative examination of the core-ring dynamics for the three periods considered allows the classification of the demographic and settlement transitions of the urban systems between the 1970s and the 1990s. These transitions are included between the two relatively stationary states of *extensive urbanisation* and *demographic stagnation*. Between these two extremes, four evolutionary curves can be identified (see Figure 3.6 in Appendix 3):

- *peri-urbanisation*, when demographic growth is supported by the rings so that the evolutionary dynamics, included between demographic stagnation and extensive urbanisation, pass through the stages of relative or absolute sub-urbanisation;
- *urbanisation*, when demographic growth is supported instead by the cores, so that the evolutionary dynamics, included between demographic stagnation and extensive urbanisation, pass through the stages of relative or absolute urbanisation;
- *dis-urbanisation*, when the slowdown in growth is checked by the resistancc of the rings and the evolutionary dynamics, with trajectories thus between demographic stagnation and extensive urbanisation, passing through the stages of relative and absolute sub-urbanisation;

- *urban decline*, when the slowdown in growth is instead checked by the resistance of the cores and the evolutionary dynamics, included between demographic stagnation and extensive urbanisation, pass through the stages of relative and absolute urbanisation.

Figure 3.4 illustrates the results of this analysis. For ease of understanding, the urban systems that remain in the stationary state of extensive urbanisation have been grouped with those that have started on the road to peri-urbanisation, while those that are on the trajectory of dis-urbanisation but that have halted this dynamic in the stage of absolute sub-urbanisation are indicated in a different shade. This representation, which also considers the demographic size of the urban systems, allows the identification of a more accurate typological division of them and thus the interpretation of their transitions as an indirect indicator of the development processes.

Two different types of urban system come under the trajectories of *dis-urbanisation*. The first includes those urban systems that show a net loss of population and that are therefore headed for the stages of relative sub-urbanisation and demographic stagnation.

In this situation, more common in the Centre-North, we find all the main single-centred and multi-centred urban agglomerations and many intermediate and minor urban systems located principally in the proximity of the former. In the main urban agglomerations, where the reduction of the population in the central cities is accompanied by the development of the tertiary, quaternary and innovative industrial sectors, dis-urbanisation does not limit but reinforces the dominion of the centre over the surroundings, where the extension of demographic growth is usually found.

In the intermediate and minor urban systems, dis-urbanisation is instead the outcome of rather different phenomena.

In the case of medium-sized urban systems, it can be ascribed, as above, to phenomena of selective change of the employment base, or to phenomena of polarisation of economic activities, not compensated for by other local growth processes.

In minor urban systems, the same phenomenon can indicate instead different processes.

In the Centre-North, there are urban systems in which the decline of the main centre is compensated at least in part by the presence in the rings of towns that remain vital from the point of view of demography and production structures; in the South, there are cases in which the demographic density and the degree of urbanisation of the rings are quite similar to those of the cores, so that the central city does not constitute a factor of territorial differentiation.

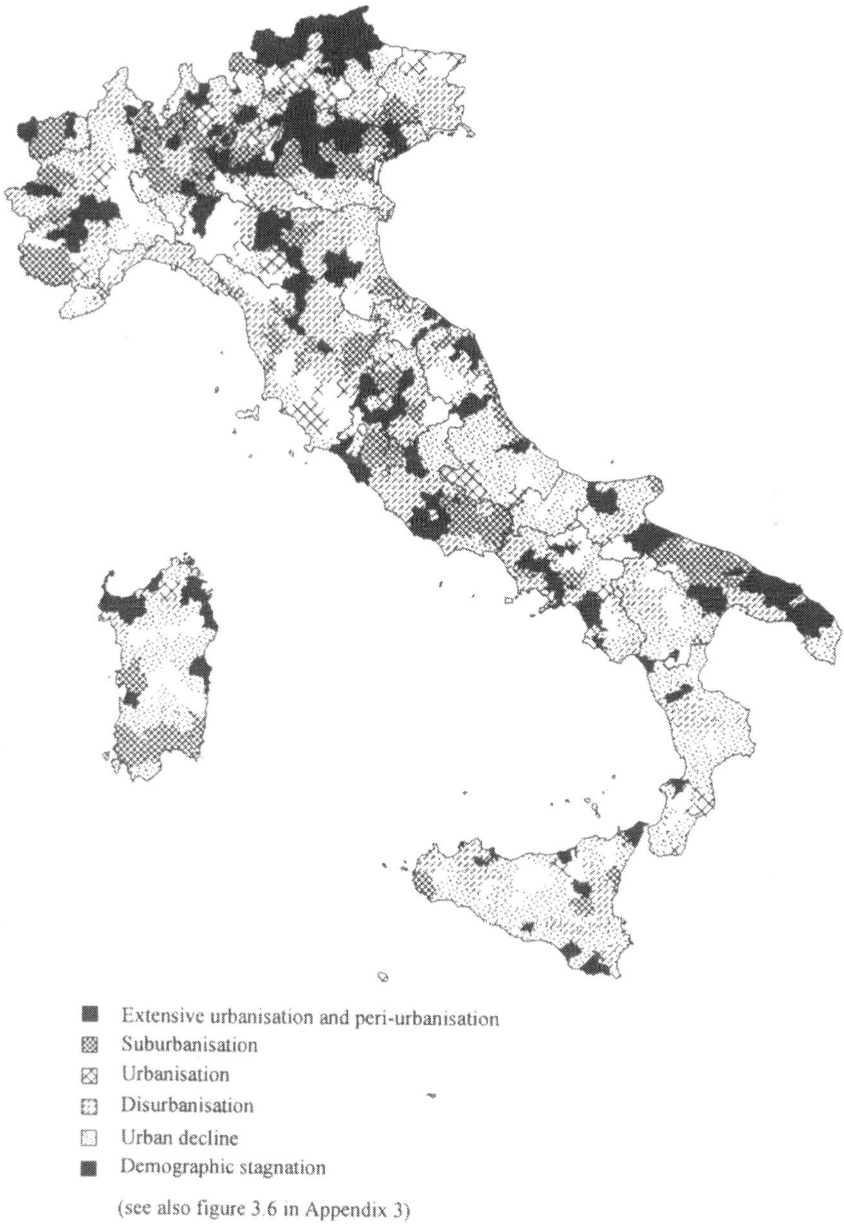

Figure 3.4 Demographic change between 1973 and 1991 by local urban system

One last case is represented by the urban systems contiguous to the peri-urban areas: the demographic resistance here can derive from the diffusion of limited forms of decentralisation, above all of housing.

The second typology includes the intermediate urban systems where the dis-urbanisation has stopped at the stage of *sub-urbanisation*. This class generally covers intermediate and large urban systems that show demographic growth. In the South, this type of growth characterises the urban systems of Cagliari and Bari, but more in general marks those urban systems that constitute the intermediate urban environment between the main cities and the areas of diffuse growth. In their central cities, declining demographically, there are phenomena of decentralisation on the regional scale of metropolitan activities that indicate high levels of centrality, or phenomena of local growth of these activities for peripheral and scattered users in the surroundings.

The trajectory of *peri-urbanisation* generally includes small and medium-sized urban systems in which the decentralisation of the major urban systems is combined with dynamics of local development and the demographic effects are distributed over a widespread settlement fabric. It should be noted how in the Centre-North this typology includes the more peripheral urban systems that have only recently started to recover, passing from situations of demographic stagnation to ones of relative or absolute sub-urbanisation, due to the effects of the spread from the major urban systems or the development of diffuse production activities. In the South, their diffusion is limited to the areas around the major urban systems, which attract the decentralised housing and the movement to the towns from the more peripheral areas.

The trajectories of *urbanisation* include the urban systems that, in contrast to the previous ones, are in a phase of growth with the prevalence of demographic growth in the central city. The relatively limited number of cases found here is, however, indicative of processes of local growth not supported by an adequate peripheral settlement fabric. They can in fact be identified in the parts of the Alpine areas, the Apennine valleys and the sea coasts where the peripheral settlement fabric, the density and thresholds of local infrastructures are minimal.

In the trajectories of *urban decline*, we find instead the systems where the positive demographic dynamics are principally localised in the main cities. This typology includes a fair number of the Southern urban systems that recorded the most substantial decline of population in their rings in the course of the 1980s. In the regions of the Centre, the trajectories of decline affect almost exclusively minor urban systems, while in the North they also characterise intermediate ones, mainly located between growing systems and others in demographic stagnation. Their proximity to the more central urbanised areas seems to have slowed their decline, and especially that of their cores. In contrast to the cores in the South, however, these tend to be headed for a gradual end to their demographic drive. With no reversal of their demographic dynamics, their transition towards negative demographic transition seems to be close. In the Northern regions, this last condition characterises both the more marginal urban systems, deprived of their endogenous strengths since the early post-World War II decades, and the more significant urban realities, in which the processes of industrial restructuring seem to be the most critical.

The new patterns of the urban network

The analyses of the demographic transitions alone do not allow further in-depth investigation of urban dynamics. They do, however, highlight how in Italy fairly extensive urban patterns came to be produced on the regional scale; after the ones that had marked metropolitan development, these helped to further change the image of the city as a single-point, geographically circumscribed phenomenon. At the centre of these vast urban agglomerations we now find the most significant urban systems. We have already seen how, in these cases, the processes of dis-urbanisation are not an indicator of decline, but on the contrary of innovative transformations generally destined to strengthen their territorial domination and to provide substantial outflows of population and economic activities. In the areas around these stronger urban systems, the positive dynamics are transmitted to medium-sized urban systems which thus assume the role of urban sub-centres, immersed in the much vaster areas of peri-urban urbanisation. In the even more external urban systems, the diffusive drives of the major urban systems tend to die out, instead, and therefore also to limit growth, which is, consequently, more limited and usually capable of affecting certain rings or the central cities according to the cases. Mixed in with these urban systems, or in even more marginal positions, there are then others that form the new regional peripheries in demographic stagnation where the endogenous resources were depleted some time ago.

Some signs of the changes described here had already emerged in the 1970s, when the first forms of demographic, economic and settlement diffusion outside the main cities were described as the 'exploded city' (Dematteis *et al.* 1986), 'dispersed city' (Indovina *et al.* 1990) and 'network city' (Gambino 1990) etc. It can therefore be said that in the course of the 1980s, despite the weakening of demographic growth, the redistribution of the population and economic activities completed these patterns, now manifest in a general and evident manner.

These new forms of settlement are also fashioned, however, on the urban networks described at the beginning of this chapter. The dynamics of recent urban development thus appear to be the result of environmental conditions generated by the historical processes of urbanisation. This acknowledgement, which may appear obvious, is however necessary, as representations and descriptions of urban change very much unconnected to ecological relations or to the historical and environmental conditions of local development have been produced even recently through the use of over-simplified conceptual and descriptive categories in the functionalist tradition.

Evidence of the weight of this conditioning is found in the role that the major urban structures play in demographic dynamics and in the processes of localisation of economic activities and functions. The high density, the physical saturation and the rigidity of these major urban structures are among the factors that determine dis-urbanisation, the selective nature of the processes of functional re-polarisation of the central areas, and thus the extension and strengthening of the urban agglomerations over the surroundings. In the multi-centred urbanised agglomerations, where these features are less pronounced, the phenomena of dis-urbanisation are less accentuated and, for the time being, mainly limited to just the central cities.

Much more complex and articulated are, instead, the effects of the recent settlement dynamics on the basic urban networks, outside or on the fringes of the urban agglomerations. They seem, in fact, to interact both with positive phenomena of local valorisation and with destabilising phenomena of 'capture' and invasion, selective splitting, and thickening and implosion of the settlement network.

Some processes of diffusion of demographic and settlement growth seem to mark the beginning of phenomena of peripheral revitalisation and re-valorisation of the networks. This can be found in the peri-urbanisation processes underway in the valleys and slopes of the Alps and Apennines. Here, in fact, demographic and settlement recovery translates in many cases into the recovery of the most marginal settlement network which would otherwise be destined either to die or to become simply a support for the growth of holiday homes, generally incapable on their own of exercising inductive effects on the processes of demographic growth.

Another type of growth occurs in the peripheral structures of the compact urban-type mesh. Here, the centrifugal dynamics that are set in motion by the selective processes of polarisation show that they generate phenomena of 'peripheral re-centralisation' capable of having positive effects not only on the dynamics of local growth but also on the reorganisation of the main centres through a strengthening of their levels of accessibility and urban image. This is generally the case with the central cities of peripheral urban systems, now in the phase of sub-urbanisation, that surround the single-centred urban agglomerations and thus tend to strengthen their multi-polar pattern. The analysis of settlement transitions demonstrates the existence of these phenomena also in the Mezzogiorno and in particular in the Naples area, where the outer urban systems adjoining Naples, and the more peripheral ones, are also going through the phase of sub-urbanisation.

Yet, there are also cases of dis-urbanisation, which characterise for example many medium-sized urban systems in the multi-centred Emilian and Tuscan urban agglomerations. The quite dense peri-urban rings around Bologna and Florence tend, in fact, to stand out from the more peripheral areas of these structures, such as the cities localised along the 'via Emilia' and in the lower Arno valley. In all these cases, metropolitan sub-systems are formed in which the processes of dis-urbanisation are not accompanied by parallel processes of peri-urbanisation. They may indicate phenomena of recession and possibly, in time, implosion of local growth and development. Similar characteristics can be traced in the urban systems that form the Northern Tyrrhenian and the Udine-Trieste urban agglomerations.

The demographic and settlement pressures that give rise to peri-urbanisation generate a progressive thickening of the mesh of the networks. This phenomenon encourages the spread of urban effects to the urban systems, but it also generates serious environmental problems due to the development of widespread, low density settlement that occupies land intensively. The increase in daily commuting between these areas and the main cities then creates additional needs for inter-city connections which, if satisfied, produce growing congestion along the link roads. These aspects, well known in the European 'core', have now spread to the whole of the Italian network and are even spreading where peri-urbanisation affects the broad mesh settlement patterns, producing thickening that prefigures the network structures of the 'diffuse city'. This occurs above all in the plains between Rome and Naples, in the external rings of these two urban systems and along the Florence-Rome axis, especially around the node of Perugia (INU 1990).

While in more peripheral areas, peri-urbanisation recovers the heritage of diffuse settlement that had lost value following the emigration in the decades after the World War II, near to the urbanised areas the poorly controlled scattering of new buildings tends instead to alter and sometimes wipe out the specific features of the traditional settlement environments. Other forms of increase in density are also present around the major traffic routes along the piedmonts, the coasts and valleys, often with a clear-cut separation from the traditional settlement network which remains in adjacent belts (Lanzani 1991, Boeri, Lanzani and Marini 1993). Similar forms of ribbon development are also evident along the Adriatic coast. In this case, the peri-urbanisation around the main urban systems and the ongoing sub-urbanisation in the others is producing an increasingly decided mix of settlement, also favoured by a type of local development based above all on the territorial diffusion of small and medium-sized firms (INU 1990).

In the South, these alignments constitute an innovative element when, starting from the coastal towns, they tend to penetrate inland to shape new lines of industrialisation, such as the one that extends from Naples and Salerno towards inland areas. Similar lines can also be traced along the coast near Pescara and in Molise in the direction of the valleys inland and, stimulated by the improved road links, also in the proximity of the coasts of Calabria or the inland areas of Puglia bordering on Campania and Basilicata (Viganoni 1991). The urban systems involved in these processes tend to slow down their decline and to settle on trajectories of dis-urbanisation or urbanisation associated with a development of the rings or the main cores, according to the territorial extension of the urban systems themselves and the local conditions of the network.

Appendix 1

Counter-urbanisation

Counter-urbanisation is defined by Berry (1976) as a process of urban de-concentration destined to reduce the demographic dimensions of the main cities and urban agglomerations, the territorial densities of population and the disparities between urban and rural areas.

This term's capacity to evoke alternative forms of urban growth to those that dominated in the phases of settlement concentration (urbanisation) has, however, encouraged its broad and generic use in the specialised literature. It has also often been adopted to define the slowdown in urban growth and the demographic recovery of the more peripheral areas, which started in Italy in the 1970s.

Fielding (1982) has, however, provided a more precise definition from the operational point of view, as the inverse correlation between demographic growth rates and the class of size of the cities. The calculation of this relation is thus able to measure statistically the 'deglomerative' trends that appear on major territorial scales (regions and countries).

In a recent contribution on the settlement dynamics in Italy (Dematteis and Emanuel 1995), this relation has been calculated for the individual urban centres (municipalities) and has demonstrated effectively how the medium-small and medium-sized towns with between 5,000 and 50,000 inhabitants have grown in percentage terms more than large ones, thus determining a reversal of the growth trajectories that dominated in the urbanisation phase (1950-1970).

In this research, the same relation is instead calculated for the local urban systems, and the curves in Figure 3.3 show how the phenomenon of counter-urbanisation can also be found on this scale, above all because of the effect of the demographic vivacity of the local urban systems centred on medium-small and medium-sized localities.

Appendix 2

Demographic dynamic of the municipalities

This research returns to and updates the results of an investigation aimed at defining the geography of the peripheral and marginal areas of Italy from 1945 to 1980 (Cencini, Dematteis and Menegatti 1983). In order to document the spatial dynamics of these phenomena synthetically, an analysis procedure was adopted based on the calculation of the population variations in the communes in three successive periods of time: 1958-63, 1968-73 and 1973-79.

The first period includes the years of the so-called 'Italian economic miracle', in which the most marked phenomena of concentration of population and employment in the major urban agglomerations occurred. The second corresponds to the years in which the first symptoms of the employment and social 'crisis' of the urban areas appeared, and saw the beginning of an extensive process of production and residential decentralisation in peripheral areas, including ones not adjacent to the major agglomerations. The third period includes the years in which the development of the peripheral urban areas consolidated and, in particular, the migration flows from the peripheries to the major cities came to a halt.

The comparison between the positive/negative signs of the population changes of each municipality in the three periods has allowed the identification of three different types of situation, whose territorial pattern is shown in Figure 3.1.

Using the same source (ISTAT 1958-79), the same time periods and the same calculation procedures, this chapter extends and updates this analysis from 1979 to 1991. The demographic decline of this period, due above all to falls in the birth rate, did however suggest modifications in the types of demographic situations. The ones felt meaningful for this purpose are given in the key to Figure 3.2: diverging partially from the previous analysis, they group the situations of persistent growth and demographic recovery that occurred in the 1980s, indicate situations of passage from growth to decline, while they confirm those of persistent depopulation. Figure 3.2 gives the territorial pattern of these types and, if compared with Figure 3.1, it provides an indication of the changes that have occurred in the decade in the geography of urban dynamics. The analysis of such changes is developed in this chapter.

Appendix 3

Demographic dynamic of the local urban systems

Investigations of the demographic-settlement dynamic of the local urban systems adopt the calculation procedures and descriptive categories of the *city life cycle model*, although with some variations compared to the original given in the CURB project by the *Vienna Centre* (van den Berg *et al.* 1982).

This model describes the evolutionary trajectories of the urban systems, defined as *functional urban regions* (FUR), through the comparative examination of the demographic changes of their cores and rings. In fact, a FUR is made up of an agglomeration that includes a *core* (or central city), with more than 200,000 inhabitants, and by a *ring* of surrounding towns, not less than 15% of whose population daily commutes towards the central city.

The left part of Table 3.3 and the lower part of 3.5 visualise the content of this model, showing respectively the typological classification of the demographic changes (positive or negative) of the core-ring of an urban system and the diagram of their evolutionary trajectory.

As can be seen above all in Figure 3.5, the city life cycle model identifies a cyclical sequence of eight different types of demographic change, in turn grouped into four different phases of urban development (urbanisation, sub-urbanisation, dis-urbanisation, re-urbanisation).

These development phases, according to the authors of the model, do not concern just the spatial distribution of the population, but also that of employment, economic activities and, more in general, the forms of organisation of the territory.

Although formally simple and elegant, the urban dynamic defined by this model corresponds only partly to the cases empirically verified. While the first three phases are usually found in medium and large urban systems in advanced countries, the fourth has so far only been found in a few cases (Cheshire 1995). Furthermore, inquiry into the behaviour of the minor urban systems has produced few confirmations even though, according to the model, similar forms of development and decline should exist, just delayed in time.

Table 3.3
Types of urban demographic change according to the Vienna Centre classification and our analysis

Phases	**Types of demographic variation of the urban system**	**Characteristics of demographic variation**			**Types of demographic variation in the urban system**
	Vienna Centre classification	Centre	Ring	Urban system	Our classification
Urbanisation	Absolute centralisation (a.c.)	+	-	+	Urbanisation
	Relative centralisation (r.c.)	++	+	+	Extensive urbanisation
Sub-urbanisation	Relative decentralisation (r.d.)	+	++	+	Extensive urbanisation
	Absolute decentralisation (a.d.)	-	+	+	Sub-urbanisation
Dis-urbanisation	Absolute decentralisation (a.d.)	-	+	-	Relative sub-urbanisation
	Relative decentralisation (r.d.)	--	-	-	Extensive decline
Re-urbanisation	Relative centralisation (r.c.)	-	--	-	Extensive decline
	Absolute centralisation (a.c.)	+	-	-	Relative urbanisation

The model can be used effectively, however, for a comparative analysis of urban dynamics. Its application to the Italian local urban systems has, in fact, provided significant results after an 'adjustment'.

In particular, the analysis of the demographic changes of the cores and rings of the local urban systems in the periods 1973-79, 1979-85 and 1985-91 allowed the definition of six different types of demographic behaviour for each period (extensive urbanisation, extensive decline, urbanisation, relative urbanisation, sub-urbanisation, relative sub-urbanisation) and their classification into two relatively stationary states of extensive urbanisation and demographic stagnation, and four evolutionary trajectories, oriented respectively towards growth (urbanisation and peri-urbanisation) or decline (dis-urbanisation and urban decline).

The right hand side of Table 3.3 and the top part of Figure 3.5 indicate the urban systems' six different types of demographic behaviour.

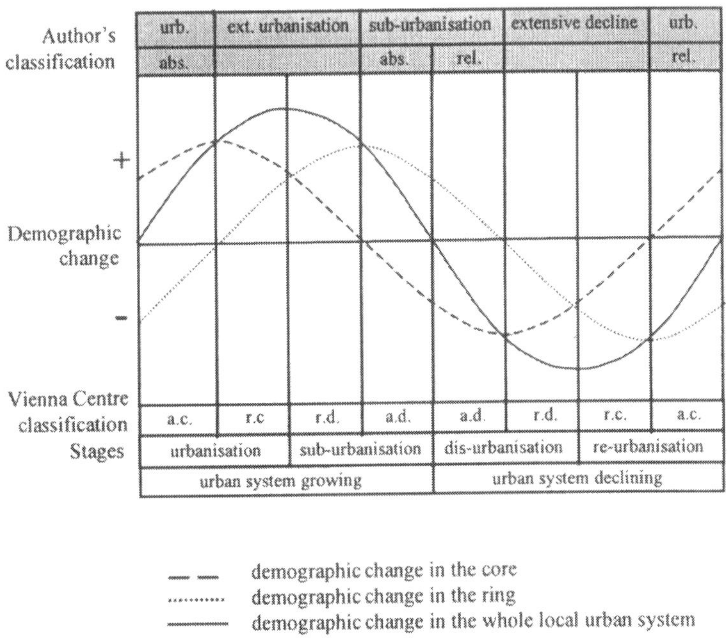

Figure 3.5 Stages of demographic change

Figure 3.6, finally, represents the four evolutionary trajectories; as can be imagined, the operative definition of these trajectories was reached through the reading of the types of demographic change in the urban systems for the three successive periods.

In the cases where the types of demographic change indicated a clear transition from situations of decline to extensive urbanisation or vice versa, and thus not allowing the attribution of the urban systems to one of the possible evolutionary trajectories, this was done through the examination of the values of the demographic balance between the core and the ring; the greater demographic resistance of one of the two elements guided the attribution to one of the trajectories in these cases.

The results obtained from this analytical and methodological extension are represented in Figure 3.4, which gives the localisation of the types of transition, highlighting settlement patterns and urban dynamics difficult to deduce from analysis only at the municipality scale.

From the methodological standpoint, we can add that through the 'adjustments' made to the original model, the description and representation of the urban dynamics are freed from the pre-conceptualisations imposed by the type of approach based on cycles or phases. Above all, the categories that define the demographic-settlement transitions can use a terminology more appropriate to the nature of the phenomena described and sometimes already used in other analyses. The concepts of peri-urbanisation and extensive urbanisation are an example.

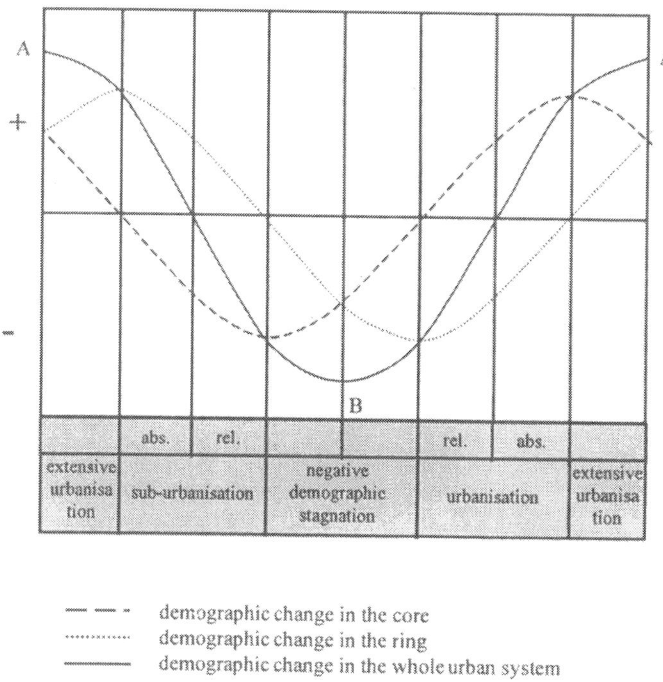

Stationary states:
- extensive urbanisation
- demographic stagnation

Transition patterns:

urbanisation	B → A'
urban decline	A' → B
peri-urbanisation	B → A
dis-urbanisation	A → B

Figure 3.6 Transition patterns of demographic change

4 The international functions

Piero Bonavero

Some concepts for the interpretation of the urban 'internationality'

The study of the forms and degrees of the internationalisation of cities allows to analyse the connections between the phenomena on a local scale and those on a supra-local one (i.e. global) in the framework of urban networks. The question has specific significance in the context of the European Community, in that international links are the factor through which the process of integration of the countries of the Union is achieved, and the cities certainly appear to be nodal elements in building these links.

Over time, therefore, a wide field of studies directed to the analysis and the transformations of the *international cities* has developed: in this framework, the main features studied have been the internationalisation of cities on the world scale and the processes of the rise of the global cities (Hall 1966, Boulding 1978, Friedmann and Wolff 1982, Chase-Dunn 1984, Knight and Gappert 1984, Timberlake 1985, Ewers, Goddard and Matzerath 1986, Friedmann 1986, Rodriguez and Feagin 1986, Feagin and Smith 1987, Moss 1987, Hall 1990, King 1990, Proulx 1990, Sassen 1991, Soldatos 1991a), but also the theme of urban internationality with specific reference to the European context (Labasse 1981, Soldatos 1990, Fabre 1991, FERE-Consultants 1991, Jeger 1991, Bonneville *et al.* 1992, Laumière 1993, Jalabert *et al.* 1993).

Even though the internationalisation process of the urban systems is a long-term one, it has been underlined, in particular, how some elements have emerged in recent years that indicate the rise of a *new generation of international cities* which characterise the end of the 20th century. This generation can be identified on the basis of three criteria:

- a temporal criterion regarding the entry of an urban system into the group of international cities, or the renewal of its international profile in recent periods (in the last fifteen or so years);

- a qualitative criterion, concerning the rise of cities whose international activity involves the fields of high technology and services;
- a criterion of the approach to international life, expressed by the fact that these cities develop a form of 'urban paradiplomacy' (public and private) that is both institutionalised (external relations offices, agreements signed etc.) and sophisticated (modern 'city marketing'), rapid and direct, even independent of the action of other government levels (Soldatos 1990).

The main characteristics of the international cities of the 'new generation' have been defined in this context. These indicate, in particular, thirteen factors concerning economic, financial, commercial and scientific relations, the position in the communication networks, the presence of international institutions, the activation of forms of 'urban paradiplomacy' etc.

It has been observed how, in reality, it is not possible to establish a clear-cut definition of an international city, because a single model of international city does not exist: there are different international levels and geographical scales. It would be more appropriate, therefore, to talk of the *cities' international functions* rather than of international cities, as various types of internationality exist: internationality is, in most cases, sectoral and incomplete (Rozenblat 1992).

This statement identifies two important dimensions of the phenomena of the internationalisation of cities: the degree of sectoral diversification of the international functions and their geographical range. The first allows to distinguish between '*complete*' *international cities*, endowed with a broad and diversified range of international functions, and '*incomplete*' *international cities*, specialised in one or few types of international functions. The second can instead lead to a differentiation between cities with international functions that are predominantly of a *continental scale* and international cities whose functions have a *global scale*.

Applying these two criteria together, a simple typology of international cities can be obtained (Table 4.1).

A third element in the interpretation of internationality concerns the relation between phenomena on the local scale of analysis and the supra-local scale. This regards the degree of *embeddedness of international functions in the urban context*, and expresses the extent of the integration of the latter with the other components of the city's economic and social system.

This allows the differentiation between two types of situations:

- those in which the international functions give rise to systematic relations of interconnection and exchange between the local and the supra-local networks of relations (situation of deep embeddedness);

- those in which the international functions tend to develop autonomously from the local networks, thus leading to the limited integration of the latter in the global circuits and the rise of phenomena of 'dualism' of the urban structures (situations of poor embeddedness).

Table 4.1
A typology of international cities

<table>
<tr><th></th><th></th><th colspan="2">Range of international functions</th></tr>
<tr><th></th><th></th><th>limited</th><th>broad</th></tr>
<tr><td rowspan="2">Geographical scale of international functions</td><td>continental</td><td>specialised continental international cities</td><td>'complete' continental international cities</td></tr>
<tr><td>global</td><td>specialised global international cities</td><td>global cities</td></tr>
</table>

The dimension of the local embeddedness of international functions can also be analysed with reference to a regional scale, i.e. distinguishing the international cities well integrated in their regional context from those that have developed their functions of excellence in the international field in relative autonomy from it. The emergence of situations of this second type has been interpreted in terms of the rise of the so-called 'city-states', and has given rise to representations of urban development on the international scale (especially in the European context) in terms of 'archipelagos' of islands of excellence, rather than of whole regions of integrated development (see, for example, Brunet 1996).

Finally, the question of the local embeddedness of cities' international functions has also been tackled with reference to the problems of *social integration*. On this point, the question has been posed of the 'inevitability' of the phenomena of social dualism in the international cities (Friedmann and Wolff 1982). Some authors have disagreed, stating that 'social synergy' can be considered as a decisive element in the processes of internationalisation of the cities, in particular for the continual renewal of the socio-economic structure that is the essential condition for the reproduction over time of their capacity to enter actively into the networks of international relations (Conti and Spriano 1990). Some studies (Tarrius 1989) have also shown how the emergence of international professional élite characterised by a high degree of geographical mobility and by lifestyles that are fundamentally independent of the specific local context of residence and work represent an important factor in the establishment of situations of social dualism in the international cities.[1]

The last important interpretative dimension concerns the ways the processes of internationalisation develop from the point of view of the attitude of local actors. On this question, two types of situation have been identified (de Lavergne and Mollet 1991):

- situations in which a 'pro-active' attitude is shown by local actors (local authorities, firms, public and private organisations of various kinds), which operate in unison, defining and implementing *explicit* strategies of internationalisation, as components of urban development policies;
- situations in which this widespread awareness of the internationalisation does not emerge, and the phenomena of internationalisation assume an *implicit* nature, in the sense that the initiatives of individual actors are not part of a general internationalisation strategy defined *ex ante*, but (may) find *ex post* coherence in the process of urban change and development.

This last interpretative dimension can be related to the previous one. It is in fact possible to imagine that the capacity of a city to define and pursue explicit strategies of internationalisation is linked to its strong or weak *identity* as local system from the point of view of its own international projection, i.e. to the extent of the internal awareness and cohesion expressed by the various local actors, which in turn appear to be directly related to the degree of embeddedness of the international functions in the urban context.

An analysis of the international functions of the Italian urban system in the European context: assumptions and methods

Studies of the phenomena of internationalisation in Italy have so far been rather limited from the geographical standpoint: in particular, no systematic studies exist on the internationalisation of the national urban system. Some information concerning the upper tiers of the urban hierarchy can be drawn from studies carried out at the European scale, such as those by Bonneville *et al.* (1992) and FERE (1991).

As far as analyses on the national scale are concerned, a recent study on the position of the Padania macro-region (i.e. the Po valley) in the European context (Fondazione Agnelli 1992) should be mentioned: this adopts a sectoral approach to the phenomena of internationalisation. The internationalisation of the economy of the Padania is examined on the basis of international trade and direct inward and outward foreign investment in the industrial sector (Alessandrini 1992). In addition, reference is not made to the local urban systems as units of analysis, as the traditional administrative divisions (regions and provinces) are used.

Information of various kinds on this issue - not only statistical and quantitative, but also qualitative - is contained in some research projects into the structure and dynamics of the metropolitan component of the Italian urban system, carried out through monographic analyses: it is worth recalling, on this point, the work on the Italian metropolitan system published in the framework of the *Progetto Milano* (IRER-Fondazione Agnelli 1986), the one on the same subject edited by Ugo Marchese (1989) and the one on the relationship between industrial dynamics and urban transformations developed in the framework of the Agnelli Foundation's research programmes (Borlenghi 1990).

Finally, the subject of internationalisation has been examined in the framework of the broad sector of monographic studies on individual cities conducted locally by research bodies, local authorities and associations of interests of various kinds.[2]

The shortage of systematic studies on the internationalisation of the Italian urban system prompted an 'exploratory' analysis of the subject, the results of which are summarised later in this chapter.

This analysis gives a breakdown both in spatial and functional terms. For the first aspect, it was decided not to limit the study to the upper tiers of the urban hierarchy, but to all centres, including small and medium-sized towns, with the intention of defining the pattern of the entire national urban system from the point of view of internationalisation, highlighting, together with the expected localisation of international functions in the major urban systems, any other local 'thickening' of functions, capable of revealing the existence of the potential for international integration.

The analysis considers a number of functions. Twenty variables were in fact examined, referring to six functional typologies: productive functions, financial functions, scientific and education functions, air links, fair and hotel functions, political and diplomatic functions.[3]

As far as the territorial unit of analysis is concerned, reference is made to the *local urban systems* used in the previous two chapters, as defined by data from the 1991 Census (ISTAT 1997). This option is justified on the basis of the considerations made in those chapters.

From the standpoint of the geographical scale of the international links examined, given the objectives of the research, reference was made to a European context where the option existed, limiting the study to relations with the *countries of Western Europe* (the 15 countries of the European Union plus Norway and Switzerland). It must therefore be underlined that the results illustrated here express the characteristics of the internationalisation of the Italian urban system with reference to this continental framework, and that an analysis referring to all the world countries could have led to different results. In effect, one of the possible developments of this analysis could be to extend it to international relations on the world scale, and to compare the results thus obtained with those relating to Europe, so as to examine in depth the phenomenon from the point of view of the interpretative dimension of the 'geographical range' of international functions, which was not taken into consideration in this research.

The study did instead examine the interpretative dimension relating to the degree of diversification of the international functions, analysing the sectoral variety in the endowment of these functions in the various urban contexts. Analysis of this aspect, although providing some interesting broad indications, did not provide results that can be considered conclusive. The set of functions examined does not completely cover the entire range of the main types of international city functions. This is because the 'exploratory' nature of the study meant making some important simplifications, in terms of not considering some functional typologies even of significant interest, ignored not due to options of a methodological nature, but because of the difficulties encountered in gathering complete and reliable statistical data for the geographical scale here adopted: this is the case, in particular, of cultural functions (museums, libraries, theatres and cultural events of international status), of functions connected to the mass media and telecommunications, and of sports events of international interest. Furthermore, particular emphasis was put on productive functions, not only because of their importance and pervasiveness for the processes of internationalisation, but also because of the greater availability of data in this field and of the relatively wider geographical diffusion of these functions compared to other functional categories.

Finally, some functional typologies were analysed only partially, again because of the problems connected to the availability of adequate statistics. Thus, for the transports, the survey was limited to air links, ignoring infrastructures and traffic flows related to other modes of transport; for the tourism only the existence of top-level hotels was taken into consideration, not considering international tourist flows; for the financial sector only banks and insurance companies are covered, ignoring other types of financial operators. A further possible line of development and deeper analysis could therefore be the broadening of the information base of urban functions, both through the integration of the range of functional typologies taken into consideration, and by enriching it with new variables not used in the present study.

The other two interpretative dimensions indicated in the introduction, that of the local embeddedness of international functions and that of the explicit or implicit character of the strategies of internationalisation, were not taken here into consideration. This is because they do not lend themselves to analyses of statistical and quantitative nature, but require a direct investigation of individual urban contexts.

The spatial pattern of the international functions in Italy

The Italian urban system from the point of view of the presence of international functions is fairly differentiated.

First of all, only just over half the local urban systems have international functions on the basis of the variables and criteria adopted: the data collected show in fact that 415 of 784 urban systems possess functions corresponding to at least one of the twenty variables considered.[4] As can be seen in Figure 4.1, these are localised unevenly throughout the country: in Northern and Central Italy, almost all the local urban systems are endowed with international functions, and only a few small Alpine and Apennine areas do not have any,[5] as well as some parts of Southern Tuscany, Northern Lazio and Umbria; in the South, instead, while there are some regions with a relatively diffuse endowment, such as along the Adriatic coast (Puglia and Abruzzo), there are others, such as Calabria and Basilicata, where most urban systems do not have international functions. An intermediate situation is found in Campania, where the existing international functions are concentrated in the central-northern coastal belt.

The localisation of international functions is also fairly limited in the Islands (Sicily and Sardinia), where they are concentrated almost exclusively in the main urban systems and in some particularly renowned tourist localities.

The general characteristics of the geographical pattern of international functions emerge from Figure 4.2, which illustrates the quantity of the various local urban systems' overall endowment with reference to all the twenty variables examined.[6] This highlights the simultaneous presence in Italy of two models of internationalisation in terms of the localisation of international functions.

The first model, which regards the urban system of the Centre-North, is characterised by the existence of widespread international functions in the fabric of small and medium-small cities, alongside the numerous ones found in the major urban systems. From the point of view of the spatial structures, axial and reticular patterns can be observed overlapping with the consolidated polarised structures.

In particular, this model is geographically structured along three main axes:

- a Po valley axis which, starting in Turin, runs through the urban systems of Eastern (and especially North-eastern) Piedmont to the close-knit network of centres in Lombardy pivoting on Milan, and continues through the very thick and articulated urban fabric of Eastern Lombardy, Veneto and Friuli-Venezia Giulia;

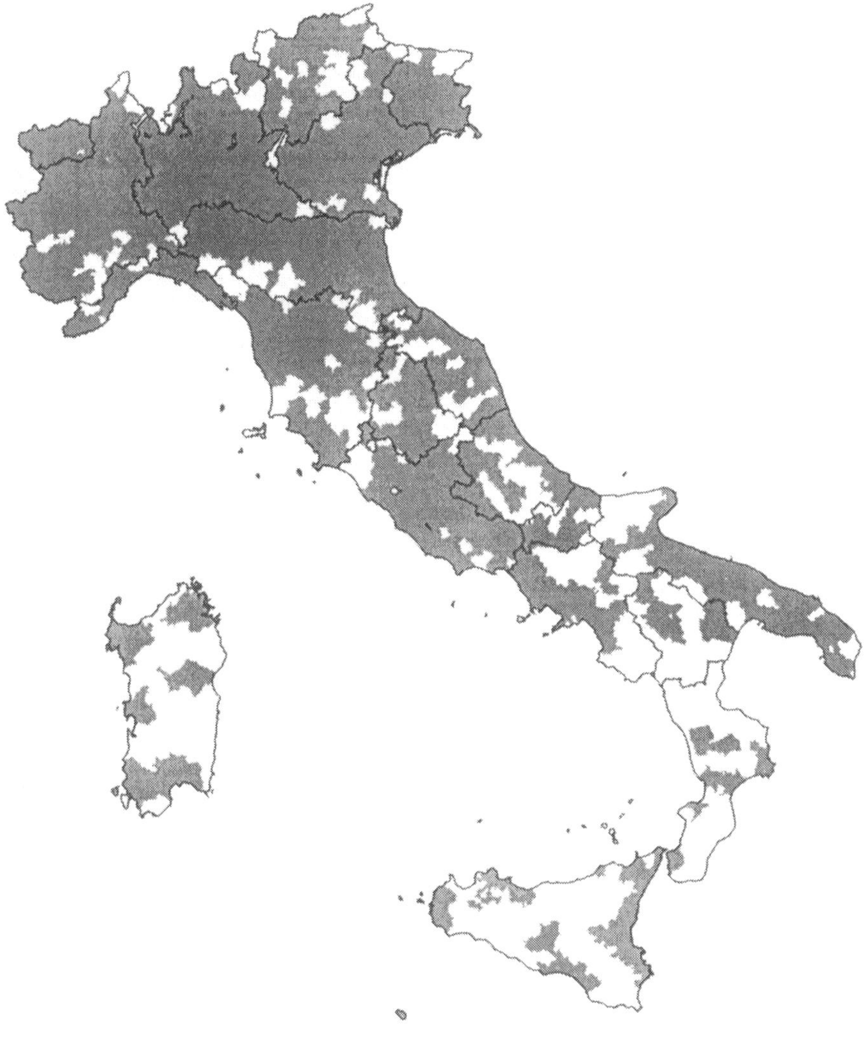

Figure 4.1 Localisation of international functions

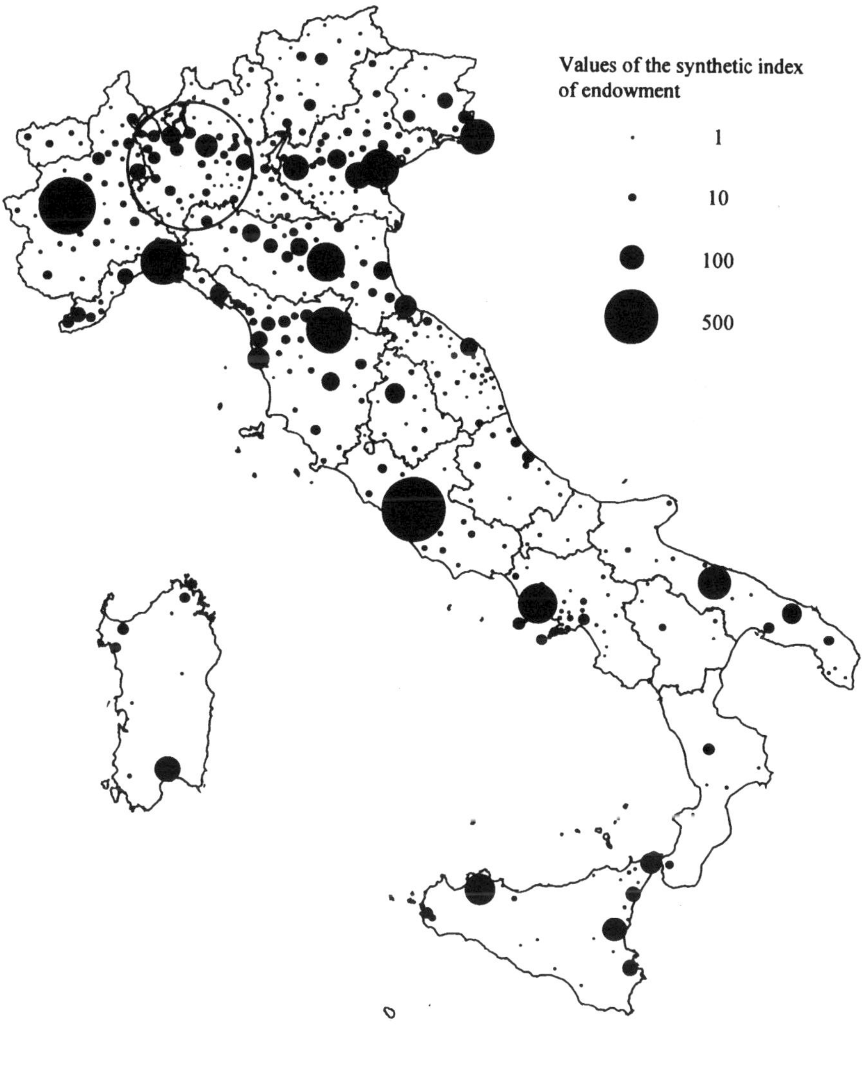

Figure 4.2 Total endowment of international functions

- an Emilia-Romagna and Adriatic axis that branches off from the previous one, involves the whole urban system of Emilia (and in particular the centres aligned along the 'Emilia Route') and the coastal belt of Romagna and Marche, reaching as far as Abruzzo;
- a Tyrrhenian axis, including the coastal belt of Liguria, the coast of Northern Tuscany and the close-knit network of medium-sized centres of the lower Arno valley as far as Florence.

A second model characterises instead Southern Italy and the Islands, typified by a more polarisation of functions in the main cities and the more limited involvement of medium and medium-small centres. The territorial structure of the international functions thus appears still to be organised more by poles than by axes or networks. Nevertheless, there is a certain variety of situations in the framework of the areas covered by this second model. For example, an axial pattern can be found along the Abruzzo coast which is, as has been said, the continuation of the Adriatic axis. Patterns of this axial type, even if essentially involving the main urban systems, also emerge in Central and Southern Puglia and in Eastern Sicily.

Urban structures tending towards the network type also emerge, even if in contexts of accentuated polarisation, in the Naples area (especially south of the urban system) and, in Lazio, in a wider area around Rome. This aspect can perhaps be interpreted as the symptom of a possible transition of the Lazio region towards a model similar to the one prevailing in the Centre-North, even if a process of this kind cannot, however, be isolated from the continuance of the phenomena of accentuated polarisation of the international functions in Rome.

Situations of greater fragmentation can instead be found - with the partial exception of Eastern Sicily - in the Islands, where the range of international functions is mainly limited to the main urban systems and those with a decided vocation for tourism.

No axial patterns crossing the country emerge to connect the Tyrrhenian and the Adriatic coast, not even the Naples-Bari line, seen by many as a key element in the future spatial structure of the Mezzogiorno. Finally, for Calabria, Basilicata and Molise, a situation of general structural weakness emerges from the point of view of international functions, with a poor level almost entirely concentrated in the main urban systems.

Observations that largely converge with what we have just noted on the basis of the analysis of the absolute endowment of international functions emerge from the examination of the *relative endowment*, i.e. the endowment in relation to the population of the local urban systems. Figure 4.3 illustrates the spatial differentiation of the values of a synthetic indicator of international functions, defined by the relation between the synthetic indicator of absolute endowment (used to construct Figure 4.2) and the population of the urban systems in 1991.[7]

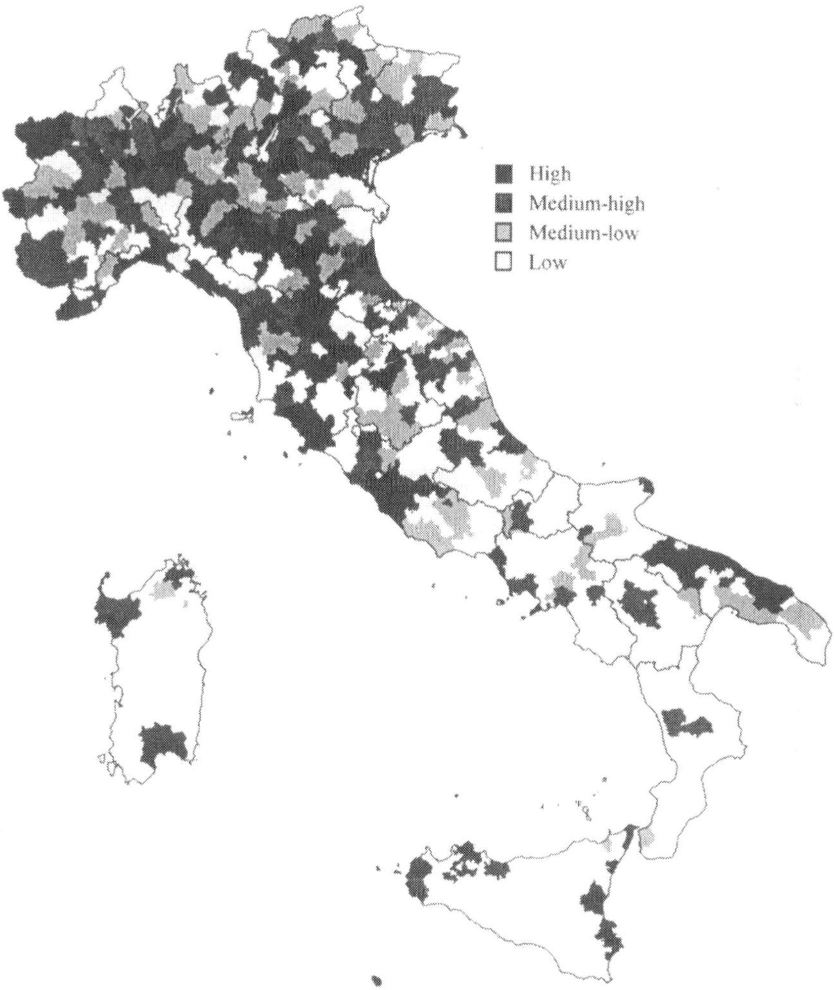

Figure 4.3 Total endowment of international functions in relation to the population

This shows fairly clearly the existence of a North-South gradient, the only significant exception to which is represented by Puglia; furthermore, most of the spatial patterns identified on the basis of the analysis of the absolute endowment are confirmed.

More detailed analysis of the relative endowment of international functions can be made through the examination of the differences between real (absolute) endowment and the theoretical endowment of the various urban systems as calculated from their demographic size.

In particular, some interesting patterns emerge from observation of the *positive or negative deviation* (Figure 4.4). First of all, it can be noted how the urban systems with a negative residue are the great majority, while there are only 72 characterised by a positive residue (17%). This is a consequence of the fact that the latter include most of the large urban systems, which have substantial residues, thus balancing the large number of smaller urban systems with negative residues. In effect, the group of urban systems characterised by a positive residue includes 12 out of the 15 urban systems that constitute the metropolitan tier of the Italian urban system on the basis of the analysis of the endowment of international functions (Milan, Rome, Turin, Genoa, Florence, Verona, Venice, Bologna, Naples, Bari, Padua, Trieste, Palermo, Catania and Cagliari: see the next section); of these, only Catania, Bari and Naples have a negative rating, and this appears particularly high for Naples.

These results demonstrate the continuing existence of phenomena of functional 'indivisibility' and 'critical mass' effects (Soldatos 1991a) for the international functions considered.

This indication is confirmed by the fact that there are also 22 main urban systems among those with a positive residue value: they are mainly distributed in the regions of the Centre-North (5 in Tuscany, 4 in Emilia-Romagna, 3 in Piedmont and Liguria, 1 in Lombardy, Veneto, Friuli-Venezia Giulia, Marche and Umbria), with only 2 in the South and Islands.

Of the group of urban systems with a positive residue, numerous have a mainly tourist-based economy: these are very largely urban systems characterised by a limited residential population, together with some more 'evolved' tourist resorts of a larger demographic size. Finally, a further 14 urban systems are identified that are marked by a positive residue value. These constitute a heterogeneous group both from the point of view of size of population and of their functional structure, and are distributed mainly in Central and Northern Italy (Tuscany, Emilia-Romagna, Lombardy, Marche, Piedmont, Liguria and Trentino-Alto Adige).

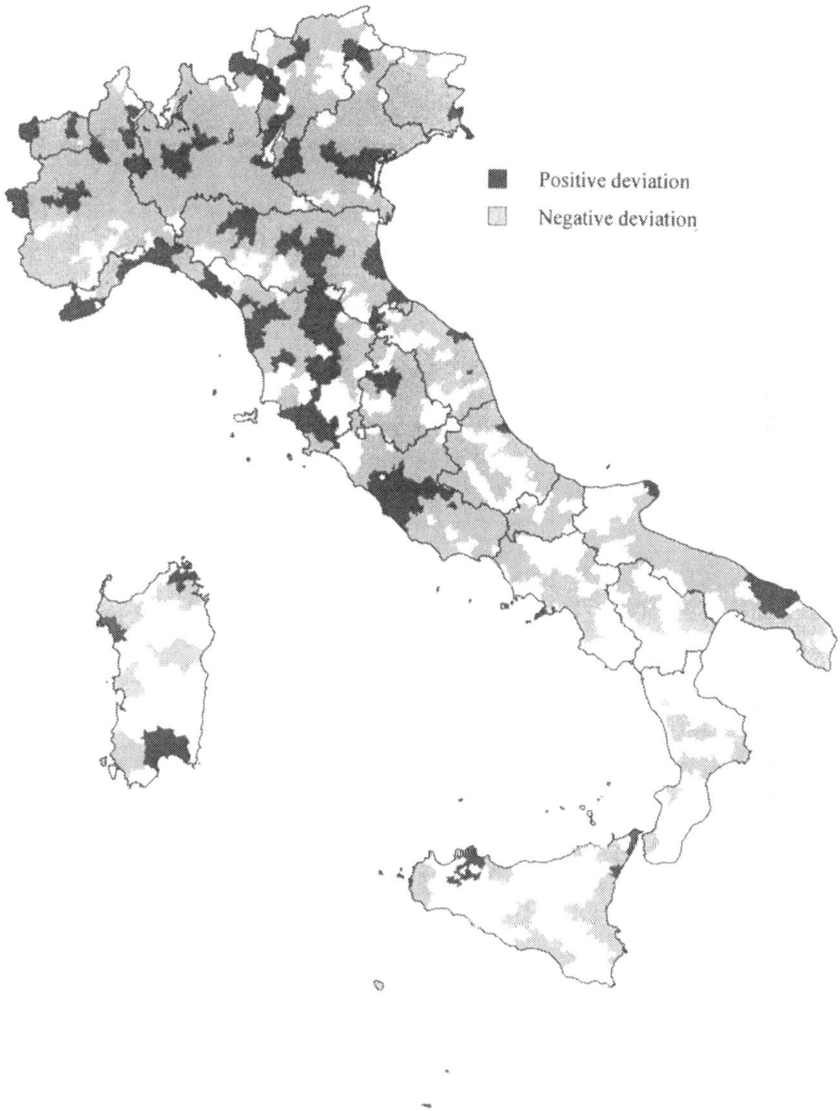

Figure 4.4 Deviations of total endowment from 'theoretical' endowment related to the population

The upper tier of the international functions: the 'metropolitan' urban systems

Table 4.2 gives the data referring to the urban systems that have the greatest range of international functions.[8] The table can be read in two ways:

- the variables are listed (by column) on the basis of their diffusion in the Italian urban system, i.e. the number of urban systems endowed with the corresponding functions;
- the urban systems are ranked (by row) on the basis of the number of variables they have.

Firstly, the existence emerges of accentuated disparity between the different variables in terms of spatial 'selectivity': the most common variables belong to the category of productive functions and regard in particular the export of commodities and services (exporting firms, and import-export companies); to these must be added the variables concerning firms' direct foreign investment (inward and outward), while the variable concerning actors participating in European Union research programmes is fairly widespread. The greater degree of selectivity emerges instead for the variables of a financial nature, in addition, naturally, for the one on international air links.

The greatest concentration of international functions is found in the twelve main urban systems corresponding to the 'metropolitan areas' envisaged in law no. 142 of the 1990.[9] The only 'extras' are represented by Verona, Padua and Trieste, confirming (and supported by the position of Vicenza and Udine) the good overall endowment of the multi-centred urban network of North-eastern Italy. These first 15 urban systems will therefore be considered by convention as constituting the *metropolitan tier* of the Italian urban system.[10]

At the *first level* there are Milan and Rome: they possess all the twenty variables considered, and thus define the *level of excellence* in the Italian urban system. The two cases are considerably different, however, both from the point of view of the overall number of functions and from the sectoral standpoint.

Milan's overall endowment is considerably more substantial than Rome.[11] The primacy of Milan is seen in sixteen of the twenty variables considered, with particularly accentuated predominance over the entire national urban system for 'market' production variables (headquarters of foreign companies, Italian companies represented abroad, exporting firms, import-export companies), for financial functions, above all incoming ones (headquarters of foreign banks and insurance companies) and for fair and exhibition functions.

Table 4.2
The international functions in the main local urban systems

Local Urban Systems	Exporting Firms	Export/Import Firms	Foreign Companies In Italy	E.U. Research Programmes	Italian Companies Abroad	Hotels	Trade Fairs And Exhibitions	Consulates	Bre Networks	Agreements Between Universities	Italian Banks Abroad	Bc-Net Networks	Scholarship Awarding Bodies	Foreign & International Institutions	Foreign Chambers Of Commerce	City Co-Operation Networks	International Flights	Foreign Banks In Italy	Italian Insurance Companies	Foreign Insurance Companies
Milan	940	978	280	133	74	24	51	15	5	84	16	9	9	20	13	4	806	45	4	32
Rome	86	491	34	90	11	22	9	14	19	30	9	10	30	66	6	1	682	8	1	6
Turin	221	119	52	57	29	5	11	14	4	60	7	3	3	5	2	7	157		3	1
Genoa	52	124	19	34	6	3	7	15		9	1	1		2	2	4	68		2	10
Florence	115	313	14	33	7	16	16	12	2	31	1	2	1	2		2	96		1	
Verona	127	86	13	1	1	3	13	1	1	2	4		1	2	1		40	2		
Venice	59	29	7	12	2	17	3	15	2	24		1	1	2	1	1	159			
Bologna	185	86	18	31	15	3	20	5	1	8	1	4		4	2	3	97			
Naples	33	164	12	22	8	4	7	14	1	19	4	2	3		3	2	66			
Bari	47	130	6	15	1	6	6	11	2	5		2		3	3	1	6			
Padova	87	53	6	11	3	10	11		2	19	2	1			1			1		
Trieste	24	267	4	19	2	2	3	11		6			1	4	3				2	
Palermo	12	12	2	4		5	6	11		5	3		3		3	1	2			
Catania	2	13	1	6		3		8		7		2	1	1	1	1	18			
Cagliari	7	11	7	10			1	9	1	3		3	3			2	11			
Bergamo	145	64	27	8	8	1	2	2	1	1	3									
Brescia	104	58	8	7	5	1	1		1	5			1	1						
Vicenza	78	37	5		2		11		1		1	1	1			1		1		
Udine	98	86	5	4	3		2		1	2		1	2					1		
Modena	63	65	4	8	1	2	3		2	3	2	1								
Ravenna	27	18	2	2	1		1	4	2			1				1				
Pisa	11	7	3	19	1	1			1	23	1		2							
Trento	20	14	6	7	2				1	5	1			1						
Parma	68	43	17	7	3	1	5	1		13										
Ferrara	10	14	2	2	1	1				4			1							1
Perugia	15	22		4		2	2	4	2	27		1								
Salerno	11	14	4	2		1		1	2	1		1								
Biella	39	12	1	4	2		4	1	1											
Varese	71	30	14	2	1		1		1				1							
Como	190	35	20	5	4	4	2							1						
Piacenza	19	35	6	3	1		4		1				1							
Reggio E.	72	76	8	3	2		2		1			1								
Rimini	13	15	1		1	5	9	6				1								
Ancona	12	13	1	4			4	5		8		1								
Lucca	39	18	5			1	1	1			1				1					
Messina	2	9		4		1	3	8		7					1					

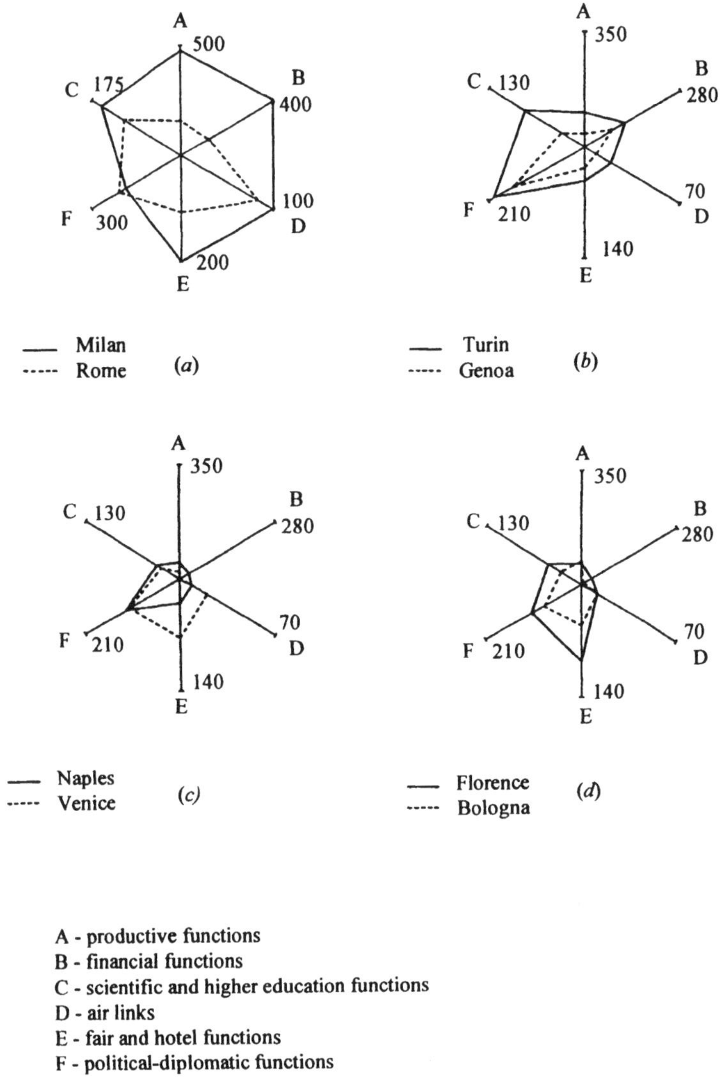

Figure 4.5 Functional profiles of the metropolitan local urban systems

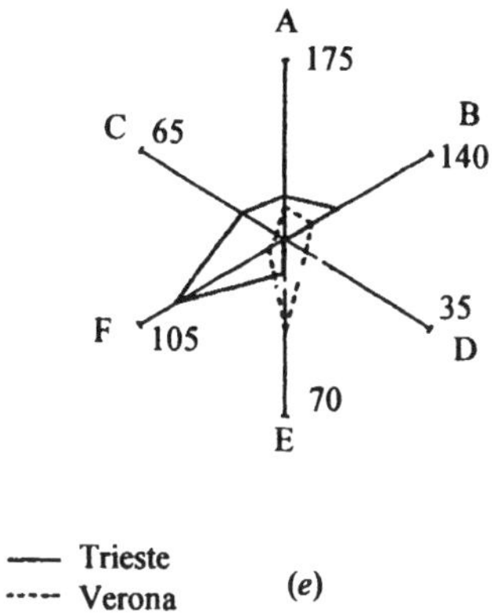

(*e*)

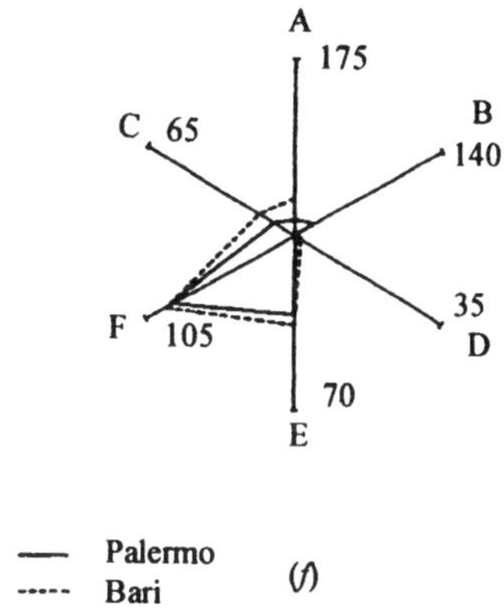

(*f*)

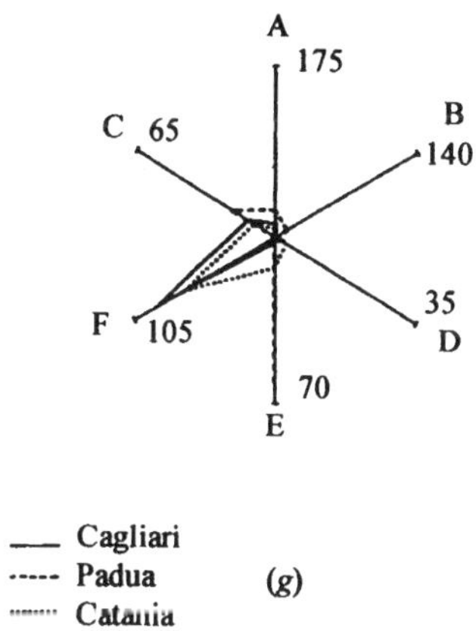

(*g*)

A - productive functions
B - financial functions
C - scientific and higher education functions
D - air links
E - fair and hotel functions
F - political-diplomatic functions

The primacy of Rome emerges instead for some variables of an institutional or quasi-institutional nature (foreign and international institutions, bodies awarding scholarships abroad, bodies participating in the BC-Net and BRE networks).

Finally, it is interesting to note how the intensity of air links with the countries of Western Europe is higher for Milan than for Rome.

From the point of view of the functional profiles, it can be seen (Figure 4.5*a*)[12] how Milan has an endowment that can be defined as 'complete', placing it with clear-cut predominance at the national level for five of the six categories considered, and overtaken by Rome only in the field of political/diplomatic functions. Rome, in addition to this last specialisation, is well endowed with scientific, training and hotel functions[13] (as well as in air links), accompanied by quite marked weaknesses in the fields of productive and financial functions.

At a *second level* we find Turin, Genoa, Florence, Venice, Bologna and Naples (Figure 4.5*b*, *c*, *d*).[14]

Turin, Genoa and Naples share a specialisation in political/diplomatic functions, as well as specialisation in the fields of scientific and training functions.[15] These elements in common are accompanied by specific characteristics of the three urban systems for other categories of functions: for Turin, a fair endowment emerges for all the other remaining four categories; in the case of Genoa, there is relative specialisation in financial functions, and a relative weakness in the other three categories; Naples shows a fair specialisation in fair and hotel and productive functions, and a particular weakness in financial functions and international air links.[16]

Florence, Venice and Bologna share a common specialisation in fair and hotel and political/diplomatic functions and a fair presence in scientific/training functions. Considerable differences emerge from a more detailed analysis of the former: Florence has a good endowment both in terms of international fairs and exhibitions and in top-level hotels; Bologna appears as the second national centre for fairs and exhibitions, but has decided weakness in the hotel sector; Venice, on the contrary, is characterised by a considerable number of top-level hotels, accompanied by only a modest number of international fairs and exhibitions. As far as the other categories of functions are concerned, Venice appears relatively well equipped in the field of international air links and clearly weak in productive functions, while Bologna and Florence are relatively less favoured from the first function but rather better endowed from the second.[17] Finally, one characteristic common to all three cities is the limited presence of financial functions, more evident in the cases of Bologna and Venice (where they are actually missing) and less accentuated for Florence.

A *third level* includes Verona, Padua, Trieste, Bari, Palermo, Catania and Cagliari (Figure 4.5*e*, *f*, *g*).[18]

The functional profiles of the first three urban systems indicate the existence of some complementary elements in the framework of the urban network of North-eastern Italy. In particular, Verona has a profile which, although in the context of an overall endowment of international functions that is decidedly more limited, appears in some ways complementary to that of Venice: in fact, while the latter has, as we have seen, a specialisation in hotel and fair facilities and political/diplomatic functions accompanied by a limited presence of productive functions and the lack of international financial functions, Verona has a relative specialisation - even if not particularly accentuated - in these last two categories. One further specialisation of Verona, this time in common with Venice, is in fair and hotel facilities. However, again in this case they are complementary cities: as we have seen, Venice's relative specialisation is in the considerable presence of top-level hotels, with a modest number of international fairs and exhibitions, while the situation of Verona for these two functions is exactly the opposite.

The pattern of the urban network of North-eastern Italy is completed by Padua and Trieste. The first urban system has neither international functions of a political/diplomatic nature nor international air links, and has a fairly accentuated relative specialisation in both hotels and fairs and exhibitions, with a fair but weaker endowment in scientific and training functions.[19] On the whole, Trieste has a fair endowment in all the categories of functions (excluding air links), with a relative specialisation in political/diplomatic functions (consulates and foreign institutions), linked to its border position and its role as gateway to some countries of Eastern Europe.[20]

Bari and Palermo have similar functional profiles, characterised by a relative specialisation in political/diplomatic functions and hotel and fair facilities. Alongside these, Bari has a fair endowment in the scientific and training functions (thanks to the variable concerning bodies participating in European Union research networks) and in productive functions,[21] while Palermo, characterised by relative weakness in the field of productive and scientific/training functions has three banks represented abroad. The two urban systems have practically no direct international air links.

The last two urban systems, Catania and Cagliari, have a rather limited endowment of international functions and fairly similar functional profiles, characterised by an accentuated specialisation in political/diplomatic functions. With reference to the other categories of functions, a certain specialisation emerges only in the scientific/training functions (with Cagliari slightly more specialised).[22]

The lower tier of the international functions: the 'non-metropolitan' urban systems

Below the upper tier, which identify the greatest concentrations of international functions, there are a further 400 local urban systems which can be considered as a *non-metropolitan tier* of the Italian urban system for the aspects examined. They represent a very mixed group, both from the sectoral breakdown of functions and from the point of view of their overall endowment, but they can be classified on the basis of these two criteria into a number of fairly homogeneous typologies:[23]

1. *complete*: endowed with five categories of functions (and missing only that of international air links);
2. *articulated*: with four categories of functions and missing only one category (other than that of international air links);
3. *relatively articulated*: endowed with three categories of functions and missing two (other than that of international air links);
4. *bi-specialised*: with only two categories of functions;
5. *mono-specialised*: with only one category of functions;
6. *exporters*: characterised by an endowment of international functions limited to the export of goods and services (i.e. only the variables concerning exporting firms and import-export companies);

The *complete* and the *articulated* local urban systems constitute a small group whose high degree of functional diversification approaches that of the urban systems included in the metropolitan tier of the national urban system. There are 24 urban systems, most of them are localised in Northern and Central Italy: 4 in Lombardy, Emilia-Romagna and Tuscany, 2 in Piedmont, Trentino-Alto Adige and Marche, 1 in Veneto, Friuli-Venezia Giulia and Umbria; while in Southern Italy there are 1 in Campania, Sicily and Sardinia.

The *relatively articulated* local urban systems is a group of 34. A fair number of them are localised in Southern Italy: 4 in Puglia, 1 in Abruzzo, Basilicata and Calabria. Nevertheless, the largest amount of urban systems are in Northern Italy. It is worth noting the presence in this group of industrial urban systems of small and medium-sized firms, such as Prato, and of important tourist resorts, such as San Remo.

The *bi-specialised* local urban systems are made up of two sub-groups: those bi-specialised in productive and scientific/training functions and those bi-specialised in productive and in fair/hotel functions.

The first sub-group consists of 60 local urban systems, scattered mainly in Central Italy (including part of Lazio), as well as in Piedmont and Western Lombardy and in some areas of Western Emilia-Romagna; there is a more sporadic presence of this type of urban systems in North-eastern Italy, along the Adriatic coast and in Southern Italy (although in

Sardinia they represent, in reality, a very high proportion of the total number of urban systems with international functions).

The second sub-group is more heterogeneous, including on the one hand medium-sized local urban systems whose fair endowment of productive functions is flanked by the presence of specialised tourist and/or fair functions, and on the other mainly tourist centres characterised by the, sometimes minor, presence of productive international functions. The group of local urban systems *mono-specialised* in fair and hotel functions is rather more uniform, made up of towns centred decidedly on tourism, such as Capri, Bardonecchia, Limone sul Garda and Fiuggi.

The *mono-specialised* local urban systems are mainly specialised in productive international functions. They include about half of the 'non-metropolitan' local urban systems and can in turn be subdivided into groups of the same size: those systems with international functions *not limited to exporting activities*, and the *exporting* urban systems.

The first includes about one hundred local urban systems, with considerable differences in the size of their endowment. The geographical pattern nation-wide of this type of urban systems shows considerable localisation in North-eastern Italy, and in particular in Eastern Lombardy, Veneto and Trentino-Alto Adige (to which should be added some areas of Emilia-Romagna), but also significant diffusion in Piedmont. There is also a certain presence in a limited area between Marche, Abruzzo and Lazio, as well as in Molise. Some typical industrial urban systems of small and medium-sized firms are also included in this group, such as Carpi, Santa Croce sull'Arno and Montebelluna.

The *exporting* local urban systems also constitute a group of about one hundred, distributed nationally in a rather more uniform manner, if compared to the previous typology: although there is a certain diffusion of this type in Northern Italy (especially in the North-east), a significant presence can also be observed in some regions of the Centre (such as Marche) and the South (such as Puglia, Campania and Sicily).[31]

Finally, some particular types of urban systems emerge, characterised by their *a-typical specialisations*, being bi-specialised in productive and political/diplomatic functions, in productive and financial functions, in scientific/training and fair and hotel functions; and mono-specialised in financial functions, in scientific/training functions, in political/diplomatic functions.

Models of internationalisation in the Italian urban system: an interpretation

The geography of the international functions in Italy appears to be characterised by the simultaneous presence of two different models of integration in the European context.

The first characterises Northern and Central Italy (excluding Lazio). In this areas, the diffusion of international functions in the framework of a dense and articulated pattern even of small and medium-sized urban systems marks the rise of the spatial model that prevails in the 'European semi-peripheries undergoing integration': that of 'interconnected networks' (Dematteis 1996), in which small and medium-sized cities are capable of gaining direct access to the international networks without necessarily passing through the regional and national major urban systems.

In Southern Italy and in Lazio, there is instead a high concentration of the international functions in the main urban systems and only a limited spread to small and medium-sized urban systems. This situation allows the assumption that, in this part of the country, the dominant model in the 'poorly integrated European semi-peripheries' continues to exist: that of the 'hierarchical networks' (Dematteis 1996), in which the small and medium-sized cities do not have direct access to the international networks, but need the mediation of the closest regional and national major urban systems.

Figure 4.6 gives the overall representation of the Italian urban system from the point of view of the geographical distribution of the various typologies of urba systems that emerge from the previous analysis, which are the basis for some synthetic observations.

A certain differentiation emerges in Northern Italy, seen in a tendency towards greater sectoral variety of the international functions in the North-West (Piedmont, Liguria and Western Lombardy) compared to the North-east (Eastern Lombardy, Veneto and Trentino-Alto Adige), characterised as a whole by greater sectoral specialisation, in particular in productive functions, and by a sectoral diversification of the international functions that is essentially limited, with a few exceptions, to the main urban systems. The other regions of the Centre-North show, as a whole, a fair sectoral variety of international functions; this is more evident in Emilia-Romagna, Tuscany and Friuli-Venezia Giulia and less marked in Umbria and Marche.

In Southern Italy the situation of Puglia stands out: it appears characterised by a fair degree of sectoral variety of international functions (and still with a good overall endowment in the field of productive functions). In other regions it also possible to identify the symptoms of a possible development of processes of internationalisation based (wholly or in part) on functions other than productive or political/diplomatic ones: this emerges clearly in Lazio with reference to scientific/training functions, but is also true in the cases of Campania, Sicily and Sardinia for tourist functions, even if in a context of lesser general diffusion of international functions.

Figure 4.6 Local urban systems according to their endowment of international functions

It is also possible to draw from Figure 4.6 elements for a tentative identification of certain *general models* of spatial organisation of the international functions in the framework of the Italian urban system.

In some areas there is a tendency to structure the distribution of international functions in *concentric circles*, seen in the presence around the 'metropolitan' urban systems of a number of surroundings endowed with a gradually declining degree of variety of international functions: according to the classification introduced, these are respectively *complete* and *articulated* urban systems, *relatively articulated* urban systems, *bi-specialised* ones (above all in productive and scientific/training functions) and *mono-specialised* ones (especially for productive functions).

This type of pattern combines (and is modified as a result) with two further models that appear to be emerging, that can be expressed in terms of gradients. Firstly, there is a *negative West-East gradient* in Northern Italy, in terms of continuity of the concentric circles indicated. Secondly, there is a *negative North-South gradient*, that regards not only the continuity of concentric circles but also their 'thickness', as well as the 'density' of urban systems at the metropolitan tier and their reciprocal interconnection.

This last gradient marks the gradual passage from models characterised by greater articulation and spatial integration to ones that are spatially more fragmented: from the network model, to that of interconnecting axes, to that of simple axes, to that of 'archipelagos and islands'.

It appears clear how these general trends are not obeyed rigidly in the geographical distribution observed, but how, on the contrary, there are considerable distortions and deviations from the expected patterns. While joint consideration of them can provide useful elements for the purpose of reaching an initial, synthetic interpretation of the phenomena examined on the macro scale, these should be considered, however, simply as provisory hypotheses deriving from some repeated features observed, and thus as a starting point for further checks and analyses.

Problems and prospects for the European integration of the Italian urban system through international functions

The existence of a remarkable geographical differentiation in the Italian urban system about its international openness in the European context emerges both from the point of view of quantity (i.e. in terms of the size of the endowment of international functions) and of quality (i.e. in terms of the predominance in different parts of the country of different models of integration on the continental scale).

Although the differentiation observed may to some extent be emphasised by the nature of the variables taken into consideration, it is clear that it implies different problems and prospects for the various geographical components of the Italian urban system from the point of view of European integration through international functions.

The overall image emerging from the analysis confirms the nodal position of Milan in the framework of the urban system of Southern Europe: it appears, in fact, as quite clearly the most 'European' Italian city, benefiting from its dual role as the southern tip of the continent's 'central backbone' and as a fundamental element of the new south European axis. The latter seems to involve not only the Po valley in the narrow sense, but all of Northern Italy and most of the Centre, structuring itself locally on axes and networks. Rome remains a city of European rank, but it appears to have a smaller variety of international functions, and it is characterised by a profile that is linked to its institutional role. For Southern Italy, the role is confirmed as part of the European periphery, essentially characterised by a marginal position compared to the main lines of European spatial integration, even though some significant development potential is emerging in given regional structures.

In general terms, the medium and long term prospects for the different regional urban systems in the processes of international integration on the continental scale seem to be bound, as well as to the overall quantity of international functions possessed, to the *degree of polarisation* of the functions around a dominant centre and their level of *sectoral articulation* (see the previous section).

On the first aspect, it is possible to hypothesise that the situations of non-accentuated polarisation, characterised by a significant capacity of direct access to the international circuits for a number of centres, show elements of advantage if compared to more markedly polarised situations. This is because in these situations, the resources of a multitude of local actors are activated, which in turn is a condition for the full valorisation of the endogenous development potential of the region as a whole. As the reaching of positions of excellence in the international urban hierarchies requires the presence of a given 'critical mass' of factors (Soldatos, 1990), it is possible to identify the most favourable situations in the regional contexts that, alongside the presence of a range of centres characterised by international functions of a certain importance, have a higher level international city.

As far as the sectoral structure is concerned, it can be presumed that a broad diversification of international functions also represents a factor of advantage for the areas concerned, if compared to situations where there is a tendency towards specialisation in one (or only a few) sectoral types of functions: openness of a 'multi-dimensional' kind undoubtedly represents a factor of 'stability' for the international integration of a given regional system, in that it can generate a greater capacity to conserve its own position in the supranational context when faced with the changes, the disturbances and the competitive challenges that emerge continually on the scale of the international networks and circuits.

On the basis of the previous considerations, a hypothesis of differentiation of the various regional urban systems can be put forward, combining the three analytical criteria used so far, i.e. the overall endowment of international functions, their degree of polarisation around a dominant centre, and their degree of sectoral diversification.

The most favourable prospects obviously seem to be for the regional systems with a conspicuous overall endowment of international functions, accompanied on the one hand by a wide distribution of them in the regional urban network, and on the other by a high degree of sectoral diversification. This type of situation is exemplified by the case of Lombardy, which can add to these characteristics the presence of a pole of absolute excellence.

Intermediate situations are found where there is an overall endowment of international functions of a significant size accompanied by a high degree of polarisation of functions on a single centre (and by the consequently limited involvement of the small and medium sized cities in the urban network), or by their poor sectoral diversification. A situation that appears to be of the first type emerges in Piedmont, while the second type can be exemplified by the case of Veneto.

Finally, a lower degree of 'preferability' can be associated with situations which have a good overall endowment of international functions with a high degree of polarisation of them on a single dominant city as well as a limited level of sectoral diversification: this type of situation can in part be exemplified in the framework of this study by Lazio.

The same typologies of situations can also refer to contexts with a more limited overall endowment of international functions. Thus, it is possible to identify regional urban systems with a not particularly large endowment of international functions, but characterised by a low degree of polarisation around a single dominant centre and by a fair level of sectoral diversification: to a certain extent, Puglia has these features. In the same way, in other contexts with a limited overall endowment of international functions, it is possible to differentiate situations with high polarisation associated with a fair sectoral articulation from ones of limited polarisation on a single centre but with poor sectoral diversification: they can to some extent be exemplified, on the basis of the analysis carried out, respectively by the cases of Campania and Sicily. Finally, the least favourable mid and long term prospects seem to be linked to situations of relatively limited endowment of international functions accompanied by a high degree of polarisation and poor sectoral diversification: these characteristics are in part seen in Sardinia.

Faced with these geographical disparities in the situation observed and in the prospects for the European integration through international functions, the problem is posed of the opportunities and the forms of promotion of the processes of strengthening the areas that are currently disadvantaged from the aspect in question, especially the South of Italy.

On this point, it seems necessary, first of all, to exploit the potential that, as we have seen, can be identified in certain spatial contexts, i.e. activate processes to enhance existing specialisation in the field of international functions.

While the prospects of greater European integration of the South appear to be linked to the opportunities of enhancing existing specialisations (and the creation of new specialisations on the basis of the natural vocations of the various areas), it should also be underlined that they cannot be separated from infrastructural factors, and in particular from the processes of updating the communications networks so as to reduce the accessibility gap compared to the continent's central and semi-peripheral areas.

On this, it has been suggested that rather than giving priority to 'heavy' infrastructures such as the gradual extension of the high-speed rail network or further intensification of North-South road and motorway system it would be more appropriate to give priority to other forms, such as air and telecommunications links. It has been said (see BfLR 1994) that, while improvement in the rail and road networks in terms of reduction in travelling times could help the integration of semi-peripheral areas into the European context, this will not be enough to bridge the geographical gap of the truly peripheral areas (such as the South of Italy), and will thus tend to perpetuate the continental 'core-periphery' model (an expression of 'hierarchical networks' in the urban system), instead of supporting the transition towards a 'multi-centrality' model (the expression of 'interconnected networks'; see Chapter 1).

These two components, the valorisation of existing specialisation (and the development of new ones on the basis of local vocations) and the upgrading of the infrastructural system, could thus help to promote a process of progressive integration on the European scale of the regional urban systems that are currently most disadvantaged in the Italian urban system. On the one hand, this process could mean a general intensification of the international connections of the parts of the national urban system that are the weakest in terms of the aspect considered; on the other, it could lead to the launching of a transition process from a model of international integration of the 'hierarchical networks' type to one of the 'interconnected networks' type in the contexts where the situation is already relatively more structured from the point of view of the endowment of international functions.

Notes

1 For a general interpretation of the effects of the processes of internationalisation on the social structure of the metropolises, see Martinotti (1993).

2 As an example, the case of Milan can be quoted. Numerous studies exist on this question and some refer specifically to the problems of international integration in the European context: among these are the research of the Progetto Milano as a whole, and some more recent analyses, such as those by AIM (Secchi and Alessandrini 1992), and the Associazione MeglioMilano (Camagni *et al.* 1994).

3 A - *Productive functions*: (A1) number of branches of foreign companies represented in Italy (Source: Reprint data bank, R&P Torino and Politecnico of Milano, 1994); (A2) number of headquarters of Italian companies represented abroad (Source: Reprint data bank, R&P Torino and Politecnico of Milano, 1994); (A3) number of exporting firms with a turnover of over 5 billion lire (Source: Cerved, 1994); (A4) number of foreign and mixed Chambers of Commerce (Source: *Guida delle Regioni d'Italia*, 1993-94); (A5) number of Italian bodies participating in the BC-Net networks (Source: figures supplied by Eurosportello of Turin at the Chamber of Commerce); (A6) number of Italian bodies participating in the BRE networks (Source: figures supplied by Eurosportello of Turin at the Chamber of Commerce); (A7) number of import/export companies (Source: *Annuario SEAT Finanza e credito 1995*).
B - *Financial functions*: (B1) number of branches of foreign banks in Italy (Source: *Annuario ABI* 1994); (B2) number of headquarters of Italian banks represented abroad (Source: *Annuario ABI* 1994); (B3) number of branches of foreign insurance companies in Italy (Source: *Guida delle Regioni d'Italia*, 1993-94); (B4) number of headquarters of Italian insurance companies with branches abroad (Source: figures supplied by ANIA).
C - *Scientific, technological and training functions*: (C1) number of Italian bodies participating in European Union research programmes (both as prime contractor and as partner) (Source: Cordis data bank, 1995); (C2) number of research agreements and contracts stipulated by Italian universities with foreign universities or bodies of the European Union (Source: data supplied by Conics, 1992); (C3) number of bodies providing scholarships abroad (Source: Noopolis data bank, January 1995).
D - *Transport*: (D1) number of weekly flights with international destinations (Source: *ABC World Airways Guide*, November 1994).

E - *Trade fair and hotel functions*: (E1) number of fairs and exhibitions of an international nature (Source: *Fiere e esposizioni 1993-94 in tutto il mondo*, Torino, Centro Estero Camere di Commercio Piemontesi, 1994); (E2) - number of top-level hotels (Source: *Guida Pirelli agli Alberghi d'Italia*, 1994).
F - '*International bureaucracy*' *and* '*urban paradiplomacy*' *functions'*: (F1) number of consulates (Source: *Guida delle Regioni d'Italia*, 1993-94); (F2) number of foreign and international institutions and United Nations and European Union bodies (Source: *Guida Monaci*, 1994); (F3) number of co-operation networks between cities promoted by the European Union (Source: *European Co-operation Networks*, Commission of the European Community, 1993).
The BC-Net (Business co-operation networks) is a network of company consultants and intermediaries created by the European Commission, in the framework of action aimed at facilitating contact between companies involved in international co-operation (DG XXIII). The purpose of the initiative is to enable companies to identify rapidly and confidentially potential partners in other member countries or other regions. The Bureau de rapprochement des entreprises (BRE) is an instrument created by the European Commission (DG XXIII) to promote non-confidential transational co-operation between small and medium-sized firms, using a network of correspondents in all member countries and in several others. Values for variable B2 were obtained by attributing differing importance to the various banks according to the size of their network of branches abroad and their type. Variable F1 includes honorary consulates.

4 For the two most common variables (exporting firms and import/export companies) a minimum endowment threshold was set: among local urban systems with only these variables (one or both), only those characterised by the presence of at least three exporting firms with the features envisaged (that is those with a turnover of between 5 and 10 billion lire and exporting over 50% of turnover, those with a turnover of between 10 and 50 billion lire exporting over 20% of turnover, and all exporting firms with a turnover of over 50 billion lire) and/or two import/export companies were considered.

5 The number of local urban systems truly without international functions could, in the area of the Eastern Alps, actually be lower than what emerges from the map because of the lack of availability of some information concerning exporting firms for certain areas of Trentino-Alto Adige.

6 Three different indicators were used to express the endowment of international functions of the local urban systems with reference to a number of variables considered together:
- a synthetic indicator of absolute endowment,
- a synthetic indicator of relative endowment and
- sectoral indicators.

Synthetic indicator of absolute endowment. The variables, which had originally been on different scales, were normalised, bringing them all into a scale of values between 0 and 100. The normalised values for the twenty variables were then added up for each local urban system, differentiating the variables by weighting coefficients, the expression of the different importance attributed to each one. In particular, the following weighting coefficients were used: for variables A1, A2, A3, A7, B1, B2, B3, B4, C1, D1, E1, E2, F1, F2, F3 coefficient 1, for variables A4 and C2 coefficient 0.5, for variables A5, A6 and C3 coefficient 0.25. The synthetic indicator of absolute endowment was thus defined by the sum of the normalised values of the twenty variables considered, multiplied by their respective coefficients.

Synthetic indicator of relative endowment. The synthetic indicator of relative endowment is defined simply by the relationship between the value of the synthetic indicator of absolute endowment of each local urban system and its 1991 census population. The 'residues' were instead defined by the difference between the value of the synthetic indicator of absolute endowment and a value expressing the 'theoretical' endowment associated with each urban system, based on its demographic size. The values of this theoretical endowment were obtained by multiplying the size of the population of each urban system by the total value of the synthetic indicator of absolute endowment for all the urban systems, and then dividing the result by the total populations of all the urban systems (with international functions).

Sectoral indicators. The sectoral indicators were constituted by partial sums, i.e. the total value (normalised and multiplied by the coefficients given above) for variables belonging to the same functional typology for each local urban system. It appears clear how the synthetic indicator of absolute endowment can thus be obtained as the sum of the sectoral indicators. Figure 4.2 illustrates the values of the synthetic indicator of absolute endowment. The value for the urban system of Milan is represented just by its circumference, so as not to hide surrounding systems.

7 See note 5. Figure 4.3 was constructed on the basis of the division into quartiles of the distribution of the values of the synthetic indicator of relative endowment.

8 Only the local urban systems possessing at least eight variables are included in the table and not all the 415 urban systems with international functions according to the criteria adopted.

9 The national law no. 142 of the 1990 and regional laws of the Sicilian Region define the municipalities which are the core of metropolitan areas, but without identifying their surroundings. The municipalities are those of Turin, Milan, Genoa, Venice, Bologna, Florence, Rome, Naples, Bari, Cagliari, Palermo and Catania.

10 These are also the 15 urban systems which show a value of over 100 on the synthetic indicator of absolute endowment.

11 The value of the synthetic indicator of absolute endowment of international functions is 1524 for Milan and 789 for Rome.

12 The diagrams with polar co-ordinates in Figures 4.5*a-g* give a representation of the values of the sectoral indicators that express the various urban systems' endowment of the six types of functions considered (see note 5). The scale of the axes is proportional to the maximum 'theoretical' value of each sectoral indicator, i.e. the value associated with a hypothetical urban system with a value of 100 in all the variables that contribute to the definition of the indicator in question.

13 For fair and hotel functions, it can be seen that for Rome there is a clear gap between a position of excellence in the field of top-level hotels (second only to Milan), while it shows serious weakness in the field of fair and exhibition functions.

14 Note the reduction in scale on the axes compared to Figure 4.5*a*, necessary to make the diagrams easily legible.

15 The specialisation of the three urban systems in political/diplomatic functions is determined above all by the variable concerning the presence of consulates (but also, especially in the case of Turin, the one concerning the membership of European Union networks of co-operation); the specialisation in scientific/training functions, as can be seen in the figure, is more accentuated in the case of Turin (where it is determined by the variable concerning research networks promoted by the European Union and by the one for

inter-university agreements) and is less marked in the other two cities.

16 In particular, in the field of productive functions, Turin is in the second position - even if at some distance from Milan - in the ranking concerning three variables (headquarters of foreign companies, headquarters of Italian companies represented abroad and exporting firms). It should also be observed that the specialisation of Genoa in financial functions is characterised by a clear gap between the accentuated weakness in the banking sector and strength in insurance. Finally, it can be noted that the fair endowment of Naples in the field of productive functions can be attributed to the variables concerning the headquarters of Italian companies represented abroad, the foreign Chambers of Commerce and import-export companies, and how the variable concerning Italian banks represented abroad is an exception compared to the overall weakness of the city in the field of financial functions.

17 In particular, Bologna is in a position of excellence for the variables concerning the headquarters of Italian companies represented abroad, exporting firms and companies participating in the BC-Net networks, while the same is true for Florence for the variable of import-export companies.

18 Note the further reduction in the scale of the diagrams.

19 This situation derives from the good endowment emerging both in terms of bodies participating in the European Union research networks and in terms of inter-university agreements.

20 This city shows a type of specialisation connected to this role also for productive functions, with a good endowment of foreign Chambers of Commerce and import-export companies. Finally, it should be noted that two of the thirteen Italian insurance companies represented abroad are based in Trieste.

21 This last feature is linked to the functions expressed by the variable concerning import-export companies and the three variables of an 'institutional' or 'quasi-institutional' nature (foreign Chambers of Commerce, companies participating in the BC-Net and BRE networks).

22 This situation is determined in both cases by the presence of some bodies that participate in the European Union research projects, and, for Cagliari, by the variable concerning bodies that provide

scholarships for abroad, and for Catania by the one concerning inter-university agreements.

23 The *complete*, *articulated*, *relatively articulated*, *bi-specialised*, *mono-specialised* and *exporting* urban systems are those endowed respectively with all productive, financial, scientific and training, fair and hotel, political/diplomatic functions, with four, three, two or only one category, and only with exporting functions (expressed by the variables of exporting firms and import/export companies). In classifying the 'non-metropolitan' local urban systems, the quantitative level of the endowment of international functions was taken into account together with the number of categories possessed, identifying different levels of size for each typology. This was done by subdividing the 'league table' of the local urban systems into quartiles for the productive, scientific/training, and fair and hotel functions, analysing the position of each urban system in these sections (while for financial and political/diplomatic functions, characterised by relatively limited diffusion, only the presence or absence was considered).

24 This group also includes a certain number of industrial districts such as Castelgoffredo, Solofra, Montegranaro and Bovolone.

5 The local milieu

Cesare Emanuel and Francesca Governa[1]

The role of the milieu and local networks in urban change

The change of a national urban systems is not only and directly related to the flows of relations and exchanges that circulate in the supra-local networks, but depends significantly on all of the resources of milieu characterising each local urban system.

To give a basic definition, the concept of milieu denotes the set of environmental conditions in a given urban system. The reference is not, however, exclusively to the conditions of the natural environment, but to all the social, cultural, political and economic characters that have accumulated in a certain place over the course of time and which can be understood as being specific properties of the place itself. The reconstruction of the process of stratification of the milieu's components thus allows us to grasp the diversities that characterise the urban system and that give each urban system exclusive features. However, if we want to understand the meaning and the role of the milieu in spatial change, reference only to the local dimension is not enough. Indeed, it is necessary to take a broader view and ask how the urban system fits into the socio-economic development processes at a global scale or, in other terms, how the specific properties of a certain place can be translated into the competitive advantages of the individual locality.

The milieu is a concept on two levels. On the first level, the set of the socio-cultural properties and features that make it up is the common heritage of local society, the territorial foundation of its identity. On the second level, the constituent characteristics of a specific milieu define not only the uniqueness and identity of each urban system, but also the local endowment of resources and development potential. Interacting with changes at wider scales through the action of local actors, the components of the milieu can help to determine the urban system's trajectories of change and evolution. The local potential that constitutes a given milieu works as a catalyst of the development process, but cannot be produced easily or rapidly according to the needs of the moment.

In this second meaning, the concept of milieu recalls the notion of *grip* (Berque 1990). This notion is proposed as keystone for the study of the relations of a given society with the physical and symbolic characteristics of the natural environment. It implies the acknowledgement of social relativity and 'subjectivity': the potential expressed by a given urban system, to become a resource in the development process, must be recognised as such and thus valorised by the action of local actors. Consequently, the components of the milieu do not have an absolute value, because it is not possible to talk about local attitudes and vocations expressed and defined once and for all. But they are constituted as resources in the development process only if and when they are recognised, interpreted, 'used' by a given social organisation.

In this process, local actors play a fundamental role. Particularly important is the set of co-operative or conflicting relations that is established between actors for the use, enhancement and reproduction of the components of the milieu. This set of relations is defined as a *local network*.[2] This network consists of 'pure' local actors, who act almost exclusively within the urban system, and of 'multi-level' local actors, who operate simultaneously at the local and the supra-local levels. In the change of a national urban system, the local network exercises a dual function of mediation: it acts both inside each urban system, as an element of cohesion in local network/milieu interaction, and outside, as a linking element with the supra-local level. The local network thus operates as a selector and decoder of the stimuli that arrive from outside, but also, and at the same time, as the gatherer and encoder of the potential that characterises the specific milieu of the urban system considered. The interaction between the local network and the milieu defines the specific local 'responses' to stimuli from the higher supra-local levels. The interesting thing is to identify how these stimuli are translated locally, determining specific ways in which actors and interests are organised and activating different components of the milieu. The analysis of the development of urban systems allows the identification of the interdependence between the concept of milieu and the concept of local networks, and between the endowment of endogenous potential and the organisational dimension of local actors.

The analysis of the milieu

The complexity that characterises the concept of milieu has many implications for the problem of empirical analysis and, in the end, for the very purposes of the analysis. The milieu of a given urban system, understood as a set of 'grips' or potentials which must be recognised and grasped through the action of local actors, reveals both an 'objective' and a 'subjective' nature. As an 'objective' fact, the components of the milieu define the specific properties of a given place; in 'subjective' terms, the value and the meaning given to these properties depends to a large extent on a social process expressed by the local networks and by their organisational changes. The same milieu's component and the same 'objective' fact can have, in different urban systems or in the same urban system at different times, a different value and meaning and therefore a different 'subjective' nature. The relation between these two aspects is clearly extremely complex to study: the (objective) facts are also always (subjective) values, and the values are also always the facts, or, in other terms, the quantity can never be completely isolated from quality (Berque 1990).

The elements that make up the ambivalent nature of a milieu can be referred, on the one hand, to the 'thickness' of the cultural and material accumulation that composes it, to illustrate local *endowment* of resources and possibilities; on the other, to the *organisational* forms of local actors, to outline the value and the meaning attributed to the specific local features in the milieu/local networks interaction process. The analysis of these two aspects clearly requires the preparation of channels of interpretation which, although complementary, can be separated, at least in an initial analysis.

The first channel aims at investigating and describing the differences that characterise a national urban system on the basis of the quantitatively and qualitatively unequal endowment distinguishing the milieu of its constituent urban systems. The analysis of this endowment, through a procedure of a quantitative nature (developed in the following paragraphs), allows the identification of the 'thickness' and the constituent features of the milieu of the urban systems considered.

The second channel focuses on the way in which the recognition and activation of the specific local features within the change of an urban system is achieved. The reconstruction of the milieu/local networks interaction process in two case studies (see below) allows the observation of the ways in which the urban systems function and evolve and, more specifically, the role played within them by the milieu and the local networks.

One way of looking at urban change that has useful indications for tackling the problem of the empirical analysis of the milieu is that of P. Soldatos (1990). Discussing a possible strategy to encourage the international expansion of cities, he notes the importance of a 'connective fabric', in other words of an internal environment of a multidimensional type whose various parts have harmonious reciprocal inter-relations. This connective fabric is the 'launching pad' that may be more or less favourable to the international expansion of an urban system in that it guarantees a more or less solid internal base. The concept of connective fabric can therefore be traced back to the concept of milieu: the analysis of the milieu can thus begin from study of the various parts, i.e. the various environments which make it up. In particular:

- an *environment connected to the quality of life*, that outlines the specific features of the urban system both from the point of view of its physical characteristics and from the styles of life within it;
- a *social environment*, concerning the demographic and social characteristics of the urban system as the basis for the identification of the presence or absence of links and synergies between the components of the various environments;
- a *cultural and scientific environment*, which involves the modes of production, reproduction and circulation of culture, the identification of the dominant cultural models and the ways in which professional technical and innovation skills are formed;
- a *labour market environment*, concerning the needs and strategies of enterprises, the state of the education system, the quantity and quality of the human resources;
- an *economic environment*, which outlines the organisation of the economic system and the diversification of the local productive fabric.

Each environment will be divided into a series of components that attempt to bring out the 'atmosphere' and the 'quality' specific to each urban system. The subdivision into environments and components is to be understood solely in terms of our purposes here: the specific features which characterise each urban system are expressed in the combination of the various factors and not in the simple listing of individual differences.

An empirical analysis: the 'metropolitan' milieu and its components

Assuming the analysis of the 'environments' described above as the starting point for the empirical study of the local milieu, the problem arises of the availability of adequate statistical sources from which to extract the data and variables required. In fact, not only do the later analytical passages depend on them, but also the very definition of the 'environments' in which the local milieu can be divided. The 1991 Census and the annual surveys of population, cultural consumption and school education are the source to define about one hundred variables that concern the characteristics of property assets and primary and secondary infrastructures, the dimensions of cultural provision and expenditure, demographic characteristics, economic position and employment status.

Much of this data is available only at the province level, and so this administrative unit has been adopted for the empirical analysis that follows. It concerns twelve cities indicated as 'metropolitan areas' by the national law no. 142 of 1990 - although not yet formally established - and by the regional law of the Sicily Region: Turin, Milan, Venice, Genoa, Bologna, Florence, Rome, Naples, Bari, Cagliari, Catania and Palermo. Trieste has been included in the group of the metropolitan areas because of the importance of its international role as highlighted in Chapter 4.

Five 'environments' have been considered: an *environment connected to housing and settlement conditions,* a *cultural and scientific environment*, a *socio-demographic environment*, a *labour market environment* and an *economic environment*. A factorial analysis applied to the variables concerning each of these environments has allowed the identification of sixteen factors, or components, interpreted on the basis of their correlation with the same variables. The pattern of these components allows the illustration of the basic features of each 'environment' in the thirteen metropolitan areas considered.

Housing and settlement conditions

This environment is defined by three components that give a picture of the morphological characteristics, the housing conditions and the services.

The first component is the expression of a pronounced compactness and vertical nature of the built-up area; it derives from the environmental characteristics connected to the *physical image of the built environment.* Its association with the formal qualities and the historical heritage constitutes a rather important feature of the cityscape, capable of influencing the processes of contemporary development and, above all, in localisation decisions for tertiary and quaternary activities. This characteristic is very different in the thirteen metropolitan areas: that of Naples is quite distinct from the others, but a pronounced image also distinguishes Milan, Rome, Genoa and Trieste. This derives both from the post-World War II building growth (stronger than elsewhere in Naples, Rome and Milan) and the physical morphology of the sites, which, in the cases of Trieste and Genoa, limits the availability of building land.

The second component is an indirect indicator of *housing quality* and the nature of housing stock. The distribution of the scores for this component in the Italian metropolitan areas is on medium and medium-high values, except the extremely high value of Catania. They are results have been achieved in the last twenty years through intense restructuring of the housing stock in Northern Italy and the construction of new housing in Southern Italy. They point out the gradual reduction in residential polarisation, overcrowding and, mainly in the South, the backlog of need accumulated during the decades of rapid urbanisation. A further confirmation of the improvement in metropolitan housing conditions can be seen in the third component that outlines the *provision of basic public services*. The scores for this component are quite high on the whole, even if Southern metropolitan areas are lower than the others.

Joint observation of the scores of the components that define this environment constitutes a synthetic, but in any case significant, indicator of the quality of metropolitan life. From this point of view, conditions of relative housing and social deprivation continue to exist above all in Southern metropolitan areas, like Catania, Palermo and Cagliari, where either housing quality or basic public services has a fairly low score. The improvements that have been made in the housing and infrastructures of these areas seem to be defective, and thus shortcomings still exist in terms of the efficiency and overall quality of the urban space.[3]

The cultural and scientific environment

The cultural and scientific environment is defined by three components: *cultural provision, local identification of university structures and their attractiveness*.

Publishing and the number of theatrical and musical performances represent the first indicator of cultural provision and vitality in the metropolitan areas. Indirectly they also represent a measure of the organisational and leisure capacities developed locally in these activities. This component shows the effects of the rather unequal distribution of publishing, with the highest scores in Milan, Rome, Bologna and Turin, where the major Italian publishers are located, although Naples and Venice also achieve good scores. The cultural identity of these metropolitan areas is also reinforced by the presence of major theatres and museums and by a consolidated 'cultural image'.

The second and third components refer more specifically to the characteristics of the scientific environment, in which the universities play a leading role.

The second component, defined by the high number of students, explains in this context the 'visibility' and the weight of universities in the metropolitan areas. These features are particularly pronounced in the minor metropolises, and especially the Southern ones, where the more limited diversification of the structures for scientific and cultural activities bring out local attachment to this institution. The role of the universities as a socio-cultural pole is lesser in the larger metropolitan areas, where there are more numerous opportunities of access to non-university bodies with the same educational purposes.

This component is to be interpreted together with the third one, given above all by the percentage of graduates in the course of the 1991-1992 academic year resident outside the region where the university is located. These data define the degree of attractiveness of some universities at the supra-regional level, linked to specific educational capacities and careers opportunities offered by some faculties, and to the relations between them and the economic environments. From this point of view, the scores obtained by the metropolitan areas differ partially from the previous ones. Venice and Bologna have the greatest university attraction; also above the average are Florence, Naples, Rome, Trieste and Bari. In North-western Italy, the presence of some decentralised dynamic and innovative universities outside the metropolitan areas considerably reduce the attraction of the larger and more 'central' ones: this explains, at least in part, the low scores obtained here by Milan and Turin.

Joint observation of the scores given for the three components confirms the marked connotation of the scientific and cultural environment of Bologna compared to the other metropolitan areas. There is also, however, a fair endowment of resources in Trieste, Rome, Milan, Florence, Venice and Naples.

The socio-demographic environment

This environment is defined by two components.

The first defines a *positive demographic change* that is maintained by the presence of extended families, by a substantial younger population, by a limited number of older people and single-member households. This demographic change is the expression of a natural increase in the population and characterises above all, as we have seen in other chapters, the more peripheral surroundings of the vast metropolitan agglomerations. The scores in this component are, however, especially pronounced in Southern Italy, where social values and customs continue to prize large families and their central role. On the contrary, the lowest figures are found in the metropolitan areas of Northern Italy, excluding Milan. In these areas, the natural trend is now negative, and economic and socio-cultural changes are encouraging the formation of smaller and smaller households.

The second indicator shows the *quality of human resources* and the demographic polarisation exercised by the metropolitan areas. High scores are found above all in the areas of Central and Northern Italy. In particular, in Rome and Milan the features of the demographic and social environment seem to be linked to the specific dynamism of their economic structures and functional specialisation.

Comparative examination of the scores for the two components confirms the presence of a particularly dynamic socio-demographic environment, capable of interacting positively with the other components of the local milieu, in Rome and Milan. In contrast, the metropolitan areas of Turin, Trieste, Venice and Genoa, where there is a weak endogenous demographic growth, modest inward migration and a limited inflow of skilled manpower and graduates, reveal crisis conditions.

The labour market environment

Some of the characteristics of the social environment are connected to those of the labour market. These are analysed through the economic position and employment status of population in the metropolitan areas and the features that persons in employment has acquired in each metropolitan area in relation to local productive specialisation. To identify this relation, the socio-economic groups (manual workers, self-employed, junior managers and office workers, entrepreneurs and professionals) have been sub-divided into the sectors of industry and services, and, within these, between those belonging to the 'intermediate' and 'innovative' manufacturing industries and the 'higher' level of services.[4] The results of the analysis reveal three distinct components that define the *manual worker structure (industry and services)*, *professional profiles of intermediate industry* and *those that concern higher services activities* and the *management of industry*.

The component of the manual worker structure has relatively high scores in almost all the metropolitan areas. The presence of manual workers remains particularly strong in the metropolitan areas where manufacture activities had been the driving force behind local development. The socio-economic pattern of these areas, although now being restructured and making significant sections of the workforce redundant, continues to be strongly marked by the presence of unskilled workers. On the contrary, the percentage of the population with a higher educational qualification and of the professionally most qualified workforce is low.

The second component is correlated mainly to those working in offices, technical and co-ordination activities in intermediate industry. It denotes quite clearly a form of local 'specialisation' of the employees. The scores show greater local selectivity for these socio-economic groups, present above all in Turin, Milan, Bologna, Genoa and Trieste, in other words in the manufacturing areas where some of the country's leading productive structures are localised.

These professional profiles, as with those of manual workers, constitute a resource created above all in major companies. In contrast to manual workers, however, their role is at present being enhanced and used in the restructuring of production based on the development of small and medium-sized firms and in the shift to services of the production processes of the large ones still in operation. In the evolution and transformation of industrial production in these areas they thus remain a main component of the labour market.

The third factor is correlated to the most innovative and elite professional profiles in the labour market. It marks the features of Milan and Rome, in which the processes of innovation and concentration of the functions connected to command and leadership of the socio-economic system have been more intense. The scores of this component point out, moreover, a deep difference between the metropolitan areas of Central/Southern and Northern Italy, which has unfavourable influences on the structure of the local milieu of Southern areas and on the quality of their change.

All the differences above mentioned are found in the total scores for the three components depicting the overall characteristics of local labour markets. In particular, one can note the continuing existence of fairly varied and qualified employment structures in the metropolitan areas of Milan, Turin and Genoa. However, the contemporary development processes, above all in Genoa and Turin, do not seem able to use fully the significant stock of human and technical resources accumulated during the post-World War II industrialisation.

The economic environment

The economic environment is defined as the share of employment in industrial and service firms. Firms are divided according to size (small, medium and large), the level of their functions (traditional, intermediate and innovative or higher) and the sector in which they operate. The analysis has allowed the definition of five components that highlight five forms of productive specialisation and organisation.

The first component derives from a group of variables that outlines an economic environment characterised by *integration between small and medium-sized industrial firms and complementary services*, and by innovative and dynamic forms of production. The scores show the presence of this productive organisation above all in the metropolitan areas of Bologna and Florence, where these activities have recently had a rapid rate of growth. The economic environment of these areas is very different from the others: only in Turin, Milan and Genoa this component show values slightly above the average. This can be attributed, at least in part, to phenomena of business 'incubation' and the development of new entrepreneurial initiatives in the more innovative sectors.

The second component explains the continuing existence of some features of a Fordist organisation of the production in some metropolitan areas. This could be defined briefly as the *characterisation in large traditional and intermediate industry*. This model of production is found above all in Trieste, Genoa and, partly, in Turin. Although offering a rich heritage of technological resources, plants and varied professional skills, it seems to constitute an element of inertia in development today, in particular for difficulties in reconverting this type of structure, as the situation of the industrial pole of Genoa exemplifies.

The third component highlights an economic environment characterised by the *integration between medium and large industrial firms and innovative services*. The scores attributed by this factor to the metropolitan areas show the existence of these features above all in Milan and Turin and, partly, in Naples and Catania. The position of Turin appears quite significant. Its economic environment seems to express new propulsive capacities in order to direct local development towards pathways of growth rather different to those of the past. Similar considerations can also be made for Naples and Catania, whose economic structure, although holding a leading position in Southern Italy, suffered seriously from the crisis and the restructuring of the state-owned firms.

The fourth component defines the *specialisation in functions of public administration*. This appears to typify in a preponderant manner only the metropolitan area of Rome. In the other metropolitan areas, the values recorded are minima.

The last component identifies the features of a not particularly evolved economic environment and a functional structure mainly linked to metropolitan tourist attractions. It has been defined as *characterisation in traditional services*. From this point of view, Venice has the highest score, followed by Rome, Naples, Florence and Milan, i.e. the places that, for various reasons, attract the greatest flows of tourists.

The joint observation of the scores of the components that outline the economic environment appears to be of little sense in that, as we have seen, rather different and sometimes not even comparable local forms of organisation and specialisation prevail. Only Milan, Rome, Bologna and Venice stand out for the more pronounced diversification of their economic environments compared to the other metropolitan areas. The absence of meaningful characterisations carries a negative weight instead in the cases of Bari, Cagliari, Catania and Palermo. Here, the economic environment appears de-structured or characterised by components not detected by the variables taken into consideration in this analysis.

Profiles and typologies of 'metropolitan' milieux

The differences and peculiarities of the thirteen metropolitan areas considered can be defined in further detail by comparing the *profile* of their own milieux. In the Figure 5.1, a profile strongly concentrated towards the centre depicts the presence of a not particularly thick and varied milieu. Vice versa, when the scores are quite high, the opposite conditions emerge of a thick milieu with considerable potential and resources usable in the local development processes. Fairly high values for only a few components indicate features of a sectorally specialised milieu.

On the basis of these results, and from the calculation of an 'index of heterogeneity', which measures statistically the form of the profile and attributes a value that falls as the variety of the components falls,[5] a typological classification of the milieu can be defined:

1. *thick and differentiated* milieu, characterised by high scores in almost all the components: Rome, Milan and Bologna;
2. *mixed* milieu, characterised by a good basic endowment and high scores in some components: Trieste and Genoa;
3. *sectoral* milieu, clearly specialised in some components: Turin, Naples, Florence and Venice;
4. *thin and fragmented* milieu, characterised by minimum scores in almost all components: Cagliari, Palermo, Catania and Bari.

It should be remembered that this classification derives from an analysis that considers only very partially and indirectly the way in which the milieu is used in the circuits of socio-economic and cultural exchange and interaction. However, it does lend itself to some concluding thoughts, bearing in mind the current development processes in the metropolitan areas.

The *thick and differentiated* milieu of Milan and Rome seem to conform to the characteristics of the development of these two metropolitan areas, expressed by their respective roles as economic, political and administrative capital cities. There emerges, in fact, not only considerable quality in the housing and services structure, in the advanced segments of the labour market and in economic specialisation, but also a high level of demographic and social dynamism suitable for reproducing and enhancing the remaining environmental components. The milieu of

Bologna, which attains points of excellence in the housing and services structure and in scientific and cultural facilities, seems capable of sustaining development change even higher than the already notable ones present in its productive and economic-cultural functions.

The *mixed* milieu of Trieste and Genoa seems to constitute a considerable potential of resources that, as a whole, are poorly valorised in the development processes of these two metropolitan areas. More careful consideration is required of the relationship between these resources and the networks of local actors in order to understand what is holding back the transformation of potential local values into active values that can be exported through the external exchange and interaction circuits.

The *sectoral* milieu of Turin, although showing a good quality of urbanisation and a clear-cut specialisation of labour, highlights some 'compression' in the characteristics of the social and scientific-cultural environment, also because of the effect of the great specialisation the metropolitan area has acquired in manufacturing industry. Nevertheless, some of the characteristics of the economic environment highlighted by this analysis - such as the growing integration between innovative large and medium-sized industrial firms and services - outline a potential trigger for processes of valorisation of many of the local resources. And these processes can bring an overall improvement in the metropolitan area. The milieu of Naples, although showing considerable 'thickness' that differentiates it clearly from the rest of the South, seems to possess a set of environmental conditions that are neither adequately valorised nor translated into available resources. Emblematic of this are the high values of the density and the physical image of the built environment which, although constituting resources potentially usable in local development processes, contribute for the time being to the formation of negative externalities connected to traffic congestion and the 'hyper-polarisation' of the city centre. Some values of the economic environment, the labour market and the scientific environment instead show positive externalities capable of favouring processes of innovative growth and transformation of the productive base. The milieu of Florence and Venice, characterised by strong sectoral features, seem instead to reflect the outcome of the more general interdependencies with their neighbouring localities. The profile of these two metropolitan areas could, therefore, be improved if they were integrated with those of the rest of the multi-centred regional urban structure to which they belong.

The *thin and fragmented* milieu of Cagliari, Palermo, Catania and Bari is probably the result of the poor capacity of the networks of local actors to recognise and valorise the local resources available. This is certainly the case with Palermo, where local resources remain in the deepest sub-layers of the milieu, which the indicators used here are not able to highlight.

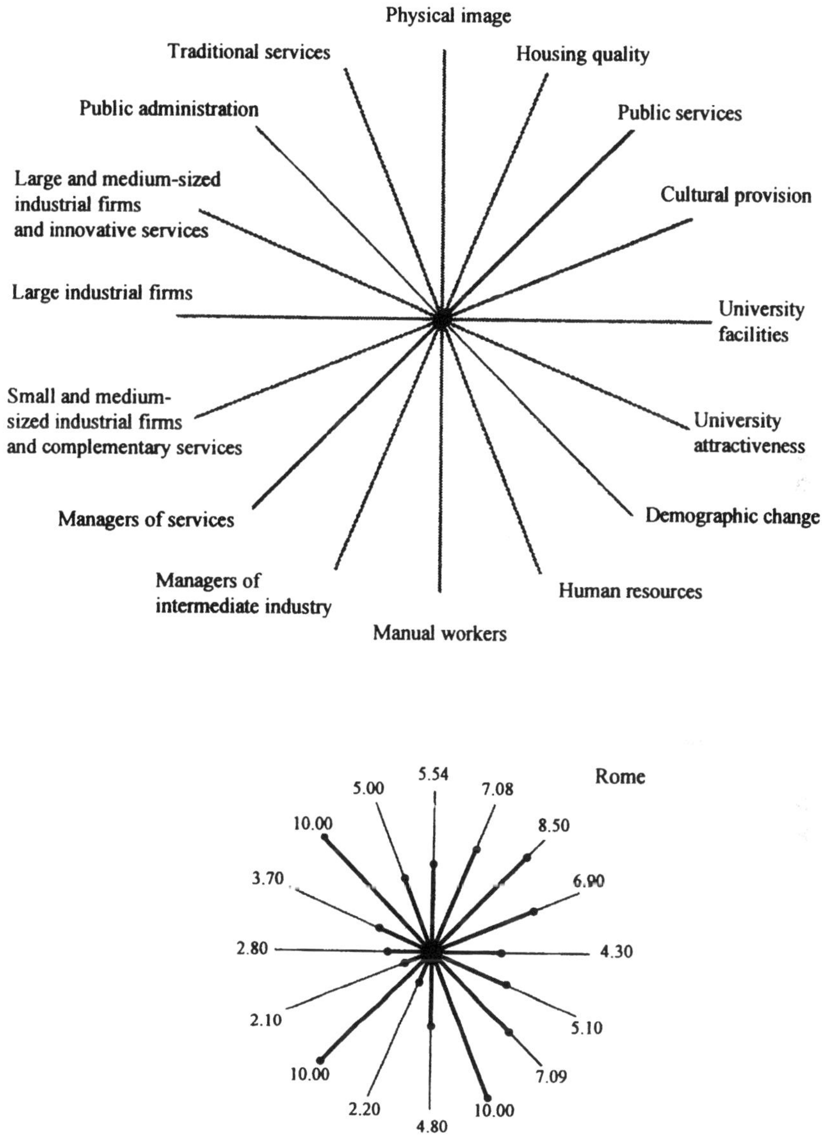

Figure 5.1 Profiles of metropolitan milieux

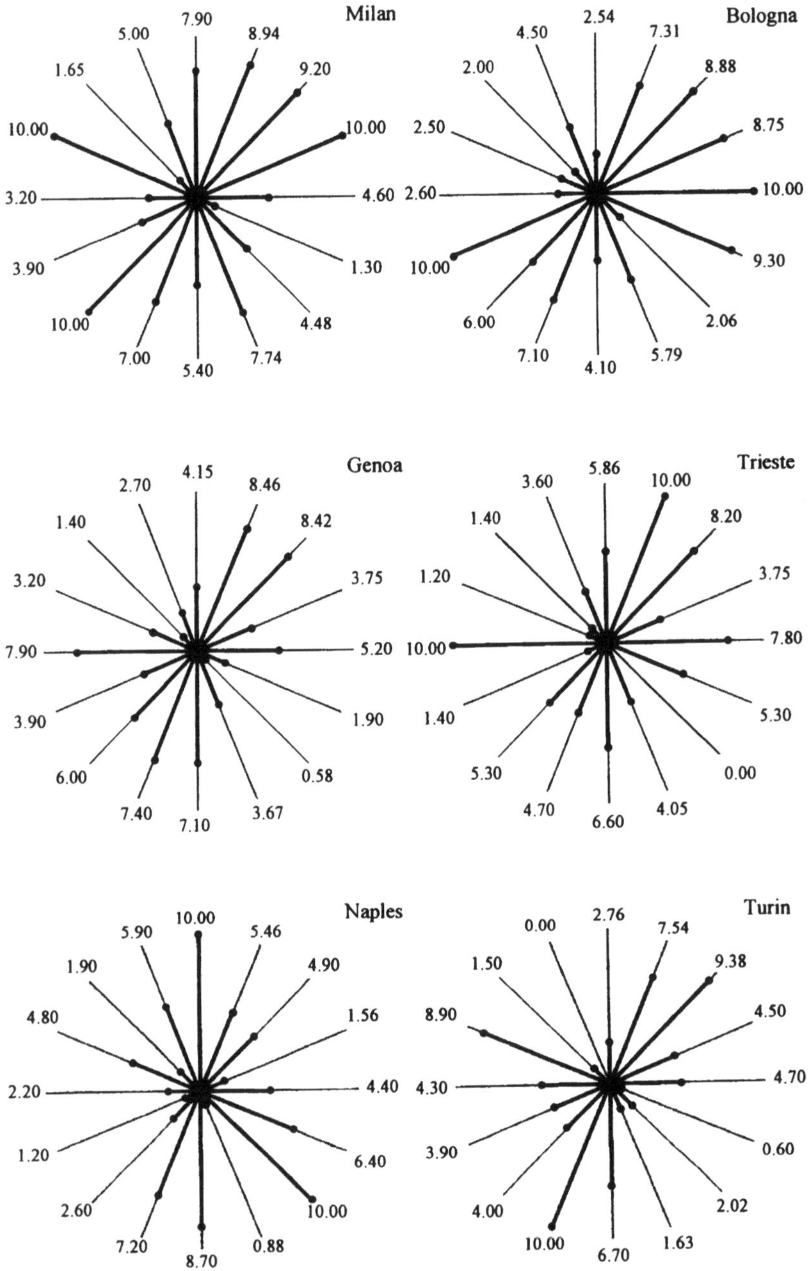
Milan
7.90
8.94
9.20
10.00
4.60
1.30
4.48
7.74
5.40
7.00
10.00
3.90
3.20
10.00
1.65
5.00
Bologna
2.54
7.31
8.88
8.75
10.00
9.30
2.06
5.79
4.10
7.10
6.00
10.00
2.60
2.50
2.00
4.50
Genoa
4.15
8.46
8.42
3.75
5.20
1.90
0.58
3.67
7.10
7.40
6.00
3.90
7.90
3.20
1.40
2.70
Trieste
5.86
10.00
8.20
3.75
7.80
5.30
0.00
4.05
6.60
4.70
5.30
1.40
10.00
1.20
1.40
3.60
Naples
10.00
5.46
4.90
1.56
4.40
6.40
10.00
0.88
8.70
7.20
2.60
1.20
2.20
4.80
1.90
5.90
Turin
2.76
7.54
9.38
4.50
4.70
0.60
2.02
1.63
6.70
10.00
4.00
3.90
4.30
8.90
1.50
0.00

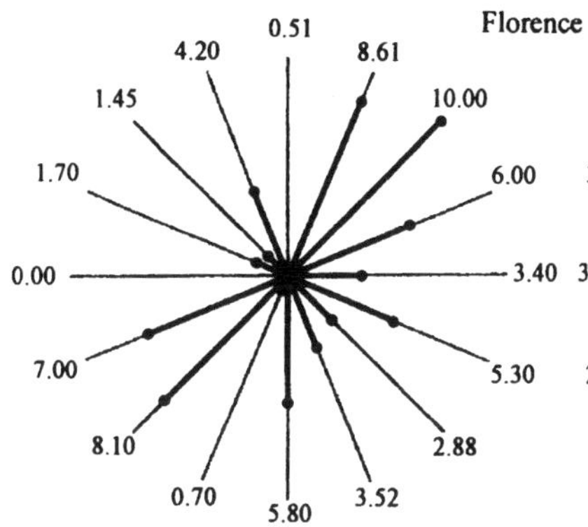
Florence
0.51
4.20
8.61
1.45
10.00
1.70
6.00
0.00
3.40
7.00
5.30
8.10
2.88
0.70
5.80
3.52

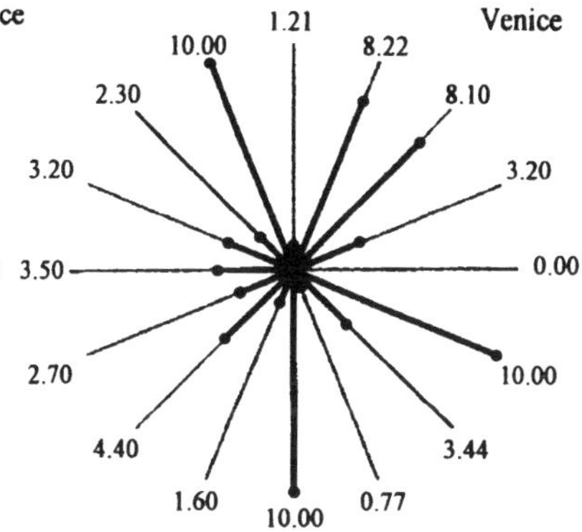
Venice
1.21
10.00
8.22
2.30
8.10
3.20
3.20
3.50
0.00
2.70
10.00
4.40
3.44
1.60
10.00
0.77

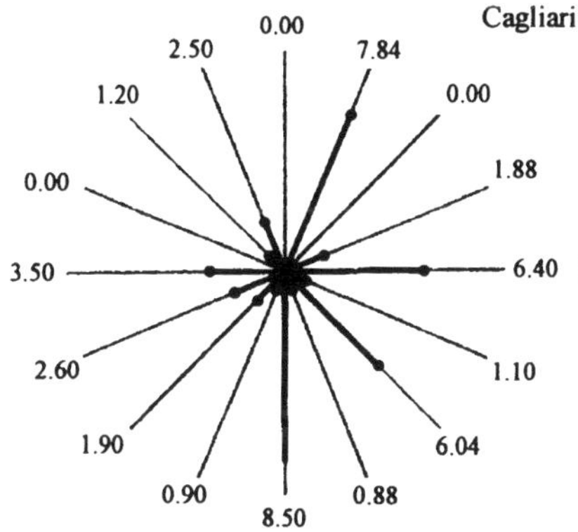
Cagliari
0.00
2.50
7.84
1.20
0.00
0.00
1.88
3.50
6.40
2.60
1.10
1.90
6.04
0.90
8.50
0.88

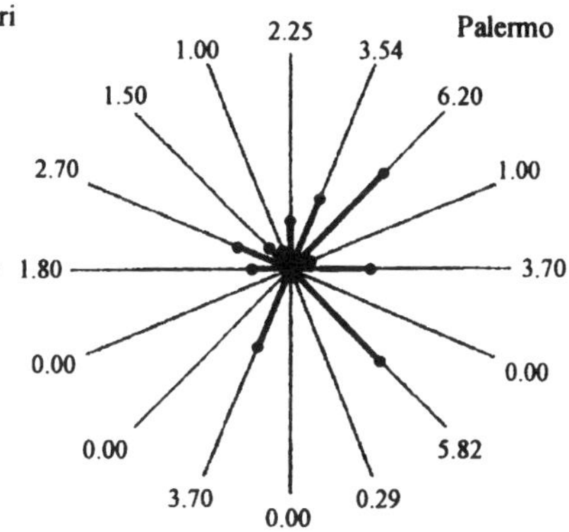
Palermo
2.25
1.00
3.54
1.50
6.20
2.70
1.00
1.80
3.70
0.00
0.00
0.00
5.82
3.70
0.00
0.29

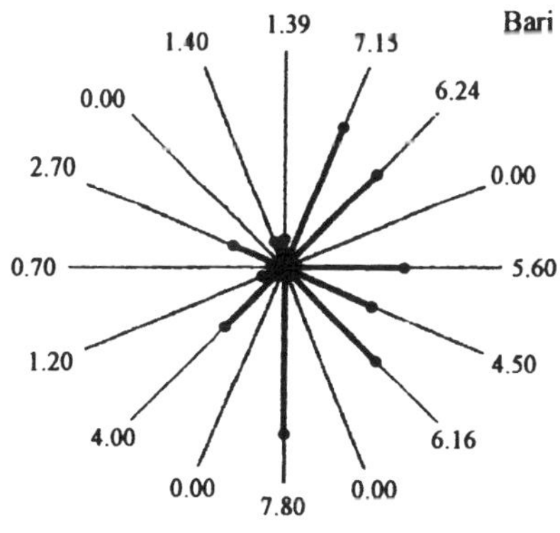
Bari
1.39
1.40
7.15
0.00
6.24
2.70
0.00
0.70
5.60
1.20
4.50
4.00
6.16
0.00
7.80
0.00

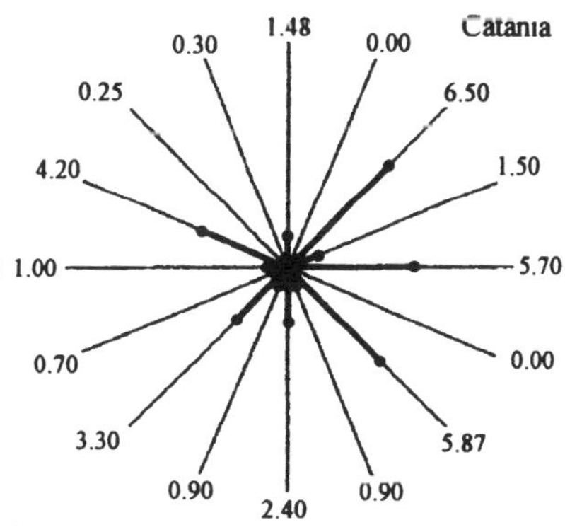
Catania
1.48
0.30
0.00
0.25
6.50
4.20
1.50
1.00
5.70
0.70
0.00
3.30
5.87
0.90
2.40
0.90

All these observations demand, however, an analysis that does not ask questions simply about the endowments of the local milieu, but also, and above all, about the complex bonds within the metropolitan areas between the networks of local actors, the milieu's endowments and the global networks.

Milieu and urban change: the case studies of Turin and Naples

The statistical analysis of 'metropolitan' milieu developed in the previous section is the basis to examine two cases, Turin and Naples. The analysis of the milieu founded on a quantitative methodology has some limits. In particular, the components of the milieu that can be measured through statistical variables are the most obvious ones, or to put it better, the most 'superficial' ones, while the potential and the urban system's specific degree of internal organisation reached or within reach are neglected.

The two case studies examined in this section intend to provide a first exemplification of the theoretical and methodological framework discussed above and, in particular, of the role of the milieu and the local networks in urban change. The reconstruction of some projects of urban transformation in Turin and Naples (Governa 1997), allow the interpretation of the urban change of these metropolitan areas from the point of view of interactive and synergistic relations that connect the components of the milieu and these to the networks of local actors.

Turin: difficulty in diversifying local actors and milieu

For a long time in the past, Turin was characterised by a strong urban identity: it was a one company town, i.e. the city of Fiat. The crisis of the Fordism is now accompanied by an identity crisis that affects not only, or better not so much, the organisation of the production, but the city as a whole. The Fordist model, as a model of social organisation, does not seem to have been replaced by a new model. The city has not yet reached a new equilibrium after the phase of restructuring and it is not clear what these balances could be and on what foundations they could be built.

According to A. Bagnasco (1986, 1990a), large-scale engineering industry still keeps a central role in post-Fordist Turin, maintaining its importance as a key resource of and for the city. Turin continues, therefore, to be interpreted and to be interpretable as a major industrial city, thus prefiguring the maintenance of the bond between economic development, industrial development in particular, and the city. Although this is true, it is however necessary to identify the anomalous and controversial bond that currently characterises the relation between economic strategies and local development. In this perspective, Turin appears a good example of the contradictions encountered by an old industrial city facing the change in the present post-industrial scenario. The phenomenon of de-industrialisation, as a phenomenon common to all the cities of early industrialisation in advanced countries (Cooke 1989, Fox-Przeworski *et al.* 1991), assumes a very particular meaning in the context of Turin. Therefore, the problem is to understand if, and above all how, Turin, without forgetting its past, but reinterpreting it, can be capable of grasping the opportunities contained in its milieu for leading its future.

As a whole, in fact, the Turin milieu expresses a fairly rich and varied range of possibilities and resources, even if not fully valorised by the city's change. The difficulty to fully exploit the considerable potential possessed seems to be connected to the tendency towards 'closure' that characterises relations between the various parts of the Turin milieu. Above all, the city's continuing industrial character and, in particular, the role played by Fiat in it, both as a 'structuring' element of the local milieu and as a leading actor in most of the city's life.[6]

The specific nature of the Turin milieu, as a city of high technology and innovation, even though continuing its industrial tradition, exposes it to some risks. This trend appears evident if we consider the division between the scientific and economic environments and the social environments. The difficulty in constructing an 'idea of the city' that involves Turin's greatest resource (the traditional of industrial work and the diffuse capacity of innovation), together with the rigidity of interaction between local actors, jeopardise the chance of exploiting the opportunities contained in its milieu. The organisational changes of the urban system, above all if they affect the economic environment in direct terms, do not manage, or manage only with difficulty, to construct shared interactive local networks. The situation is different instead in the case of other environments where an 'effervescence' of projects is present, which in some ways show a renewed vision in the city. In fact, to describe the characteristics of the Turin milieu, it is useful to add other 'latent identities' in addition to the city's predominant industrial and technological specialisation. In searching for everything that 'exists' in Turin in addition to industry, the exploration of the cultural environment is particularly interesting. 'Culture as a resource' (Bagnasco 1990b) is a catch-phrase that seems to contain, also for Turin, some possibilities and that marks the presence in the local milieu of a fairly rich and diversified set of components. The role of some local actors lies in this process: they manage to aggregate other actors and, by the intense dialogue with the components of the urban milieu, define a city 'design' aimed at exploiting endogenous potential and at opening the urban system towards the outside. So, recent changes in Turin exemplify a clear contradiction of the city, concerning the diversification of actors and milieu component in a city that was for a long time 'mono-cultural'. On the one hand, the scientific-technological features of the local milieu and the difficulty of defining around these a shared idea for the future of the city; on the other hand, the discovery of interesting dynamics of development in an environment traditionally of secondary importance to the urban identity, particularly in the cultural environment.

Naples: the new network of local actors in the organisation of urban transformation projects

The identity of Naples, understood as the expression of the city's specific character but also as its self-organising capacity, is characterised by its fragmentation. The recurring lines of interpretation indeed depict the difficulty in giving a clear interpretation of the city, proposing essentially dualistic schemes of interpretation. For example, Allum (1973) and, more recently, Marselli (1987) identify in Naples the features of a socio-economic-cultural situation in which there has been no integration between the model of society (*gesellschaft*) and the model of community (*gemeinschaft*). The components of Naples milieu and the organisational characteristics expressed by the local networks can therefore, referring to these interpretations, consider the city as the *juxtaposition* of two different socio-historical forms.

At the same time, Naples is also seen as a typical example of an urban system in which, alongside a sizeable milieu endowment, the self-organising capacity of local actors has long been wanting. The urban transformations and development processes were in fact founded more on the adaptation to exogenous choices and strategies than on the improvement of endogenous potential, mainly because of the connivance and overlapping between national and local government which were almost total for a long time (Barbagallo 1997). Power in Naples has long been organised in almost a 'circular' form, in that it was

> ramified in the fabric of the city and connected directly to the central power in Rome. [Moreover] never did any power group in Italy have under their control all the levers of power that the various politicians like De Lorenzo, Gava, Di Donato and Pomicino wielded in the 1980s (Caracciolo 1994, p. 120).

Following this reasoning, it is interesting to ask on what basis the current 'renaissance' of the city is founded,[7] what the components of the local milieu activated in this process are, and who the actors are that have enabled this activation. In this sense, this is connected to the considerable change that the city is going through, whose beginning can be identified with the preparatory work for the G7 summit in July 1994. On that occasion, a local network of actors was organised to interact actively with a common purpose: the rediscovery of a different Naples, both for tourists and, above all, for the residents themselves, and different ways of acting within the city. This strongly symbolic beginning was then followed by a series of initiatives in which it is possible to see unusual attention paid to the enhancement of specific local features through the active and direct involvement of actors traditionally absent from the city's political, civil and cultural decisions.[8]

One example that is directly connected to the strongly symbolic nature of the works for the G7 summit is represented by the initiatives to rediscover and win back possession of Naples' artistic and cultural heritage so as to re-launch the image of the city and the city as a whole.

Nevertheless, the greatest contribution of the project for the G7 summit or the other initiatives seems to be on the symbolic level, through the rediscovery and the re-assertion of a collective identity as the basis for building the present. The urgent needs of Naples increasingly clearly require a shift from a mainly symbolic level of intervention to a more concrete one, with the consequent need to go beyond the stage of discovery and demonstration to inaugurate a phase of design and construction. This trend is well demonstrated by the recent development of the Science and Technology Park. This project also links into the plans to rejuvenate the no longer used industrial sites on the outskirts of Naples and supported in the planning policies of the new city council (Bolocan and Salone 1996).

The event of the Science and Technology Park for the Naples metropolitan area shows the loss of importance and power of certain traditionally key actors in the development of the city, with the central role of actors traditionally absent in the processes of urban change. The new role assumed by these actors, first of all the City Council, but also actors from the economic, social and cultural environments, underlines the possibility of a different mode of action for the exploitation of the potential neglected for so long as resources for the city on the whole.

Notes

1 First, second and fifth paragraphs are by F. Governa; third and fourth paragraph are by C. Emanuel.

2 The reference for the analysis of the local networks, despite the multitude of theoretical and methodological approaches, is the analysis of social networks (Chiesi 1980 and 1981, Granovetter 1973, Hannerz 1980, Piselli 1995, Wellman and Berkowitz 1988). This framework of reference has to be adapted to the urban change. An interesting example referring to the case of the technopole of Toulouse is in Jalabert *et al.* (1991).

3 These results should be interpreted with some caution because of the limited capacity of the variables, relating mainly to school facilities, to express the dimension and need of basic public services. In fact, the increase in availability of school facilities derives also from the demographic slowdown that has occurred in almost all the metropolitan areas. However, needs are increasing rapidly for other services which were not considered here, such as social welfare and transport, connected to the rapid ageing of the population and to the constant rise in mobility and traffic.

4 This sub-division of economic activities makes reference to the work of G. Tassinari (1983) developed according to the technological content. The 'higher' level of services includes air transport, telecommunications, banking and finance, information technology, research and development, university education, radio and television services, and publishing activities.

5 The index of heterogeneity calculated for each metropolitan area is given by the following equation:

$$Ie = \frac{\sum_{i=1}^{k} \left| S_i - n/k \right|}{2n^* k - 1/k}$$

where:

K is the number of the components (16) that explain the characteristics of the milieu

n is the overall score of the components of each metropolitan area

S is the score of each component of the metropolitan milieu

i is the individual component of the milieu
The index assumes the value of 1 when the scores of the 16 components are highest and therefore give rise to maximum heterogeneity and diversification of the local milieu, and 0 in the opposite case of the concentration of scores in only one component. These results have been transformed into a scale from 0 to 100. Zero value corresponds to the 'thinnest' and least diversified metropolitan milieu (Catania), while 100 corresponds to maximum heterogeneity and diversification (Rome). Values of other urban milieu are: 92.7 for Milan; 86.2 for Bologna; 80.5 for Genoa; 75.2 for Trieste; 71.5 for Naples; 63.6 for Turin; 53.9 for Florence; 45.0 for Venice; 30.7 for Cagliari; 30.5 for Palermo and 7.40 for Bari.

6 The pervasive role of Fiat is emblematically demonstrated by the re-conversion of the Lingotto from the obsolete Fiat car factory to a modern multimedia centre (Bobbio 1990, Fondazione Agnelli 1995, IRES 1995).

7 The 'renaissance' of Naples seems to be connected principally to the new political and administrative phase that began in December 1993 with the election as Mayor of Antonio Bassolino. The recognition of a specific event as the beginning of a new phase in the cities' life can be seen as the 'turning point' identified and described by R. Knight (1993). It is clear that the main interest lies in the understanding of the way in which an individual urban system pursues this change. See, for a first opinion on the work of the new Naples Council, the thoughts of P. Macry (1994); on the local government programme, see Caracciolo (1994), and Bassolino (1995).

8 The historic lack of a responsible middle class or of the highest representatives and institutions of the Naples cultural environment is pointed out by Allum (1973). For observation from 'within' the productive middle classes of Naples, see 'La Fabbrica Vivente. Conversazione con Antonio D'Amato', while for reflection on the reluctance of Neapolitan intellectuals to assume political leadership directly, or even to give a lead in society, see 'Non potete massacrarmi Napoli! Conversazione con Massimo Cacciari', both in Velardi (1992).

6 Regional cohesion and global networks

Giuseppe Dematteis

Criteria for a comprehensive classification

In Chapters 2, 3 and 4, the local urban systems were classified on the basis of individual economic/functional and demographic/spatial attributes. This chapter will propose a comprehensive classification[1] of the 148 local urban systems of medium, medium-large and large size.[2]

In line with the initial research hypotheses, this classification must take into account two major types of spatial relations:

1) long-distance ones, in which the local urban system acts as a 'node' of supra-regional[3] networks of interaction, that we shall refer to in brief as *network relations*;
2) relations of physical proximity, by which the local urban system interacts at the regional and sub-regional scale with the closest local urban systems, that we shall refer to as *territorial relations*.

The first belong to a *virtual space* (or global network space), in which the interactions are influenced little, if at all, by physical distance; they reflect the division of labour at the supra-regional scale and thus indicate the *degree of globalisation* of the local urban systems. The second type of relations occur in a *territorial space* where the 'friction of distance', physical forms (high land, plains, coasts etc.) and historical legacies have a significant influence; they reflect the *degree of regional cohesion* of the local urban systems.[4] Although acting on different levels and in different ways, these two groups of relations do not rule each other out, but, as we shall see, interact in their respective spheres: the network interactions transform the physical space and the structures of the latter condition network connections.

The indicators used here to describe the two types of spatial relations are illustrated analytically in the notes to Table 6.2 at the end of this chapter.

Conceptually, they can be defined as follows:

1. *Network interactions* (degree of globalisation)

   1.1 Size of the local urban system (resident population and jobs). The assumption is that network interaction grows with size.
   1.2 Structure of the economic base. Here, the assumption is that network interaction, and thus the dynamism of the 'nodes', grows with the social division of labour, the range of specialisation, the degree of tertiarisation and the integration between services and industrial activities.[5]
   1.3 Degree of internationalisation. Interaction grows with the number of localised international functions.

2. *Territorial interactions* (degree of regional integration and cohesion)

   2.1 Intensity and level of interaction within the regional network to which the local urban system belongs. The assumption is that interaction grows with the number of hierarchical/functional levels characterising the network, the density of the nodes and the intensity of connections.
   2.2 Position of the local urban system in the regional network. The assumption is that interaction grows with the hierarchical/functional level of the local urban system considered and of the other local urban systems with which it has relations of domination, dependency and complementarity.
   2.3 Diffusive demographic dynamics: demographic growth induced by the local urban system considered in the contiguous minor local urban systems. Interaction is expected to be proportional to the extent of diffusion.

For each of these indicators, the 148 local urban systems considered were organised into classes to which scores were attributed. For the single urban system, the sum of the scores of the indicators 1, 2 and 3 offers a rough measure of the *functional openness* of the local urban systems in a global network space. By adding up the scores of indicators 4, 5 and 6, instead, we obtain a rough measure of the regional cohesion of the local urban systems. As we shall see in the following sections, the ratio between these two measures (functional openness and regional cohesion) enables enquiry into the relationships between network (global) interactions and territorial (proximity) interactions. The same measures also offer a useful method for a comprehensive classification of the local urban systems. It should be noted that, like the measurements on which they are based, these indicators are largely approximations, in the sense that they allow the identification of large aggregates, while the attribution of them to some individual cases presents margins of arbitrariness and uncertainty.

The local urban systems as nodes of global networks

Combining together the indicators regarding size, the structure of the economic base and the degree of internationalisation reveal the following classes of local urban systems. These are ranked in decreasing order of intensity of network relations with the supra-regional scales (the local urban systems belonging to each class are found in col. 5 of Table 6.2).

A1 *Major dynamic and open systems.* These have a population of over 500,000 inhabitants and/or employment for over 150,000 jobs. They have an evolved industry/services specialisation and a complete, or almost complete, range of international functions. It includes 7 local urban systems: Milan, Rome, Turin, Florence, Bologna, Padua and Verona.

A2 *Major open systems.* These have a population of over 500,000 inhabitants and/or employment for over 125,000 jobs. Compared to group A1 they have less differentiation in the economic base and a slightly more restricted range of international functions. It includes 7 local urban systems: Naples, Genoa, Palermo, Venice, Catania, Bari and Cagliari.

A3 *Dynamic and open medium-large systems.* These have a specialised industry/services structure and a range of international functions immediately below that of the two previous classes. Included here are 19 local urban systems.

B1 *Open specialised systems.* These have less than 250,000 inhabitants and/or 100,000 jobs. Economic structure specialised in industry or services or both. They also have fairly well developed international functions. Includes 28 local urban systems.

B2 *Weakly open specialised systems.* These are generally of medium size. Economic structure specialised in industry or services or both, and a limited range of international functions. Includes 41 local urban systems with important functions on the regional and sub-regional scale.

C1 *Open non specialised systems.* Despite their size, they have a weak or poorly differentiated economic structure, and international functions range from average to weak. Includes 7 local urban systems.

C2 *Mono-specialised systems.* These are medium-sized urban systems, usually specialised in manufacturing and limited to the export of goods. Includes 10 local urban systems.

C3 *Non specialised systems.* Medium-sized urban system without productive specialisation and with only one or no specialised international functions. Includes 28 local urban systems.

Figure 6.1 illustrates the geographical distribution of the 148 local urban systems belonging to the classes described above. The map offers a synthetic picture of the functional urban structure of the country.

The first two classes, corresponding to the metropolitan level, are more numerous in Northern Italy, but are relatively well distributed throughout the country. However, while in Northern and Central Italy there are numerous local urban systems of mid to high functional size categories (classes A3, B1 and B2) around and between the metropolitan nodes, in Southern Italy these are completely missing in the metropolitan surroundings and very scarce elsewhere. In the North this is, relatively, the most numerous (62% of the Italian total) and best distributed class. So, it has to be concluded that the most serious spatial unevenness does not concern the metropolitan level but the regional pattern of the mid to upper tier of the Italian urban system. In other terms, while in Northern Italy and, to a large degree, the Centre, the supra-regional and international networks find connections in nodes even of medium size, in Southern Italy these nodes are localised above all in the few nodes of the metropolitan level. On this point, the comparison between Milan and Naples is significant: both of them are surrounded by local urban systems of medium-large and medium size, yet, while those around Milan are almost all in the medium-high range, those around Naples all belong to the medium-low.

The local urban systems as nodes of regional networks

The degree of regional integration of the local urban systems (Table 6.2, col. 10) shows a consistent correspondence between the values of these indicators, which concern interactions of territorial proximity, and those for supra-regional network interactions. This suggests that the local urban systems belonging to dense, articulated and cohesive regional networks participate within them in a division of labour that favours their access to the global networks.

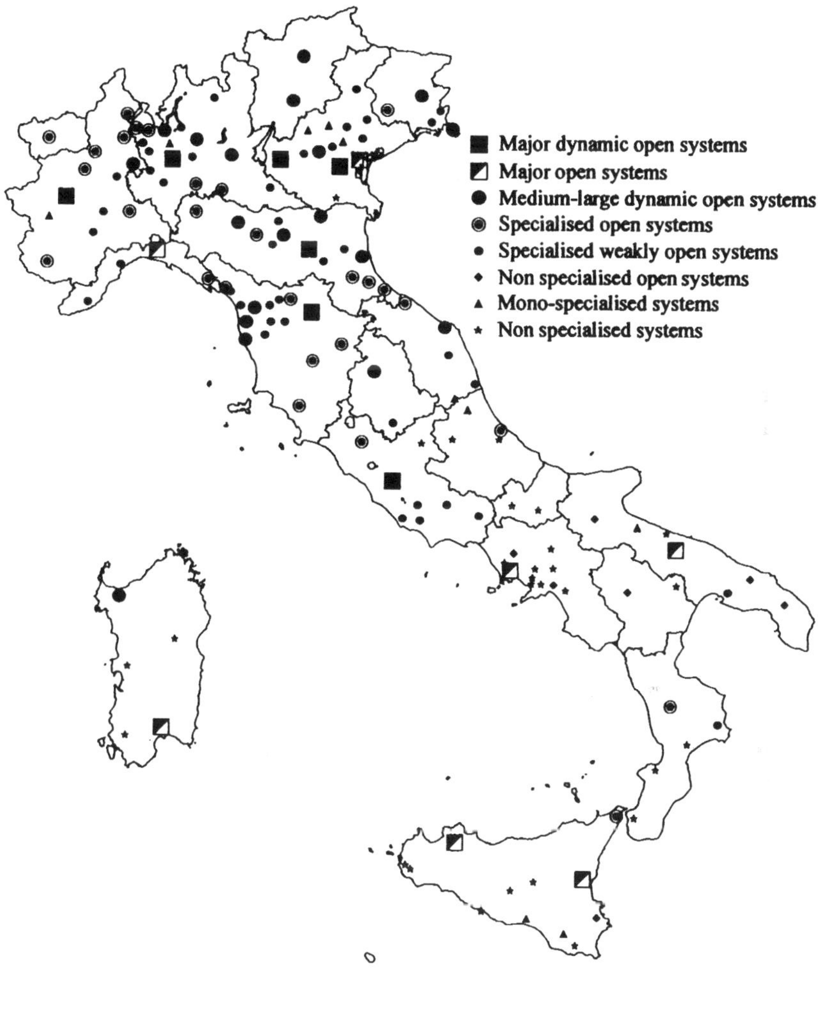

Figure 6.1 Major urban systems classified by their degree of integration into European networks

The reciprocal effect is also probable, i.e. that usually the local urban systems that fit best into the global networks receive and transmit impulses within their regional structure that tend to strengthen and expand. The competitive advantages of the cities would thus lie not only in their relationship with a local milieu, but also in their relations with the regional structures to which they belong. The latter are represented in Figure 6.2, which illustrates settlement patterns that influence supra-regional network connections.

The better integrated territorial structures are the *metropolitan functional regions* followed by the *urban functional regions*. The functional regions are the upper tier of urban regionalisation of Italy, while the local urban systems are the lower tier.[6] The metropolitan functional regions are the most regionally cohesive, while the urban functional regions are again cohesive but usually smaller. They include one or more of the 148 urban systems considered here, surrounding a large 'non-metropolitan' urban system (or two as in the case of Trieste and Udine). There are then areas such as that of the Po valley (from Novara to Trieste), that of Emilia-Romagna (from Parma to the Adriatic) and that of Northern Tuscany, where the *metropolitan* and *urban* functional regions are connected together by a dense and articulated settlement pattern on various functional levels, linked by relations of hierarchy and complementarity.

A lower degree of regional integration is shown by the 'dense fragmented' settlement patterns in which the mesh of medium and medium-high urban systems, although relatively dense, does not have the same intensity of connections. Finally, there are vast peripheral or marginal zones in which the same mesh, as well as being fragmented, is also often much thinner and more discontinuous, with only few, relatively isolated urban nodes.

The indicators of regional integration given in Table 6.2 (cols. 7, 8 and 9) take into account both the urban systems' membership of the above mentioned regional structures and the hierarchical (functional and dimensional) position that each of them occupies and also the diffusive effects on neighbouring urban systems. These effects can be observed in Figure 6.4. They consist in the spread of demographic growth from the more central and dynamic systems (usually in stages of dis-urbanisation) to neighbouring ones going through sub-urbanisation, peri-urbanisation or peripheral urbanisation. This demographic dynamic does not only derive from residential spillovers (mainly contained within the surroundings of each individual urban system). It indicates instead that a spatial redistribution of activities is occurring at the regional scale.

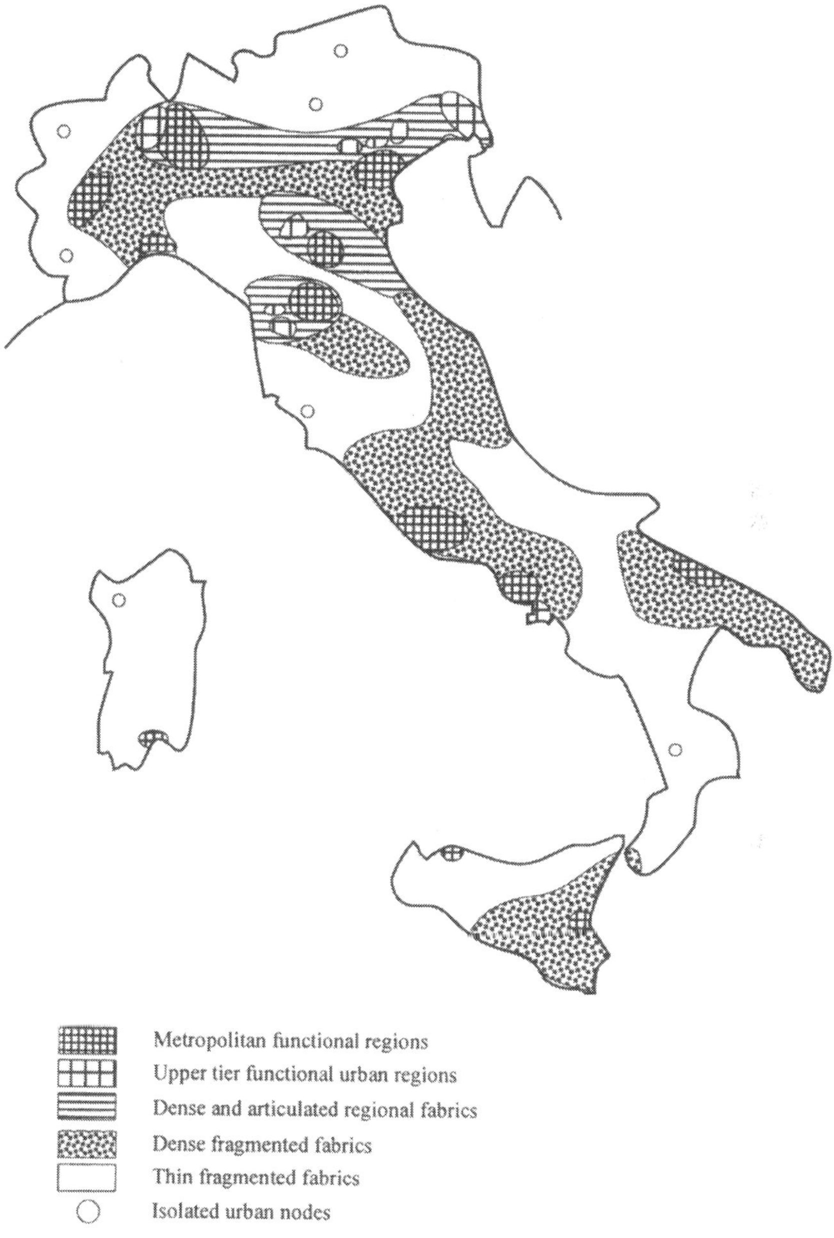

Figure 6.2 Regional urban structures and types of settlement fabric

According to the different cases, this may depend on the de-localisation of activities from the major urban/metropolitan nodes or on local development with endogenous components (i. e. the industrial urban systems of small and medium-sized firms, or the industrial districts).

Global networks and regional cohesion: a synthetic classification

The diagram in Figure 6.3 offers an assessment of the relationship that exists between the degree of territorial integration (regional cohesion) of the local urban systems and their degree of supra-regional openness (globalisation). The axes represent the scores that give a synthetic measurement of the two components, as calculated from the indicators illustrated previously and given in Table 6.2 (cols. 5 and 10).

Notwithstanding the approximation and the relatively arbitrary nature of a measurement through scores, the result is interesting, above all because the dispersion of the scores reveals a positive correlation between the two groups of indicators. In addition, the various areas of the diagram offer the possibility of reaching a comprehensive classification that takes into account both the projections of the urban systems into the virtual network space and their integration into regional space. It should also be observed that the most numerous and greatest deviations regard local urban systems with a relatively strong degree of international openness and a relatively weak degree of regional integration. In these cases, we have to presume that the network relations are rooted principally in the urban system's local milieu and that their positive effects finish within it.

The major sets of urban systems that can be observed in the diagram are the following:

1A *Metropolitan*: 12 major urban systems (in decreasing order of scores): Milan, Rome, Florence, Turin, Bologna, Bari, Naples, Palermo, Venice, Cagliari, Catania, Genoa. While the first seven are far ahead of the other urban systems, both in terms of network and territorial interactions, the last five have similar scores to the other local urban systems in groups 2A and 2B in one or other of the groups of relations.

1B *Para-metropolitan*: 9 major urban systems (Padua, Verona, Vicenza, Brescia, Bergamo, Udine, Trieste, Parma and Modena) that support the network system of the eastern Po valley, Veneto and Emilia. Although smaller than the metropolitan systems, their degree of network and territorial interaction is the same as some of them.

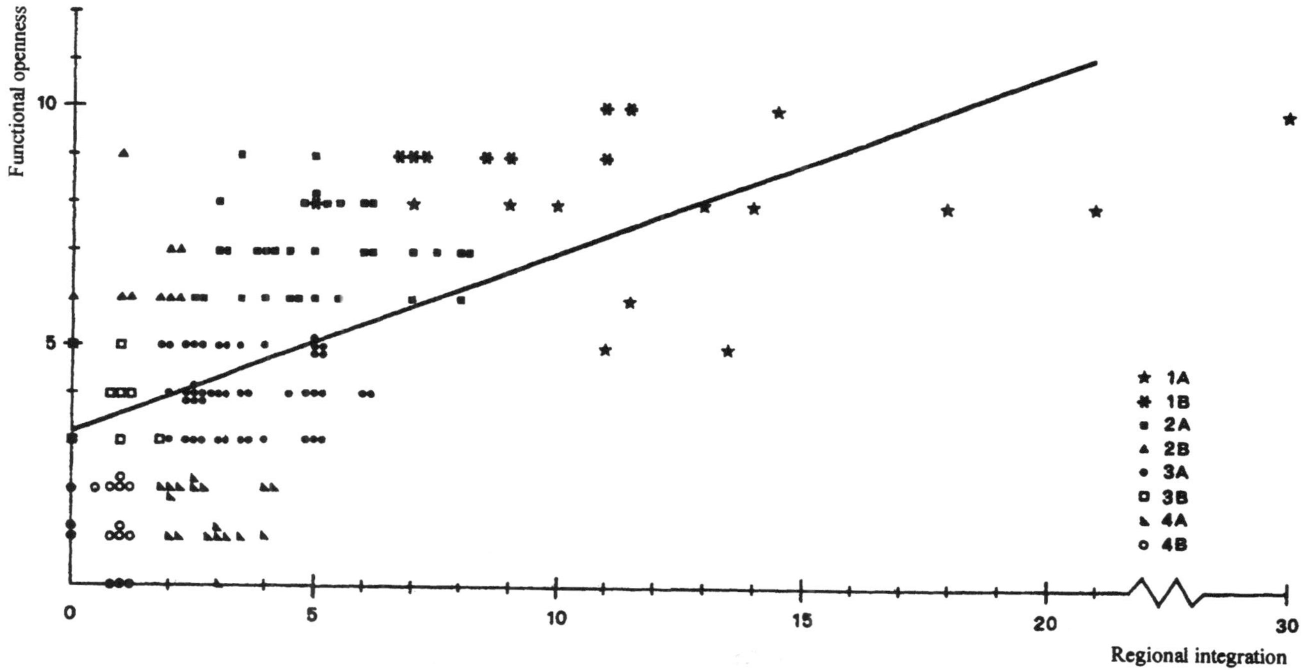

Figure 6.3 Position of the local urban systems in terms of regional interactions and functional openness (based on the two indicators of table 6.2, cols 10-11)

2A *Integrated urban systems:* 32 urban systems, all in the Centre-North (see list in Table 6.2), which are part of metropolitan surroundings or articulated regional systems or which, like Perugia, Ancona, Bolzano, Trento and Pescara, are poles of 'peripheral' regions.

2B *Integrated urban systems with a weak territorial component:* 9 urban systems, all from the Centre-North (with the exclusion of Sassari), which have a serious weakness in territorial cohesion compared to the relatively high levels of supra-regional interaction.

3A *Fairly integrated urban systems.* This is the most numerous and heterogeneous group (45 urban systems). It includes urban systems of the metropolitan surroundings, urban systems with a strong manufacturing or tourism specialisation and some urban systems that are poles of sub-regional importance.

3B *Fairly integrated urban systems with a weak territorial component.* 8 urban systems whose territorial integration is decidedly inferior to their network integration.

4A *Weakly integrated urban systems:* 18 urban systems, all in the South, belonging to metropolitan surroundings or with sub-regional territorial functions usually more important than network functions.

4B *Very weakly integrated urban systems:* 15 urban systems localised in Southern Italy (with the exception of Rovigo) with access to local networks that ranges from weak to nil and with a very limited role in territorial organisation.

The regional pattern of the urban network

One of the initial ideas in this research was that urban cities have shifted in recent decades from their original *nuclear* shape to more extended *areal* forms and, more recently, to *network patterns* recognisable on various scales. The dimensions and physical shapes of settlement thus change, and above all the spatial structure of the flows and interactions that link them together changes. This occurs at the same time in the virtual spaces of the global networks, in the physical spaces of the territorial networks and in the social spaces of the local milieu.

Mapping the classification of the previous section, which summarises the urban systems' different forms and connections (Figure 6.4), it is easy to see the spatial pattern of the urban network in relation to a typology of its nodes that, to some degree, also reflects the other dimensions of the phenomenon. Interpretation of the map thus allows us to give an overall evaluation of the Italian urban system in its regional patterns. In particular, the following typologies can be recognised:

Figure 6.4 Regional pattern of the major urban systems according to the relationship between functional openness and regional integration

- *Metropolitan regional systems*: some are strongly monocentric (those centred on Turin, Milan, Rome and Naples), others organised around dominant poles in a more balanced regional urban system (Bologna, Florence and Bari), others still with a multi-polar metropolitan structure (Padua and Venice). The bi-polar system of Trieste-Udine also prefigures a metropolitan structure of this type.
- *Sub-regional metropolitan systems:* these have a more limited capacity for control of the regional urban network. They are Genoa, Cagliari, Palermo and Catania, all monocentric systems.
- *Dense and articulated urban systems*: areas with a high density of metropolitan, para-metropolitan and urban systems of different levels, partially connected by commuter flows. These are the three areas (already illustrated in Figure 6.2): Po valley-Veneto, Emilia-Romagna and Northern Tuscany. The area around Latina and Campania, which is tending to merge with the functional regions of Rome and Naples-Salerno, comes close to these characteristics.
- *Wide-mesh regional grids*. These are less dense and less hierarchically articulated regional structures than the previous ones, but without the great gaps of the following group. The main one is that of Eastern Piedmont and the central Po valley, which separates the metropolitan systems and the 'dense networks' of Northern Italy. Other regions of this type are the mid-Adriatic between Pesaro and Pescara, the Puglia system and that of South-western Sicily. The mesh of the central Apennines of Umbria and Abruzzo is only partially continuous. The premises also exist for the formation of meshes of this type in the Alpine area of Veneto and Alto Adige and in the inner Southern Apennines, between Campania, Abruzzo, Molise and Puglia.
- *Fragmented regional grids*: these can be recognised in peripheral parts of the North (inner Alpine zones, South-western Piedmont and Liguria), of the Centre (the Tyrrhenian coast and inland from it), in the South (Calabria) and the Islands (Sardinia, North-western Sicily).

The Italian urban network and the European network

Beyond stereotypes

The image of Italian urbanisation that emerges from our study, while it confirms some well-known lines, underlines trends and potential conditions capable of throwing new light on the relationship to the European urban system.

The polycentric nature of the Italian urban system is confirmed at all its levels, a structure inherited from the pre-unification period which should still today be taken into account to explain densities, rarefaction and spatial discontinuities. Its shape also reflects the morphological conditions that favour linear coastal development and hinder cross-peninsula and cross-border connections and links with the Islands. The effects of the negative North-South gradient are also clear. Going from Lombardy to Sicily, the number of urban systems decreases and the links between them become looser. As a whole, these structural conditions seem to underline the peripheral nature and the imbalance of the Southern urban pattern compared to the 'European' one of the Centre-North, and in particular that of the Po valley.

But an interpretation of this kind, although containing elements of truth, concedes too much to the stereotype, which makes the ills of Southern Italy (the Mezzogiorno) depend on geographical and environmental factors against which little can be done. These arguments are not enough to justify the marginalisation of a region like the Italian South that, with a population of 20.5 million and 17 urban systems with more than 200,000 inhabitants, has the demographic and urban dimensions of a medium-sized European country. Furthermore, it would be an excessive simplification to reduce the discussion of the Italian urban system to terms of North-South dualism.

In reality, the image of urban Italy that is emerging in the 1990s contradicts this simplification and highlights a variety of elements and characteristics to exploit in order to improve the cohesion of the national urban network and to promote its integration into the European urban context.

The identity of the nodes explains the development of the network

The great municipal traditions, the 'thickness' of the local milieu and the strong identity that characterises many Italian cities are the components of a historical and cultural substratum that explains many aspects of the urban vitality of contemporary Italy and which represents a resource that should not be neglected.

Particularly striking is the dynamism of the medium-sized and medium-large urban systems. While in other European situations the medium-sized cities are penalised by the polarised growth of the major cities (EC-DG XVI 1995), in Italy, as has been seen, the intermediate urban level is instead characterised by an evolved structure of the economic base and by the intensity of its international connections. These features often coincide with the development of industrial urban systems of small and medium-sized firms. The dynamic nodes of the Italian urban system are, therefore, in the majority of cases, local systems with a strong endogenous component, linked to specific components of their local milieu. It is in these substrata that the diffuse presence of international relations highlighted in our study is rooted.

These conditions indicate that the fundamental task of urban policies is to promote networks of complementarity and synergy (Camagni 1992) which bring together and strengthen local development areas and enable access to higher technological and organisational levels. It would in fact be an error to neglect these 'natural' competitive advantages and to accept standard models of development, held to be more advanced because they have proven to be successful in other contexts. Typical 'made in Italy' goods, the economy of cultural resources, tourism and similar 'traditional' activities are not necessarily 'mature' sectors. While drawing on resources accumulated in the past, they lend themselves to innovative upgrading no less promising and competitive than in sectors that are normally considered as high tech ones. Obviously, the latter should be supported and developed in the individual urban systems where they are rooted and to which they ensure competitive advantages at the international level.

Connections are more important than size

Although it is true that the development of the urban network depends on the capacity for autonomous development of the individual urban systems, it is also true that the latter draw advantages from their integration into strong regional networks, dominated by metropolitan systems. While in the 1950s and 1960s the growth of the metropolitan nodes drew resources from the minor centres, slowing their growth, the last twenty years have seen the opposite occur. The proximity of the metropolitan nodes now stimulates the division of labour between the nodes of the regional networks, with threshold and development effects at all the levels of the urban hierarchy. Similar effects are also found in regions like Veneto where, although lacking major metropolitan poles, highly connected networks have been formed. The most favourable conditions would seem to be those in which, such as the case of Lombardy, the two typologies - the hierarchical, monocentric one and the network, polycentric one - overlap and combine together.

In any case, these dense and dynamic urban systems, where complementary and synergetic relations already tend to develop spontaneously, appear to be particularly right for implementing network policies on the regional and sub-regional scale (to which we shall return in the next chapter). Moreover they are an alternative to the uncontrolled sprawl of the 'dispersed city'.

The regional systems replace the metropolitan areas

Almost all the Italian regional systems are now tending to evolve towards interconnected structures. In Piedmont, the monocentrism of Turin is balanced by the emergence of non-centripetal connections and networks. Lazio, from being a typical example of a region poorly integrated with its metropolitan core (i. e. Rome) and even deserted by abnormal growth of it, is gradually changing into a multi-polar urban system and branching into neighbouring regions. The dense and articulated networks of Emilia-Romagna and Northern Tuscany improve their cohesion with the rise of Bologna and, even more, Florence as dominant metropolitan nodes. The role of Naples in the network of Campania is in many ways similar to that of Rome in Lazio. We can also expect positive effects from a further strengthening of Bari in a regional urban network that is already well outlined.

Other large urban systems, both in the North (Genoa) and in the South (Cagliari, Catania and Palermo) are going through an implosive phase, and the regional networks are feeling the effects. In fact, these large but isolated systems show weak values of functional openness when compared to other systems such as Vicenza and Brescia (and the 'para-metropolitan' group in general) which are smaller but integrated into strong regional systems.

We must recognise that the driving structure of regional development is no longer the metropolitan area by itself. The concept of 'metropolitan area' as it is commonly understood and applied in Italy and other European countries, refers more to the urban concentration of the 1960s than to the current phase of selective polarisation. Yet, more to the old form of compact agglomeration and sub-urbanisation than to the new networked regional structures, no longer based on continuous settlement expansion.

By their very nature, the latter escape purely territorial control, and so it would seem illusory to imagine governing the new forms and articulations of the urban network by multiplying the levels of local government. And not even by defining new administrative partitions or adjusting the borders of existing ones to adapt them to the evolution of the regional structures. Given that urban and regional spaces cannot be taken for granted, but change continuously with the geometry of the networks, the spatial forms of local and regional government must also have a variable geometry and be based on networks of co-operation between public actors with different functional and spatial responsibilities. This theme will also be taken up again in the next chapter.

The North-South backbone unifies and organises the Italian urban system

Another important consideration concerns the substantial unity of the Italian urban system, whatever the variety and complexity of its regional components. There is no urban network of the North, or even of the Po valley, with uniform features that differentiates it from other networks found in the peninsula or in the South. Giving a rough sketch of this, an alignment along a central backbone seems to emerge in line with the European '*dorsale*'. It includes the strong regional systems centred on Milan, Bologna, Florence, Rome and Naples. To the east and west of this backbone, the urban structures are relatively weaker: in the Po region, there are those of Veneto and Piedmont; in peninsular Italy one can make out an Adriatic alignment parallel to the central one to the east, but with only one metropolitan pole (Bari). To the west, on the Tyrrhenian coast, there are the weak urban networks of Liguria, Southern Tuscany, Calabria, Sardinia and Sicily.

The connection of the regional systems does not imply their merger

The recognition of axial patterns in the Italian urban system at the national level is, however, an over-simplification, in that there is hardly continuity even between the various regional systems. Even the strong regional systems appear separated by zones of rarefaction which, as we saw in Chapter 3, are also areas of negative demographic trends, without being poor. In particular, the line of the Po creates a border effect, which is anything but negative in that it limits the network expansion of the settlement patterns, thus offering a support for desirable policies to limit urban sprawl. The Apennine backbones, the inland mountains of Sardinia and the Alps chain are all precious natural conditions for similar policies of containment, which obviously do not exclude an increase in functional connections and flows between regional urban systems.

Even the concept of 'corridor', as the line preferred both by traffic and linear urban expansion should be applied cautiously to Italy. Along the existing great axes (the Northern one at the foot of the Alps, the Emilia, Adriatic and central peninsular one etc.) the urban centrality is not distributed uniformly, but concentrated, as can be seen in Figure 6.4, in regional systems. The image of the 'corridor' could be applied, therefore, only to the physical continuity of urbanised space. But this continuity is neither necessary nor useful; in fact, it is damaging as it reduces and segments open spaces, or even eliminates them where their environmental value is greatest, such as along the coasts.

The Italian urban system is already European

As a whole, the Italian urban system, because of its structure and its recent trends, is more similar to that of the continental core than to that of the other European 'peripheries'. The density of the cities, their regional linkage and articulation is not very different to that of the central European backbone, of which it is the extension.

The Po regional systems rival in terms of centrality, density and continuity the parallel and symmetrical ones on the other side of the Alps. The Po systems, together with that of the upper Tyrrhenian appear as a whole more articulated and cohesive than those of the Western Mediterranean arc (Catalonia and the French Midi), of which they are the natural continuation towards Central and Eastern Europe.

In the demographic transition analysed in Chapter 3, the Italian urban systems follow trajectories that are now the same as and almost contemporary with those of the urban regions of Central-Western Europe. In the 1960s and 1970s, Italy showed some backwardness in the passage from the phase of urbanisation to that of dis-urbanisation (van den Berg *et al.* 1982). But the next process of counter-urbanisation and the more recent one of peri-urbanisation appeared in Italy in ways and at times not dissimilar to those of Europe's 'old core' (Cheshire 1995).

That the Italian urban system can now be considered structurally homogeneous with the most advanced part of Europe does not mean that its integration into the European network has already been completed. Despite a close-knit network of connections, much remains to be done, above all for the urban systems of the Mezzogiorno.

The great urban potential of the Mezzogiorno is underused

The problem of Southern Italy has rightly been identified with that of its cities and, on the spatial level, with the weakness of its urban structure. The indicators used in this study give a dramatic confirmation of this. The determining factors should not, however, be sought only in the shortcomings of the territorial structures. As can be seen in Table 6.1, the urban endowment of the Mezzogiorno is not especially inferior to that of other parts of Italy. The differences become greater, instead, when we go on to look at the other indicators, which measure connections, in other words the capacity to valorise the urban endowment through network connections at the various levels, from the global to the regional. This means that the potential offered by the present Southern urban spatial structures is not adequately used. It is not a question, therefore, of increasing the current endowment so much as of improving economic and social productivity with decisive action on other levels, such as that of social cohesion, the creation of competitive advantages linked to the local milieu, networks of co-operation between cities etc.

Table 6.1
Urban endowments and performance indicators for standard geographical areas

	Main urban systems		Residents in the urban systems		Functional openness		Functional openness and regional cohesion	
	No.	%	Population (thousands)	%	Scores	%	Scores	%
NW	34	23.0	11,010	28.2	205	28.7	379	27.8
NE	35	23.6	7,221	18.5	212	29.6	395	28.9
North	69	46.6	18,231	46.7	417	58.3	774	56.7
Centre	31	21.0	8,087	20.7	172	24.1	316	23.2
South	48	32.4	12,726	32.6	126	17.6	275	20.1
Italy	148	100.0	39,044	100.0	715	100.0	1,365	100.0

Source: calculated by the author on ISTAT data.

How to be central in the European periphery

More serious and practically insuperable are the obstacles that the urban systems of Southern Italy face in order to adapt to the continental-type rationale, which still guides the development of the European network. This development, being based on the expansion of the connections of proximity with the core, tends to marginalise the 'periphery'. It spreads its benefits to a semi-central zone, which in Italy, even when the necessary high-speed rail links through the Alps are in place, will not go far south of the Po and would increase the dependency of the peninsula's urban systems on its regions.

This logic can be overcome in two complementary ways:

- with strong external cross-border openings, such as the one across the Mediterranean, and
- with a distribution of centrality between the major European metropolitan systems, following a network rationale not conditioned by distance, according to the models of 'decentralised concentration' and 'distributed multicentrality'. This means helping the peripheral metropolitan systems participate in the close-knit network of exchange

of services, technology, information, capital and culture that characterises the cities of the European 'core', expanding its mesh to Mediterranean Europe.

This means implementing very complex policies that involve the European level (Mediterranean geo-politics, transport and telecommunications infrastructures and tariffs), the national level (infrastructures, services, tax and socio-institutional policies) and the local level (competitiveness, valorisation of the milieu, social cohesion, self-organisation, identity and image).

In the South, the local conditions that can be exploited for projects of this kind are present above all in the urban systems of metropolitan level. These already today are in a position to play a role as active 'exchangers' (*gateways*, in the definition of P.K. Kresl 1991) between the national and European level, the trans-Mediterranean level and the local-regional one.

This and other considerations suggested by the analysis carried out so far are worth further in-depth examination concerning the possibility offered by the urban network policies in the processes of territorial integration from the local/regional scale to the European one. The following chapter deals with this subject.

Table 6.2
Indicators for the 148 local urban systems of large, medium-large and medium size*

	1	2	3	4	5	6	7	8	9	10	11	12
Local urban systems	Population 1991 (thousands)	Jobs 1991 (thousands)	Economic specialisation (classes)	International openness (classes)	Supra-regional interaction (classes)	Demographic transition (classes)	Diffusive dynamic (score)	Regional urban structures (classes)	Position in the regional structures (classes)	Regional integration (scores)	Functional openness (scores)	Synthetic classification
Rome	3,314	1,057	B2	A1	A1	A	9	A2	A1	21.0	8	1A
Milan	2,890	1,252	A	A1	A1	A	11	A1	A1	30.0	10	1A
Naples	2,381	479	D	A1	A2	A	4	A2	A1	13.5	5	1A
Turin	1,545	595	A	A1	A1	A	5	A2	A1	14.5	10	1A
Bari	1,123	270	B2	A2	A2	B	5	A2	A1	13.0	8	1A
Florence	877	316	B2	A1	A1	A	7	A2	A1	18.0	8	1A
Palermo	818	183	B2	A2	A2	A	3	A3	A3	10.0	8	1A
Genoa	796	244	D	A1	A2	A	0	A3	A3	7.0	8	1A
Bologna	683	288	B2	A1	A1	A	5	A2	A2	14.0	8	1A
Venice	611	203	C2	A1	A2	A	3	A2	A2	11.5	6	1A
Catania	608	133	D	A2	A2	A	4	A3	A3	11.0	5	1A
Cagliari	461	126	B2	A2	A2	B	2	A3	A3	9.0	8	1A
Padova	506	189	A	A2	A1	B	4	B	A2	11.5	10	1B
Verona	470	167	A	A2	A1	B	4	B	A2	11.0	10	1B
Bergamo	456	175	A	B1	A3	B	5	B	B1	9.0	9	1B
Brescia	381	153	A	B1	A3	B	7	B	B1	11.0	9	1B
Udine	357	123	A	B1	A3	D	2	B	B1	7.0	9	1B
Trieste	262	88	B2	A2	A3	D	0	B	B1	5.0	8	1B
Parma	258	104	A	B1	A3	D	3	B	B1	7.0	9	1B
Modena	243	103	A	B1	A3	B	2	B	B1	7.0	9	1B
Vicenza	234	93	A	B1	A3	B	4	B	B1	8.5	9	1B
Como	400	135	B1	B1	A3	B	0	A1	B2	6.0	8	2A
Busto Arsizio	357	118	B1	C1	B2	B	0	A1	C1	5.0	6	2A
Lecco	286	97	B1	C1	B2	B	1	A1	B2	7.0	6	2A
Reggio nell'Emilia	254	97	A	B2	B1	C	2	B	B1	6.0	8	2A
Varese	254	86	B2	B2	B1	B	2	A1	B2	8.0	6	2A

	1	2	3	4	5	6	7	8	9	10	11	12
Treviso	247	91	A	C1	B2	B	4	B	B2	8.0	7	2A
Pescara	246	75	B2	B2	B1	B	2	C1	B3	4.5	6	2A
Prato	240	87	A	B2	B1	C	0	A2	B2	5.0	8	2A
Pordenone	222	79	B1	B2	B1	B	0	B	B1	4.0	7	2A
Ferrara	196	62	B2	B1	A3	D	0	B	B1	4.0	7	2A
Perugia	190	70	B2	B1	A3	B	5	C1	B2	7.5	7	2A
Leghorn	187	54	B2	B1	A3	D	0	B	B1	4.0	7	2A
Pisa	179	58	B2	B1	A3	D	1	B	B1	6.0	7	2A
Ravenna	172	61	B2	B1	A3	D	2	B	B1	6.0	7	2A
Novara	170	59	A	B1	A3	E	1	B	B1	5.0	9	2A
Ancona	164	61	B2	B1	A3	D	3	C1	B3	5.0	7	2A
Bolzano	157	59	B2	B1	A3	D	6	C2	B3	7.0	7	2A
Lucca	156	54	B1	B1	A3	D	1	B	B1	5.5	8	2A
Trento	155	60	B2	B1	A3	C	7	C2	B3	8.0	7	2A
Cesena	155	49	B2	B2	B1	B	0	B	C2	2.5	6	2A
Forlì	150	52	A	B2	B1	D	1	B	B1	5.0	8	2A
Ivrea	150	47	A	B2	B1	D	1	A2	C1	5.0	8	2A
Lodi	142	43	B1	B2	B1	B	0	A1	C2	4.5	7	2A
Cremona	137	45	C1	B1	B1	E	3	C2	C3	4.0	6	2A
Arezzo	136	53	A	B2	B1	B	1	C1	B3	3.0	8	2A
Viterbo	133	37	B2	B2	B1	B	2	A2	C2	5.5	6	2A
Pistoia	120	40	A	C2	B2	D	0	B	C1	3.0	7	2A
Aprilia	114	30	B1	C1	B2	D	0	A2	C2	3.5	6	2A
Sassuolo	110	46	B1	C1	B2	C	2	B	C2	4.5	6	2A
Pesaro	109	41	A	B1	B1	D	1	B	C2	3.5	9	2A
Siena	101	36	B2	B1	B1	D	2	C1	C3	3.0	7	2A
Carrara	75	20	B2	B2	B1	D	0	B	C2	2.5	6	2A
Cosenza	238	57	B2	B2	B1	D	0	C2	B3	1.0	6	2B
La Spezia	216	66	B2	B2	B1	D	0	C1	B3	2.0	6	2B
Sassari	204	58	B2	B1	A3	C	1	C2	B3	2.0	7	2B
Piacenza	167	57	B2	B2	B1	E	0	C2	B3	2.0	6	2B
Cuneo	150	49	B2	B2	B1	B	2	C1	C3	2.0	6	2B
Mantova	139	49	A	C2	B2	D	1	C2	C3	2.0	7	2B
Asti	129	35	B1	C1	B2	C	0	C1	C3	1.0	6	2B
Biella	124	45	A	B1	B1	D	0	C1	C3	1.0	9	2B
Grosseto	93	29	B2	B2	B1	C	0	C2	C3	0	6	2B
Taranto	492	112	C1	C1	B2	B	1	C1	B3	3.0	4	3A
Desio	482	146	C1	D	C2	C	0	A1	C1	5.0	3	3A
Lecce	399	85	D	B2	C1	C	1	C1	B3	3.0	3	3A
Brindisi	367	76	D	B2	C1	C	1	C1	B3	3.0	3	3A
Salerno	294	75	D	B1	C1	D	4	C1	B3	6.0	4	3A
Frosinone	259	67	C1	C1	B2	B	1	A2	B2	5.0	4	3A
Messina	236	59	C2	B1	B1	C	1	C1	B3	3.0	5	3A
Vigevano	225	71	B2	C1	B2	B	0	A1	C1	5.0	5	3A
Rimini	218	67	C2	B1	B1	B	1	B	B1	5.0	5	3A
Velletri	198	42	C2	C1	B2	C	1	A2	C1	5.0	3	3A
Pavia	197	62	C1	C1	B2	B	0	A1	B2	6.0	4	3A
Treviglio	191	55	B1	D	B2	B	0	A1	C1	5.0	4	3A
Gallarate	186	70	C1	C1	B2	B	0	A1	C1	5.0	4	3A
Foggia	176	47	D	B2	C1	D	2	C1	B3	4.0	3	3A

	1	2	3	4	5	6	7	8	9	10	11	12
Latina	171	55	B1	D	B2	C	1	A2	C1	5.0	5	3A
Terni	170	48	C1	C1	B2	D	2	C1	C3	3.0	4	3A
Cassino	151	35	C1	C1	B2	B	1	C1	C3	2.5	4	3A
Alessandria	151	55	B1	B2	B1	E	0	C1	B3	2.0	5	3A
Potenza	136	39	D	B2	C1	D	0	C1	B3	2.0	3	3A
Bassano del Grappa	131	47	C1	D	C2	C	1	B	C2	3.5	3	3A
Monfalcone	130	36	C1	C2	B2	D	0	B	C2	2.5	4	3A
Sesto Calende	117	38	C1	B2	B1	B	0	A1	C1	5.0	5	3A
Pinerolo	116	32	C1	D	C2	B	1	A2	C1	5.0	3	3A
Cittadella	114	36	C1	C2	B2	C	1	B	C2	3.5	4	3A
Castelfranco Veneto	111	34	C1	D	C2	C	0	B	C2	2.5	3	3A
Imola	110	37	B1	D	B2	C	0	B	C1	3.0	5	3A
Montecatini Terme	109	33	C1	C2	B2	B	0	B	C2	2.5	4	3A
Viareggio	107	28	C2	C2	B2	D	0	B	C2	2.5	3	3A
Conegliano	103	37	B2	D	B2	B	1	B	C2	3.5	4	3A
Montebelluna	100	37	B2	D	B2	C	0	B	C2	2.5	4	3A
Pontedera	100	35	B2	C1	B2	B	1	B	C2	3.5	5	3A
S. Benedetto del Tronto	100	31	B2	D	B2	B	2	C1	C3	3.0	4	3A
Lugo	97	31	B2	C1	B2	E	0	B	C2	2.5	5	3A
Thiene	96	34	C1	D	C2	C	1	B	C2	3.5	3	3A
Borgomanero	92	31	C1	B2	B1	E	0	B	C2	2.5	5	3A
Empoli	91	30	B1	D	B2	C	0	A2	C1	4.0	5	3A
Santa Croce sull'Arno	88	32	B2	D	B2	D	0	B	C2	2.5	4	3A
Carpi	82	33	B2	D	B2	C	0	B	C2	2.5	4	3A
Massa	76	20	C2	C2	B2	B	0	B	C2	2.5	3	3A
Arzignano	75	34	C1	C1	B2	C	2	B	C2	4.5	4	3A
Macerata	74	24	B2	C1	B2	D	4	C1	C3	5.0	5	3A
Gorizia	72	24	B2	C2	B2	D	0	B	C2	2.5	5	3A
Aosta	70	24	C2	B2	B1	B	2	C2	C3	2.0	4	3A
Sondrio	55	18	B2	C2	B2	D	2	C2	C3	2.0	5	3A
Verbania	53	15	C2	B2	B1	C	0	B	C2	2.5	4	3A
Savona	133	37	B2	C2	B2	D	0	C2	C3	1.0	5	3B
Teramo	112	35	C1	D	C2	E	1	C1	C3	2.0	3	3B
Ascoli Piceno	107	34	C1	D	C2	C	0	C1	C3	1.0	3	3B
Crotone	98	17	C2	C1	B2	E	0	C2	C3	0	3	3B
Alba	91	32	B2	D	B2	D	0	C1	C3	1.0	4	3B
Belluno	83	28	C1	C2	B2	D	1	C2	C3	1.0	4	3B
Vercelli	77	25	B2	D	B2	E	0	C1	C3	1.0	4	3B
Imperia	52	17	B2	C2	B2	D	0	C2	C3	0	5	3B
Caserta	364	79	D	C1	C1	C	1	A2	B2	4.0	2	4A
Siracusa	258	58	D	C2	C1	E	0	C1	B3	2.0	2	4A
Aversa	234	27	D	D	C3	B	0	A2	C1	3.0	1	4A
Reggio Calabria	222	47	D	C1	C3	E	1	C1	C3	2.0	2	4A
Nola	184	28	D	D	C3	C	0	A2	C1	3.0	1	4A
Nocera Inferiore	184	32	D	C1	C3	C	1	C1	C2	2.5	2	4A
Torre Annunziata	167	26	D	D	C3	D	1	A2	C1	4.0	1	4A
Barletta	161	34	C1	E	C2	C	1	A2	C1	4.0	2	4A
Avellino	159	41	D	C2	C3	B	1	C1	C3	2.0	2	4A
Gela	159	24	C2	D	C2	D	1	C1	C3	2.0	2	4A
Bisceglie	114	20	D	D	C3	D	0	A2	C1	3.0	1	4A

	1	2	3	4	5	6	7	8	9	10	11	12
Campobasso	113	30	D	D	C3	E	2	C2	C3	2.0	1	4A
S. Giuseppe Vesuviano	110	17	D	D	C3	C	0	A2	C1	3.0	1	4A
Battipaglia	105	28	D	D	C3	C	2	C1	C2	3.5	1	4A
Benevento	103	28	D	E	C3	D	2	C1	C3	3.0	0	4A
Chieti	101	32	D	C1	C3	C	1	C1	C2	2.5	2	4A
L'Aquila	95	30	D	C1	C3	E	1	C1	C3	2.0	2	4A
Ragusa	90	25	C2	E	C2	E	1	C1	C3	2.0	1	4A
Agrigento	177	33	D	E	C3	E	0	C1	C3	1.0	0	4B
Caltanissetta	155	28	D	D	C3	E	0	C1	C3	1.0	1	4B
Catanzaro	144	37	D	D	C3	E	0	C2	C3	0	1	4B
Trapani	136	31	D	C2	C3	D	1	C2	C3	1.0	2	4B
Marsala	135	23	D	C2	C3	B	0	C2	C2	0.5	2	4B
Iglesias	129	28	D	C1	C3	B	0	C2	C3	0	2	4B
Modica	108	21	D	E	C3	C	0	C1	C2	1.0	0	4B
Rieti	98	25	D	D	C3	E	0	C1	C3	1.0	1	4B
Enna	94	16	D	E	C3	E	0	C1	C3	1.0	0	4B
Rovigo	90	28	D	D	C3	E	0	C2	C3	1.0	1	4B
Nuoro	80	22	D	C1	C3	E	1	C2	C3	1.0	2	4B
Oristano	77	20	D	C1	C3	B	1	C1	C3	1.0	2	4B
Vibo Valentia	67	14	D	D	C3	C	1	C2	C3	1.0	1	4B
Matera	65	20	D	C1	C3	C	0	C1	C3	1.0	2	4B
Isernia	47	13	D	D	C3	E	1	C2	C3	0	1	4B

Source: calculated by the author on ISTAT data.

* The rows show the 148 local urban systems which at the 1991 Census satisfied at least one of the following three conditions: a) to have more than 100,000 residents; b) to have more than 30,000 jobs; c) to be the capital city of a province. They include 19.8% of the Italian local urban systems and are grouped as they appear in the comprehensive classification (col. 12); and, within each group, by demographic size.

The columns are sorted as follows:

1 *Population*: residents at the 1991 Census (ISTAT 1997).

2 *Jobs*: employment at the 1991 Census (ISTAT 1997).

3 *Economic specialisation* (according to Chapter 2).

- A - Local urban systems with location quotient (LQ) higher than 1.00 in business services and in manufacturing employment
- B1 - Local urban systems with LQ higher than 1.00 only in manufacturing, but with a harmonic mean between this and the LQ for business services, higher than 1.00
- B2 - Local urban systems with LQ higher than 1.00 only in business services or in business services and consumer services

C1 - Local urban systems with LQ higher than 1.00 only in manufacturing
C2 - Local urban systems with LQ higher than 1.00 only in consumer services
D - Local urban systems with LQ higher than 1.00 in any of the sectors considered.

4 *International openness:* range of the international functions (according to Chapter 4).

A1 - Local urban systems of the 1st and 2nd metropolitan level
A2 - Local urban systems of the 3rd metropolitan level
B1 - Local urban systems *complete* and *articulated* non-metropolitan
B2 - Local urban systems *relatively articulated* non-metropolitan
C1 - Local urban systems *bi-specialised* in productive or research/training functions or *mono-specialised* in the latter
C2 - All the other *bi-specialised* local urban systems and those *mono-specialised* in functions other than production
D - Local urban systems *mono-specialised* in productive functions
E - Local urban systems in which the minimum threshold is not reached in any international function.

5 *Supra-regional interactions* (connections to global networks): the classes are those illustrated in this chapter, identified by combining the indicators in columns 1, 2, 3 and 4.

6 *Demographic transition*: each local urban system has been classified according to its position in the trajectories of demographic transition identified in Chapter 3.

A - 'Metropolitan' local urban systems in the final stage of *dis-urbanisation*
B - Local urban systems in *dis-urbanisation*, in the stage of *sub-urbanisation*
C - Local urban systems in *peri-urbanisation* and *urbanisation*
D - Local urban systems in *dis-urbanisation*
E - Local urban systems in *demographic decline*.

7 *Diffusive dynamic*: this phenomenon is measured according to the regional pattern of Figure 6.4, attributing to each local urban system one point for each contiguous local urban system in a positive demographic phase (B and C: in column 6). The latter were counted only once, so when a positive local urban system was contiguous to two or more local urban systems in the table, the corresponding point was attributed to the larger one, or divided between two local urban systems belonging to the same class of size.

8 *Regional urban structures*: (ref. Figure 6.2). Each local urban system has been attributed to a class according to its membership of one of the following regional structures (irrespective of the size and the hierarchical position it occupies):

A1 - *1st level metropolitan functional regions*: those including one 'metropolitan' local urban system and others classified A3 in column 5 (functional regions are the upper tier of the urban regionalisation of Italy; thus they are aggregates of local urban systems: ISTAT-IRPET 1986)

A2 - *2nd level metropolitan functional regions*: those including local urban systems classified (at most) as 'B' in column 5, surrounding a local urban system of metropolitan level

A3 - *3rd level metropolitan functional regions*: those including local urban systems surrounded by other local urban system which are not listed in the table

B - *Dense and articulated regional fabrics*: zones with a high density of large, medium-large and medium-sized local urban systems, amalgamated each other by linkages within a number of 'metropolitan' or 'urban' functional regions. Three areas have these features (see Figures 6.2 and 6.4): Po valley-Veneto, Emilia-Romagna and Northern Tuscany

C1 - *Dense fragmented fabrics*: zones with an average density of large, medium-large and medium local urban system, belonging to different functional regions, with reciprocal distances and from A1, A2 or A3 structures of less than 50 km

C2 - *Thin fragmented fabrics*: zones like C1 but with greater distances between the local urban systems.

9 *Position in the regional structures*: the local urban systems have been assigned to different classes according to their hierarchical position in their regional structures.

A1 - *Dominant metropolitan poles*: large local urban systems at the centre of a functional region (as defined by column 8) including at least two local urban systems listed in the table

A2 - *Integrated metropolitan poles*: as above with less than two local urban systems but part of a 'dense articulated regional fabric' (see col. 8)

A3 - *Isolated metropolitan poles*: large local urban systems that do not satisfy the conditions of either A1 or A2

B1 - *Integrated urban poles*: medium-large local urban systems (non-metropolitan, over 200,000 residents and/or 50,000 jobs) included in 'dense articulated regional fabrics' (see col. 8), excluding those sub B2

B2 - *Urban sub-poles*: medium-large local urban systems in 'metropolitan' functional regions (see col. 8)

B3 - *Isolated urban poles*: medium-large local urban systems that do not satisfy the conditions of either B1 or B2

C1 - *Dependent medium-sized urban systems*: medium-sized local urban systems (less than 200,000 inhabitants and/or 50,000 jobs) in 'metropolitan functional regions' (see col. 8)

C2 - *Integrated medium-sized urban systems*: medium-sized local urban systems not in 'metropolitan' functional regions but in 'dense articulated regional fabrics' (see col. 8)

C3 - *Isolated medium-sized urban systems*: medium-sized local urban systems that do not satisfy the conditions of either C1 or C2.

10 *Regional integration*: the numerical indicator that synthesises those of territorial integration in columns 7, 8 and 9, attributing to each of them a score and adding up the points obtained by each local urban system. The points are as follows:

- Index of diffusive dynamic: the number of contacts as seen in column 7
- Index of membership of regional structures (col. 8) A1 = 4, A2 = 3, A3 and B = 2, C1 = 1, C2 = 0
- Index of position (col. 9): A1, A2 and A3 = 5 points to which is added half a point for each large, medium-large or medium-sized local urban system included in a functional region; B1 and B2 = 2 points, to which is added half a point if there are local urban system in a functional region as above; B3 and C1 = 1. C2 = 0.5. C3 = 0.

11 *Functional openness*: numerical indicator that synthesises the indicators of supra-regional interactions in columns 3 and 4 to make them comparable with those of territorial interaction in columns 7, 8 and 9 (see Figure 6.3). This is obtained by attributing a score to each class and adding up the points obtained by each local urban system. The points are as follows:

- Index of economic specialisation (col. 4): A = 5, B1 = 4, B2 = 3, C1 = 2, C2 = 1, D = 0
- Index of international openness (col. 5): A = 5, B1 = 4, B2 = 3, C1 and C2 = 2, D = 1, E = 0.

12 *Comprehensive classification*: as illustrated in this chapter.

Notes

1 This classification, like the drawing up of the chapter, is the result of remarks and suggestions of the authors of the other chapters.

2 The classes are defined as follows, using the 1991 Census data: *large*, more than 500,000 residents and/or 125,000 jobs; *medium-large*, more than 200,000 residents and/or 50,000 jobs; *medium*, more than 100,000 residents and/or 30,000 jobs, or even less if the urban system is focused on the capital city of a province.

3 By 'regional', we mean the territorial scale immediately below the national one. In Italy, it corresponds to the administrative regions (see Figure 2.3 in Chapter 2).

4 This concept should be distinguished from the *internal cohesion* of the local urban system (Chapters 1 and 5). The latter cannot be considered here, as the data used is aggregated for each urban system, and thus without the possibility of assessing the differences in the internal structure (territorial, social, economic, of milieu etc.), although they are noteworthy.

5 These characteristics are in line with the hypothesis of post-Fordist development described in Chapters 1.

6 The reference is to the *functional regions* defined in ISTAT-IRPET 1986; the figures are from the 1991 Census.

7 Towards European integration

Carlo Salone

Introduction

The empirical studies carried out have highlighted the territorial patterns that characterise the Italian urban system. They also allowed us to focus on some questions crucial to the formulation of policies that set up the objectives of an integrated development of the European urban network and the socio-economic cohesion of the EU. The need to produce consistent policies on the different geographical scales has already been felt by many of the institutional actors that operate in the European context (EU, member countries, regions and local authorities) and in some this has already stimulated the definition of forward-looking documents at the national level.

In the light of what has emerged in the course of this study, this final chapter will underline some aspects of the Italian experience that demand special attention, helping also to define, although in general terms, the main guidelines for public intervention aimed at solving problems.

The analysis will start from the local scale, to then move progressively up to higher ones, presenting some measures desirable to:

- strengthen the local milieux, considered above all in their function as nodes of broader networks;
- facilitate the formation of multi-centred regional urban systems through connections between the nodes and the urban systems;
- promote the network-effect between small and medium-sized cities, thus aiding re-equilibrium and, where possible, co-operation between regional urban systems and metropolitan cities;
- spread the city-effect, reinforcing the network of local urban systems at the national scale;

- tackle the problems that have been on the table for some time with new instruments: in particular, the question of the lagging development that characterises a fair part of Southern Italy and inland areas, attempting to extend the effects of metropolitan centrality to the regional 'peripheries'.

Measures to strengthen the local milieu

The theme of local urban development is not the heart of this study, which is dedicated principally to the study of the Italian urban system and its relations with European space. However, in the analysis of the relationship between nodes and networks, and thus in a rather special perspective, the question acquires significance and stimulates a number of reflections.

Almost all observers of the urban phenomenon in Europe agree that we are seeing a vigorous return of the cities onto the continent's economic and cultural scene. The weakening of guiding and governing functions, as well, at the end of the day, of the nation states' capacity for social and economic regulation, and the still uncertain role played by regional administrative institutions, leave the field objectively open to a renewed central role of the cities. In many cases, they are key localities in the present process of economic restructuring. Paradoxically, this can be seen as one of the effects of the globalisation of the economy that has gradually consolidated since the eighties.

While it is therefore important, from the national point of view, but also from that of the supra-national institutions, to take into account the network and supra-local nature of many spatial relations, it is equally decisive to give the right weight to the functioning of the local milieu. The competitive efficiency of the cities is today a consequence of the liberalisation of trade and, at the same time, the condition for attracting influxes of extremely mobile financial capital. In reference to city promotion policies from the point of view of competition, it is possible to identify two general models of approach which are worth briefly summarising.

The first model sees passive adaptation to external stimuli without innovative drive, consisting merely in attracting outside capital and producing zero sum games. A second model, grounded in self-organisation, presupposes instead continuous improvement of the attractiveness of local resources, in which positive sum games are played, utilising positive local externalities as factors capable of reducing uncertainty (Camagni 1989 and 1996b).

In the 1980s, many EU countries saw mainly the rise of urban development policies of the first type, encouraged by general economic policy more favourable to laissez-faire attitudes than was true a decade earlier. They often made reference to the principles of strategic planning, but in reality they turned out to be more *policies for the enhancement of strategic functions* (location proposals for major international capital, urban projects with high profile publicity etc.). The spread of these experiences seems to have followed at least two paths. The first corresponds to processes of competitive emulation, triggered by the need to face up to the globalisation of markets, and involved a number of major European cities such as Barcelona, Lisbon, Lyon and so on, which were very active in terms of competition to attract inward flows of financial capital and whose experiences have been widely followed in the specialist literature (Ciciotti and Perulli 1990, Ciciotti, Florio and Perulli 1994, Calvaresi 1994, Curti and Gibelli 1996). In these matters, the awareness of the technical limits and the fairly modest outcomes of traditional approaches has led local authorities and planning agencies to consider the usefulness of extending the field of planning to sectors traditionally subject to sectorial plans, and to look for more advanced forms of co-ordinating management action. The creation of new job opportunities, falling worryingly, the strengthening of the urban economic base as a response to the challenges of international competition and the need to reinforce infrastructures lead to intervention models based on strategic management.

The second path was instead conditioned by the guiding role of public central planning bodies: the French case of DATAR was paradigmatic, promoting in the course of the eighties new forms of local and city action. This meant, above all, major projects involving parts of the urban fabric with a high symbolic value. In the most extreme cases, as some experiences in France (e.g. Montpellier and Nîmes) and Great Britain (London, Glasgow, Bristol) show very effectively, these policies were developed with no general planning framework and were accompanied by aggressive advertising campaigns. It does not seem, however, that these types of city marketing have been able to produce, on their own, significant processes of local development, partly due to the recession that hit the European economy at the end of the decade. This recession affected above all the system of small and medium-sized cities, the ones that had the greatest need to free themselves from the hegemony of the major cities. Yet from this point of view, the 'diversity' of the Italian case would appear to be a positive factor, and could perhaps provide useful suggestions for action to other countries.

The negative effects produced by market-oriented urban policies, not only on the weaker elements of local societies but, in the end, also on the very efficiency of local economies, thus force an overall rethinking of the forms of public intervention. Leaving aside the unlikely return to forms of central planning with everything resolved by public intervention, it is evident that the agility of decision-making and implementation mechanisms as well as spending constraints have to be conciliated with forms of collective action open to the extensive participation of the social groups present in the local urban context. Indeed, it is exactly this acknowledgement of the decision-making autonomy of the local actors that has been one of the most interesting aspects of many innovative urban policies, even if it has not become common practice in planning.

The main elements that characterise this new philosophy of urban intervention are:

- the adoption of horizontal and non-hierarchical decision-making approaches and forms of co-ordination of actors;
- a new awareness of processes of inclusion/exclusion of 'weak' interests, i.e. marginal social actors or ones not adequately represented; some experiences in the field of local urban policies that attempt to tackle the social consequences of economic restructuring (for example, the EU *Quartiers en crise* action) appear to move in this direction; in this experience, however, the perspective seems to prevail of seeing 'weak' interests as just subjects, and not active protagonists, in the initiatives;
- the creation of flexible mechanisms to implement localised urban policies, which envisage forms of periodical monitoring of the results achieved and allow adequate margins for changes of tack;
- the explicit recognition of negotiation as an essential forum for the definition of general goals which the plan sets and of partial objectives to be reached through a gradual process;
- the opportunity to integrate sector interventions into a coherent local development plan.

  In addition, in order to pursue *integrated sustainability* in urban development, it is above all necessary to:

- redefine the local collective identity, working on the symbolic aspects of the urban image and the sharing of certain values (actions aimed at defining a shared vision of the future development scenarios and constructing consensus around the policies undertaken) (Gibelli 1996);
- give back form, recognisability and cohesion to urban agglomerations, opposing processes of uncontrolled spread of built-up areas, also through use of the infrastructure lever (internal public transport and local wide-band telecommunications networks).

Governing multi-centred regional urban systems

The multi-centred nature of numerous metropolitan systems makes it increasingly necessary today to consider the problem of 'governing' them as a question of the choice of instruments appropriate to the needs of co-operation and co-ordination between the various urban nodes that make up these systems. Historically, the metropolitan areas have been a subject of much debate, both from the standpoint of the techniques used for territorial boundary-drawing (demographic, statistical, functional, morphological etc.) and of aspects (examined less in the specialist literature) concerning the nature and content of the bodies called on to 'govern' their economic and spatial dynamics.

As was seen in the previous chapter, these territorial structures can be identified less and less today with simple 'metropolitan areas', characterised by concentrated development. They appear increasingly as 'networks' in which a close-knit fabric of small and medium-sized cities is integrated with strong metropolitan centres within the regional context.

Dialogue with the nearest metropolitan centres is required in order to exploit the capacities for openness towards networks of European excellence. These relations are, naturally, the only way to encourage spillover processes of highly-prized functions, the only ones capable of achieving the goal of 'decentralised concentration' which already characterises the European core.

To this end, the creation of physical infrastructures of communication (second level airports, interconnecting lines with the first level nodes of the high-speed networks, diffuse telecommunications networks and other measures, as well as the extension of the existing networks well beyond the linear concentration along a few privileged axes) would provide acceptable conditions of access to the great trans-European networks, and through them to the urban network of excellence, in addition to guaranteeing the required cohesion within the regional metropolitan networks (Batten 1995).

It is thus also necessary to bring up to date the government and planning instruments traditionally associated with the phenomenon, where it is characterised as a process of formation of regional metropolitan networks. The start of forms of collaboration between networks of medium-sized cities and metropolitan nodes, on the base of existing synergies, can produce much more tangible positive effects than through competition between these spatial components, at the end of which the weight of the metropolis would be dominant. In the Italian situation, for example, there are especially numerous cases in which regional networks can be associated with strong metropolitan systems.

In this case, interest is lost in the 'functionalist' conceptions of metropolitan government, i.e. the production of new *institutional* places of administration and planning, based on a 'hierarchical-areal' vision of territorial relations and which operate according to a top-down approach. The 'functionalist' conceptions have generally proposed levels of territorial government in which the prerogatives of bodies of an intermediate scale (such as the Province in Italy or, with some differences, the Department in France) are added to administrative powers and areas of responsibility typical of urban administration, but of a 'higher level'. These levels of government operate in given territorial partitions which show the typical rigidity of institutional jurisdictions.

The second type of solution seems more appropriate. We find significant examples in the French *établissements publics* such as the *Districts Urbains* or the *Communautés de Villes*. These are experiences which have a low 'functionalist' content being the result of greater flexibility of action and orchestration of local powers.

These relatively new forms of urban intervention can also be considered as the combined outcome of reform processes of the political/decision-making system and the use of instruments for strategic action, in which co-operation between the different levels of government, public-private partnership and transparency in the negotiation of the stakes are decisive elements.

These are not, however, political and administrative solutions assumed and implemented authoritatively through regional legislation (otherwise they would have been seen as the result of 'functionalist' conceptions as described above), but the outcomes of an agreed definition of the territorial boundaries and powers of action of the 'new' government institution. In a certain sense, it is the problems that define the territorial frontiers of action, and not vice versa.

In Italy, a country characterised by an overall weakness of public action in urban policy, the development of concerted forms of action and government of the metropolitan systems should therefore be encouraged through the definition of more flexible national regulatory frameworks, of a new governance framework, and not through the production of new local government institutions.

This would prevent the creation of new centres of bureaucratic power and the rationalisation of public spending commitments, as the need to find additional resources to make these institutions work would be reduced, while the search for organisational and management synergies between the existing local authorities would be fostered.

Promoting the network-effect among small and medium-sized cities

Although the empirical evidence provided in the previous chapter gives a glimpse, at least in Italy, of the growing importance of the urban systems at the regional scale, gradually being integrated more closely with the historically dominant metropolitan centres, the hegemony still exercised by the metropolises in many European regions requires a significant effort to achieve spatial re-equilibrium, redistributing at least some command functions.

The case is instead more problematic for great regional spaces without metropolitan nodes: the West of France, many inland areas of the Iberian peninsula, a good part of Greece and the North of Scandinavia. Here, a strengthening of the weak link in the urban network, i.e. the fabric of networks of intermediate cities, is of vital importance in order to avoid the marginalisation of these areas in Europe. Yet, it is also a difficult challenge.

Some member countries of the European Union launched national initiatives some time ago to encourage the establishment of voluntary alliances between medium-sized cities. The experience, whose results have been hotly debated, of the French *réseaux des villes* seems to fit into this frame (DATAR 1991). The relative ineffectiveness of many of these experiences also depends on the fact that there can be no 'metropolitan effect' without a metropolis. It cannot derive only from the co-operation and shared goals of small and medium-sized cities, but has to lean on synergical relations with existing metropolitan nodes. As an alternative, it has to be strongly supported by policies of decentralisation of command functions by the central state.

Some programmes of inter-urban co-operation included in the EU initiatives, such as some networks of Recite and Med-Urbs programmes, assume the intermediate dimension of cities as the reference for spatial re-equilibrium action.

This type of network can, however, adequately deploy its own development potential only under certain conditions: that there be easy infrastructure links between the nodes and that objectives and programmes are shared pragmatically by local political institutions and economic decision-makers (Batten 1995). It would seem that these conditions can be ensured above all by spatial proximity/connectivity and by the need to tackle challenges that are felt to be common ones.

On the infrastructure level, it is necessary to take action on: 1) connection with the nodes in the global network, 2) functional and management integration of transport modes, 3) selective strengthening of access to encourage targeted sections of demand. The promotion of forms of inter-municipal co-operation must therefore be grounded in the consolidation of the existing connections between sufficiently specialised intermediate nodes, ensured by physical infrastructures but also by infostructures, so as to constitute complementary urban networks. The marginalisation of small and medium-sized cities from the major networks can in fact be mitigated by the new role that accessibility can play. The sense of this recommendation is not to consider accessibility as a pre-requisite to be obtained wherever and however. What counts is not reaching a uniform degree of spatial proximity as much as the establishment of articulated forms of continuity of networks and fluidity of demand. The organisation of these forms cannot stem only from the application of 'rules of optimisation' (often too abstract and generalised for the diverse territorial structures), but must stem from analysis of the real possibilities of connection among networks, which can emerge above all by putting the cities' local specific features at the centre of attention.

On the institutional and management level, there can also be networks founded on inter-institutional partnership between the local authorities involved: these are networks in which co-operative action between different local authorities consists in sharing economic and organisational resources to bear the costs of the creation and co-management of large-scale collective amenities (airports, trade fair centres, waste treatment plants, water purification and distribution plants etc.).

The intermediate cities should also act with greater conviction to create forms of co-operative lobbying towards central governments and supra-national institutions, in particular the EU, with the intention of attracting greater influxes of finance and expertise. It may be useful to reflect on the experiences of interurban co-operation that have been conducted so far in Europe, especially those in the Recite Programme of DG XVI. Some authors (e.g., Figueiredo 1995) maintain, in fact, that these tend to reproduce some inter-regional inequalities in the 'grape' form. This would seem to occur because of the fact that the cities tend to dialogue with other centres characterised by at least comparable development conditions and economic performance levels. One non-negligible side effect of the classic Keynesian redistribution rationale that regulates the allocation of Structural Funds is a triggering of competition between the 'poor', in which European integration is seen only as an additional source of funding, to compensate for the long-term deficit (Hadjimichalis 1994).

EU action should therefore concentrate on the need to be selective about participation in the networks of co-operation so as to guarantee the presence of cities with reasonably varied economic profiles, thus encouraging the circulation of the 'success stories' of some cities and a more effective exchange of experience. On the other hand, in the current conditions it does not seem easy to avoid the fact that some 'opportunist' members see participation in the thematic networks merely as access to the EU levers of financial support.

Networking the local urban systems at national scale: interventions to diffuse the city-effect

Many European countries have been making an effort to produce coherent visions of their national spatial structure, following original paths strongly influenced by local planning traditions. In Italy, despite the traditional state intervention in the economy, there has been a lack of government reflection on the dynamics of territorial development and on the possible measures to direct them towards forms of re-equilibrium. Only recently has the Ministry of Public Works set up an in-depth programme of study and monitoring of the country's settlement structure. One of the aims is to promote, in the formulation of territorial policies

> the passage from a sectorial and hierarchical decision-making process to a more complex one, characterised by the complementarity and subsidiarity of diverse powers and by the need for broad agreement on choices, with particular reference to the relationship between the central administration and the local governments (Cempella 1996, p. 17).

These are important signals which need, however, to be specified more incisively in terms of policy content and harmonisation in the choices of the different levels of government involved in the processes (municipalities, provinces, regions, nation states, EU) (Di Palma and Mele 1996, Nigris 1996).

Innovative policies in the sense described above have to hinge on two main pivots: firstly, the promotion of forms of inter-sectorial co-ordination of the development programmes (infrastructures, infostructures, housing construction, decentralisation of important public functions) and, secondly, the creation of decision-making places in which the inter-institutional co-operation of a vertical type (EU-nation states-local governments) and horizontal ones (between local authorities) becomes an ordinary component of public action.

On the national level, the guidelines proposed by government bodies assume as central planks:

1) the formulation of a system of nation-wide territorial policies, linked into the development lines of the EU and other European countries;

2) the definition of a framework of consistency between the various levels of government and local planning;
3) the guarantee of effective co-ordination between the planning of major national infrastructures and territorial planning at the various levels of responsibility.

On this front, the role of central government must be less and less that of an active decision-maker and operator and increasingly an organisational pivot, capable above all of providing the various local powers with an agile regulatory framework for the construction of territorial policies based on: 1) inter-institutional negotiation and agreement with social actors, 2) construction of integrated budgets in which public resources are supported by private funds.

In the Italian case, in particular, this demands an additional creative effort which must, in any case, go in the direction of a reduction in red tape and assume a problem-solving approach.

In addition, the probable evolution towards a 'lighter' form of the state, perhaps with a federal structure, advises against the creation of a central agency endowed with broad powers on the model of other countries. The central level could instead maintain monitoring and co-ordination functions, delegating to the regional level the definition of the most suitable instruments for governing the ongoing dynamics in the various local urban and metropolitan systems.

All the institutional actors, present with varying responsibilities and active on different scales in the field of territorial policies, must thus work together to reach the goals of redistribution of the city-effect and of key functions. Among the measures necessary, the following should undoubtedly be noted:

1) as *direct intervention*:
- extension of transport and telecommunications infrastructures so as to improve the conditions of accessibility in less well-endowed local urban systems (mainly responsibility of the state, but also of intermediate institutions);
- aid for regional development, which today depends on and will depend even more in the future on EU funding; in this case, there is a dual level of intervention, because it involves both the central government and European institutions, and local communities, alone or in development associations (see paragraph below);
- environmental protection measures to safeguard against uncontrolled urban sprawl (green belts, urban re-use policies etc., the responsibility of local authorities);

2) as *indirect intervention*:

- industrial policies favourable to innovation (support for industrial districts, promotion of technopoles, business service centres, the responsibility of local government);
- vocational training policies (in which the regions should act more effectively than in the past, also in co-operation with higher scale bodies);
- tourism promotion activities, following models that abandon intensive exploitation of given environmental resources and focus on service facilities, making the most of the environment from a protectionist standpoint (action to be taken on the regional or intermediate scale);
- tax policies giving greater financial autonomy to the levels of local and regional government, connected to reform of administration.

These measures can encourage co-operation or trigger positive dynamics of competition between regional urban systems. Both processes are useful for the purpose of balancing the national networks, above all in contexts characterised by metropolitan dominance.

Areas of lagging development: new instruments for old problems

In the cases where the medium-sized cities of an urban system show conditions of particular fragility (for Italy, the reference is above all to the Mezzogiorno, where conditions of lagging development are associated with weakness and fragmentation of the local socio-economic fabric), serious consideration must be given to the adoption of alternative instruments to the traditionally ineffective ones of emergency intervention.

These instruments must touch at least three aspects.

The first concerns the performance of the infrastructure systems in a logic of connection among different networks. As we saw in the previous chapter, the regions of the Mezzogiorno and their urban systems are not, overall, affected by infrastructure shortcomings, but suffer from great inefficiencies in the capacity to built networks among the various levels and, through these, fully exploit the urban resources that characterise them. In this perspective, local and regional endowments must be enhanced through an adequate policy of interconnection within the national urban system, and in particular with the urban system of Northern Italy: impetus must therefore be given to the great networks south of Rome, to lines to connect the nodes of the port system together and to maritime and air relations with the other shores of the Mediterranean, above all the eastern and southern coasts. In addition, it is necessary to modernise the national telecommunications lines, to bring them up to

European standards and to link into the major trans-European telecommunications networks.

The second concerns cross-border relations (even if relations with the eastern and southern shores of the Mediterranean are seen in Europe more as a problem than as an opportunity). Our country's geographical position urges more incisive action on at least two territorial fronts: the first involves the hinge function that the Po valley in part already plays between the regions of the Latin Arc and central and eastern Europe, the second is the great potential of Italy from the point of view of links with the Balkans and the Maghreb countries. The first set of relations, which are effectively already deployed along the axis of Lyon-Turin-Milan-Verona-Trieste, needs above all adequate infrastructure reinforcing. The second type of relations suffers from difficulties that are of both a physical and political nature, but in any case demand an effort to overcome them. The need to establish stable relations between Italy and the African and Balkan coasts of the Mediterranean is confirmed by the initiation in other points of the European Union of initiatives with a similar goal and which could be seen as competing projects.

In other areas of Europe, for example in Spain, it is in fact easier to recognise an explicitly 'Mediterranean' dimension of infrastructure policies: for instance, the project for a Tangiers-Tarifa tunnel has been on the agenda of Morocco and Spain for some time, even though doubts and perplexities persist, particularly on the Spanish side (Fareri 1995).

In this sense, the still generic hypothesis of the 'multi-modal corridor' along the Adriatic could bring strategic consequences for Italy in the medium and long term. It could generate significant effects, however, only if it manages to link adequately with coastal Dalmatian-Montenegran-Albanian-Greek communication axis and the trans-Balkan crossing of Durazzo-Sofia-Varna proposed by the Christopherson Commission (Pavia and Palazzo 1995).

Finally, the third aspect concerns the possibility of promoting forms of self-centred development that use local resources not only for the comparative advantages linked to particular factors (labour market, availability of land etc.) but also by exploiting latent potential.

On the level of the drive to form self-organising local urban systems, the possibilities opened by forms of 'negotiated planning' should be evaluated positively, and they should assume an 'ordinary' nature and constitute a set of intervention methodologies 'exportable' to other European contexts.

This line of intervention (Gorla and Vito Colonna 1995, CNEL 1996) was introduced by legislative decree in the course of 1995 and was included in the budget for the year. It aims to make the decision-making processes and mechanisms of resource distribution more fluid. The 'territorial development pacts', promoted by the CNEL, can also play a useful role in mobilising financial, technical and institutional resources for the purposes of self-organised development on the basis of social and economic partnership between the institutions and organised interest groups (local authorities, chambers of commerce, trade associations, voluntary groups etc.).

The model of 'negotiated planning' is in some ways similar to that of the European structural policies programmes and, like it, is not faultless: it can in fact happen that an 'opportunistic' criterion of conformity to the formal pre-requisites for funding prevails over the consistency between development strategy and conditions of the local milieu. This is a challenge that has to be met, as an alternative to the traditional policies of support which have not eliminated, indeed in some cases have even strengthened, the mechanisms of external dependency of peripheral societies and economies.

The Italian urban system in the European context: the strong and weak points on which to take action

After have proposed some regulatory implications of the main questions that emerged in the course of this study, it is now useful to try to identify the weak and strong points that characterise the Italian urban system, in a perspective of its increasing integration into the European context.

These factors of development and backwardness have been summarised in Table 7.1, starting from the local scale to move on to spatial relations of a higher order (national and supra-national). Consideration of these factors can also indicate some territorial policy guidelines, both direct and indirect, that it would be advisable to pursue with the goal of governing the spatial phenomena underlined and guaranteeing greater efficiency of the various political and decision-making systems involved.

The first strong point of the Italian urban system is represented by the quality and considerable wealth of milieu that characterise its cities, including small and medium-sized ones, resources that can encourage virtuous relations between local supply and the global demand expressed by the networks to which the urban centres belong.

The second positive factor, linked to the first, concerns the economic base of Italian cities. In many of our country's urban centres, in fact, the process of post-Fordist industrial transition seems relatively advanced compared to other urban systems of the 'European periphery': the results of the analysis highlight how this phenomenon is especially accentuated in the major cities of North-western Italy.

Table 7.1
The Italian urban system: weak points, strong points and guidelines for action

Strong points	Weak points	Actions	Government levels and policies
• wealth of local urban milieux • strong historical identities	• municipalism, lack of voluntary regional networks • unused potential (esp. in Southern Italy) • difficulty in cross-border connections	• support for cross-border co-operation	*local*: paradiplomacy, urban marketing *supra-local*: multilateral EU city and region relations (CERM)
• cities in advanced stage of post-Fordist transition	• marginality compared to the major trans-European networks	• guarantee connections to physical and immaterial networks • strengthen some nodes as natural gates, in particular towards the Mediterranean	*local/supra-local*: equip nodes (ports, trade terminals etc.) *supra-local:* national scale infrastructure policies with new instruments (project financing, partnership etc.)
• network evolution of metropolitan systems	• urban sprawl • consumption of agricultural land	• control of urban sprawl • reform of planning instruments • support for co-operation between small and medium sized cities	*local:* appropriate land use policies; strategic planning; environmental protection *supra-local:* decentralisation of power; voluntary associations between cities (national and EU programmes)
• articulated urban system • interconnected network • regional systems already formed or being formed	• accentuated internal disparities • poor local/regional and national policy co-ordination • missing links • lack of governance	• strengthening of internal communication networks • co-ordination of urban and territorial policies on basis of subsidiarity	*local:* self-organisation *local/supra-local:* negotiated planning, regional co-operation networks *supra-local:* government co-ordination agencies (see below) between sector policies (esp. transport) and territorial organisation
• part of urban network of European 'excellence'	• lack of government policy for cities	• guiding role of central government bodies	*supra-local:* government agency for urban areas

This would seem objectively to favour the insertion of important nodes of the Italian urban system in the circuits of the international circulation of capital and the processes of relocation of major trans-national corporations.

Moving on from the local scale to that of interurban network relations, it is worth repeating the results of our analysis: in many areas of the country the historical antagonism between metropolitan agglomerations and medium-sized cities is being overcome. The former now show an acceptable degree of embeddedness in their own regions, while the latter have undergone a network evolution, which allows a more efficient spatial division of functions in the different regional urban systems according to organisational models patterned on complementarity. Signs of this evolution are evident in the major multi-centred metropolitan structures of Northern Italy. They can also be seen in the Mezzogiorno where, like in the Naples metropolitan system, they assume the traits of peripheral recentralisation that have a positive influence both on local growth and on the restructuring of the main cities.

Thus, it can be said that network relations, although on different scales and with different degrees of interconnection, now characterise many parts of the national urban system, and can be used as a competitive advantage in the European context.

The last two points of strength to be noted concern the Italian urban system as a whole.

First of all, the dense and articulated nature of the Italian urban system appears of great importance, placing it alongside the European 'ridge' and distinguishing it quite clearly from the urban structures of other continental 'peripheries'.

Secondly, it is important to consider that many Italian cities, even medium-sized ones, are part of the network of European excellence.

Nevertheless, the Italian urban system also displays some undeniable weak points, some of which mirror the factors of strength listed above. The most evident are described below, indicating the possible corrective action and the institutions responsible.

The first element of weakness is the difficulty underlined repeatedly in making efficient cross-border connections. Co-operation between bordering regions, in addition to demanding the overcoming of natural barriers, also imposes paradiplomacy and city marketing initiatives at the local level while, on the higher government levels, impetus has to be given to multilateral relations on the model experimented by the European Council of Regions and Municipalities and also by other international bodies.

Secondly, but closely linked to the previous point, we should remember the marginal position of the Italian urban system as a whole compared to the major European infrastructure networks. Connections with these networks (physical communication and telecommunications) must also be accompanied by the strengthening of some nodes that function as 'natural bridges' towards countries on the southern shores of the Mediterranean and the Balkans. In this case, while the equipping of the nodes (ports, trade terminals etc.) is delegated to the local level, the national level should define the network infrastructure policies to serve the 'natural bridges', guaranteeing rapid implementation times (using innovative instruments such as project financing, partnership and so on).

It is also necessary to connect the major infrastructure networks and make them complementary, with particular reference to the metropolises: this means tackling the problem of interconnection. If not solved, this could generate 'chains of marginality' which would also involve the smaller nodes.

This means supporting integration between transport modes and fostering not just speed as such but functional continuity and fluidity of service and, as far as the territorial aspects are concerned, integration with land use and city property policies. Lack of attention to these aspects risks widening the gap between new infrastructures and existing facilities, with the consequent underuse of the former and gradual decline of the latter.

Urban sprawl, a phenomenon that mirrors the progressive network articulation of much of the national urban system, undoubtedly represents, with costs due to the use of free land, an element that damages the country's competitive capacity in terms of settlement quality. Closer control of the processes of urban spread is thus needed. While at the local scale this can be entrusted to appropriate land use policies, on the supra-local level it certainly demands a push towards co-operation, above all between medium-sized and small cities, so that they can agree and co-ordinate more rationally the expansion processes of built-up areas. National and supra-national government bodies can instead provide a more flexible regulatory framework and economic incentives for voluntary association initiatives between cities.

Even though the degree of articulation of the Italian urban system is good as a whole, the analyses show the persistence of accentuated disparities, in which many areas of Southern Italy appear particularly disadvantaged. If the model of spatial reorganisation is that of 'distributed centrality', often mentioned in EU documents and ones of many member countries, it is necessary to reflect on the need to strengthen the more fragile components of the Italian urban system. To this end, it is unthinkable to intervene only on the lever of infrastructures, even if more has to be done in terms of connections between local urban systems and major networks. It is also necessary to stimulate the planning capacities of local authorities so as to activate endogenous development processes capable of producing cumulative and emulative effects. To do this, negotiated planning and territorial instruments represent an interesting step forward in the search for a 'contractual' and non-hierarchical interaction between the national level (the central government agencies that provide the instruments of co-ordination and targeted financial resources) and the local level (local authorities, understood as 'federations' of localities and economic and social actors).

In the background to this whole set of intervention measures, it is worth drawing the attention of political decision-makers to the usefulness of looking for greater co-ordination between EU bodies and Departments of the Italian government responsible for economic and urban/regional planning.

Bibliography

Alessandrini, S. (1992), 'Internazionalizzazione dell'economia padana', in Fondazione Giovanni Agnelli (a cura di), *La Padania, una regione italiana in Europa*, Edizioni della Fondazione G. Agnelli, Torino, pp. 121-194.

Allum, P.A. (1973), *Politics and society in post-war Naples*, Cambridge University Press, Cambridge.

Bagnasco, A. (1977), *Tre Italie. La problematica territoriale dello sviluppo*, il Mulino, Bologna.

Bagnasco, A. (1986), *Torino. Un profilo sociologico*, Einaudi, Torino.

Bagnasco, A. (1990b), 'La cultura come risorsa', in *La città dopo Ford. Il caso di Torino*, Bagnasco, A. (a cura di), Bollati Boringhieri, Torino, pp. 46-67.

Bagnasco, A. (1994), *Fatti sociali formati nello spazio. Cinque lezioni di sociologia urbana e regionale*, Angeli, Milano.

Bagnasco, A. (a cura di) (1990a), *La città dopo Ford. Il caso di Torino*, Bollati Boringhieri, Torino.

Bagnasco, A. and Le Galès, P. (sous la dir.) (1997), *Villes en Europe*, Paris, La Découverte.

Barbagallo, F. (1997), *Napoli fine Novecento. Politici, camorristi, imprenditori*, Einaudi, Torino.

Bassolino, A. (1995), 'Indirizzi generali di governo', *Spazio e Società*, n. 69, pp. 57-62.

Batten, D.F. (1995), 'Network cities: creative urban agglomerations for the 21st century', *Urban Studies*, vol. 32, n. 2, pp. 313-328.

Becattini, G. (1986), 'Riflessioni sullo sviluppo socio-economico della Toscana in questo dopoguerra', in Mori, G. (a cura di), *Storia d'Italia. Le regioni dall'Unità a oggi. La Toscana*, Einaudi, Torino, pp. 901-924.

Becchi Collidà, A. (1979), *Politiche del lavoro e garanzia del reddito in Italia*, il Mulino, Bologna.

Becchi Collidà, A. (1984), *La terziarizzazione urbana e la crisi delle città*, Angeli, Milano.

Berque, A. (1990), *Médiance. De milieux en paysages*, Gip Reclus, Montpellier.

Berry B.J.L. (1976), 'The counterurbanization process: urban America since 1970', in Berry, B.J.L. (ed.), *Urbanization and counterurbanization*, Sage, Beverly Hills, pp. 17-30.

Bflr (Bundesforschungsanstalt für Landeskunde und Raumordnung) (1994), *Spatial Planning Policies in a European Context*, Federal Ministry for Regional Planning, Bonn.

Bobbio, L. (1990), 'Archeologia industriale e terziario avanzato: il riutilizzo del Lingotto', in Dente, B., Bobbio, L., Fareri, P. and Morisi, M. (a cura di), *Metropoli per progetti. Attori e processi di trasformazione urbana a Firenze, Torino, Milano*, il Mulino, Bologna, pp. 101-161.

Boeri, S., Lanzani, A. and Marini, E. (1993), *Il territorio che cambia. Ambienti, paesaggi e immagini della regione milanese*, Associazione Interessi Metropolitani-Abitare Segesta, Milano.

Bolocan, M.G. and Salone, C. (1996), 'Approcci strategici alla prova. Alcune esperienze italiane', *Urbanistica*, n. 106, pp. 78-91.

Bonifazi, C. and Cantalini, B. (1988), 'Mobilità interna e migrazioni interregionali', in Irp (Istituto di Ricerche sulla Popolazione), *Secondo rapporto sulla situazione demografica italiana*, Roma, pp. 141-149.

Bonneville, M., Buisson, A., Rousier N. and Commerçon, N. (1992), *Villes européennes et internationalisation*, Programme Rhône-Alpes Recherches en Sciences Humaines, Lyon.

Bonomi, A. (1996), *Il trionfo della moltitudine. Forme e conflitti della società che viene*, Bollati Boringhieri, Torino.

Borlenghi, E. (a cura di) (1990), *Città e industria verso gli anni Novanta*, Edizioni della Fondazione G. Agnelli, Torino.

Boulding, K. (1978), 'The City as an Element in the International System', in Bourne, L.S. and Simmons, J.W. (eds), *Systems of Cities*, Oxford University Press, New York.

Brunet, R. (1996), 'L'Europe des réseaux', in Dematteis, G. and Dansero, E. (a cura di), *Regioni e reti nello spazio unificato europeo*, Società di Studi Geografici, Firenze, pp. 237-260.

Brusco, S. (1989), 'Il modello Emilia: disintegrazione produttiva ed integrazione sociale', in Brusco, S. (a cura di), *Piccole imprese e distretti industriali*, Rosenberg & Sellier, Torino, pp. 243-291.

Cabodi, C. (1998), 'Le reti della collaborazione scientifica e della mobilità interuniversitaria nel sistema urbano europeo', in Bonavero, P. and Dansero, E. (a cura di), *L'Europa delle regioni e delle reti*, Utet Libreria, Torino, pp. 393-404.

Cafiero, S. and Busca, A. (1970), *Lo sviluppo metropolitano in Italia*, SVIMEZ, Roma.

Calvaresi, C. (1994), 'Alcune note sulla pianificazione strategica: matrici teoriche e processi di piano', *Progetto e gestione*, n. 9-10, pp. 12-60.

Camagni R.P. (a cura di) (1996a), *Città in Europa: globalizzazione, coesione e sviluppo sostenibile*, Riunione dei Ministri delle Politiche Regionali, Venezia.

Camagni, R.P. (1989), 'Cambiamento tecnologico, milieu locale e reti di imprese: verso una teoria dinamica dello spazio economico', *Economia e politica industriale*, n. 64, pp. 209-236.

Camagni, R.P. (1992), *Economia urbana. Principi e modelli teorici*, NIS, Roma.

Camagni, R.P. (1996b), 'La città come impresa, l'impresa come piano, il piano come rete', in Curti, F. and Gibelli, M.C. (a cura di), *Pianificazione strategica e gestione dello sviluppo urbano*, Alinea, Firenze.

Camagni, R.P. and De Blasio, G. (a cura di) (1993), *Le reti di città. Teoria, politiche e analisi nell'area padana*, Angeli, Milano.

Camagni, R.P., Fiori, L., Guiducci, R. and Morganti, F. (a cura di) (1994), *Milano città d'Europa. Progetti possibili, risorse attivabili*, Associazione MeglioMilano, Abitare Segesta Documenti, Milano.

Campos Venuti, G. (1993), *Cinquant'anni: tre generazioni urbanistiche*, in Campos Venuti, G. and Oliva, F. (a cura di), *Cinquant'anni di urbanistica in Italia: 1942-1992*, Laterza, Bari, pp. 5-39.

Carozzi, C. and Mioni, A. (1970), *L'Italia in formazione. Ricerche e saggi sullo sviluppo urbanistico del territorio nazionale*, Laterza, Bari.

Cattan, N., Pumain, D., Rozenblat, C. and Saint-Julien, T. (1994), *Le système des villes européennes*, Anthropos, Paris.

CEC (Commission of the European Communities) (1993), *White Paper: Growth, Competitiveness, Employment*, Office for the Official Publications of the European Communities, Brussels-Luxembourg.

CEC DG XVI (1991), *Europe 2000. Outlook for the Development of the Community's Territory*, Office for the Official Publications of the European Communities, Brussels-Luxembourg.

CEC DG XVI (1993), *Community Activities in Urban Matters: The Development of the Urban System and the Urban Dimension in Community Policies*, Office for Official Publications of the European Communities, Brussels-Luxembourg.

Celant, A. (a cura di) (1988), *Nuova città e nuova campagna. L'Italia nella transizione*, Pàtron, Bologna.

Cempella F. (1996), 'Territorio, infrastrutture e ruolo dell'amministrazione centrale', in Clementi, A, Dematteis, G. and Palermo, P.C. (a cura di), *Le forme del territorio italiano. Temi e immagini del mutamento*, Laterza, Roma-Bari, vol. 1, pp. 13-42.

Cencini, C., Dematteis, G. e Menegatti, B. (a cura di) (1983), *L'Italia emergente. Indagine geo-demografica sullo sviluppo periferico*, Angeli, Milano.

Chase-Dunn, C. (1984), 'Urbanization in the World System: New Directions for Research', in Smith, M.P. (ed.), *Cities in Transformation*, Sage, Beverly Hills.

Cheshire, P.C. (1995), 'A new phase of urban development in Western Europe? The evidence for the 1980s', *Urban Studies*, vol. 32, n. 7, pp. 1045-1063.

Chiesi, A.M. (1980), 'L'analisi dei reticoli sociali: teoria e metodi', *Rassegna di Sociologia*, n. 2, pp. 291-310.

Chiesi, A.M. (1981), 'L'analisi dei reticoli sociali. Un'introduzione alle tecniche', *Rassegna di Sociologia*, n. 4, pp. 577-603.

Ciampi, F. (1994), *Squilibri e assetto finanziario nelle Pmi. Finanziamenti e società italiana negli anni Novanta*, Firenze, Banca Toscana.

Ciciotti, E. and Perulli, P. (1990), *Politiche urbane per una metropoli europea: Lione*, Quaderno Aim, n. 6, Milano.

Ciciotti, E., Florio, R. and Perulli, P. (1994), *Milano: competizione senza strategia ?*, Quaderno Aim n. 24, Milano.

Clementi, A., Dematteis G. and Palermo P.C. (a cura di) (1996), *Le forme del territorio italiano.* (vol. 1: *Temi e immagini del mutamento*; vol. 2: *Ambienti insediativi e contesti locali*), Laterza, Roma-Bari.

CNEL (Consiglio Nazionale dell'Economia e del Lavoro) (1996), *La normativa dei patti territoriali: una lettura comparata*, CNEL, Roma.

Committee for Territorial Development (1998) *European Spatial Development Perspective*, Meeting of Ministers Responsible for Spatial Planning of the European Union, Glasgow.

Compagna, F. (1967), *La politica della città*, Laterza, Bari.

Conti, G. (1991), 'La popolazione', in Fuà, G. (a cura di), *Orientamenti per la politica del territorio*, il Mulino, Bologna, pp. 25-39.

Conti, S. (1982), *Un territorio senza geografia. Agenti industriali, strategie e marginalità meridionale*, Angeli, Milano.

Conti, S. and Spriano, G. (a cura di) (1990), *Effetto città. Sistemi urbani e innovazione: prospettive per l'Europa degli anni Novanta*, Edizioni della Fondazione G. Agnelli, Torino.

Conti, S., Dematteis, G. and Emanuel, C. (1995), 'The development of areal and network systems', in Dematteis, G. and Guarrasi, V. (a cura di), *Urban Networks*, Pàtron, Bologna.

Cooke, P. (ed.) (1989), *Localities. The changing face of urban Britain*, Unwin Hyman, London.

Cori, B. (1983), 'Sguardo d'insieme al sistema insediativo italiano', in *Atti del XXIII Congresso Geografico Italiano*, Università di Catania, Istituto di Geografia, Facoltà di Lettere, vol. 2, pp. 347-391.

Costa, P. and Canestrelli, E. (1983), *Agglomerazione urbana, localizzazione industriale e Mezzogiorno*, Giuffré, Milano.

Costa, P., Martellato, D. and Van der Borg, J. (1990), 'L'economia del sistema urbano e regionale italiano. Le trasformazioni 1971-1981', in Martellato, D. and Sforzi, F. (a cura di), *Studi sui sistemi urbani*, Angeli, Milano, pp. 263-299.

Curti, F. and Gibelli, M.C. (a cura di) (1996), *Pianificazione strategica e gestione dello sviluppo urbano*, Alinea, Firenze.

DATAR (1991), *En Europe, des villes en réseaux*, La Documentation Française, Paris.

De Lavergne F., and Mollet, P. (1991), 'The international development of intermediate sized cities in Europe: Strategies and networks', *Ekistics*, vol. 58, n. 350-351, pp. 368-381.

De Roo, P. (1994), 'Quatre scénarios pour les villes d'Europe entre réseau et territoire', in DATAR, *Dossier Prospective et Territoires*, La Documentation Française, Paris.

De Santis, G. (1991), 'La distribuzione della popolazione', in Fuà, G. (a cura di), *Orientamenti per la politica del territorio*, il Mulino, Bologna, pp. 179-196.

De Vecchis, G. (1992), *La montagna italiana. Verso nuove dinamiche territoriali: i valori del passato e le prospettive di recupero e di sviluppo*, Edizioni Kappa, Roma.

Dematteis, G. (1983), 'Deconcentrazione metropolitana, crescita periferica e ripopolamento di aree marginali: il caso dell'Italia', in Cencini, C., Dematteis, G. and Menegatti, B. (a cura di), *L'Italia emergente. Indagine geo-demografica sullo sviluppo periferico*, Angeli, Milano, pp. 105-142.

Dematteis, G. (1988), 'Valorizzazione e trasformazioni territoriali. Problemi teorico-metodologici con riferimento all'Italia centro-settentrionale', in Leone, U. (a cura di), *Valorizzazione e sviluppo territoriale in Italia*, Angeli, Milano, pp. 44-69.

Dematteis, G. (1995), 'Le trasformazioni territoriali e ambientali', in Barbagallo, F. (a cura di), *Storia dell'Italia repubblicana, II/1. Politica, economia e società*, Einaudi, Torino, pp. 661-709.

Dematteis, G. (1996), 'Towards a metropolitan urban system in Europe: core centrality vs network distributed centrality', in Pumain, D. and Saint-Julien, T. (eds), *Urban Networks in Europe/Réseaux urbains en Europe*, J. Libbey / Ined, Paris, pp. 19-28.

Dematteis, G. (a cura di) (1992), *Il fenomeno urbano in Italia: interpretazioni, prospettive, politiche*, Angeli, Milano.

Dematteis, G. and Emanuel, C. (1992), 'La diffusione urbana: interpretazioni e valutazioni', in Dematteis, G. (a cura di), *Il fenomeno urbano in Italia: interpretazioni, prospettive, politiche*, Angeli, Milano, pp. 91-103.

Dematteis, G. and Emanuel, C. (1995), 'Le dinamiche dell'urbanizzazione negli anni '80', *Orizzonti Economici*, n. 75, pp. 17-28.

Dematteis, G., Gambino, R. and Coppola, P. (1986), 'Città e territorio negli anni '80. Prima analisi delle tendenze, dei problemi e delle politiche', in *Progetto Finalizzato Struttura ed Evoluzione dell'Economia Italiana*, CNR, Sottoprogetto 4, Tema 8, Working Paper n. 2, Torino.

Di Palma, M. and Mele, G. (1996), 'Tra economia e territorio: politiche comunitarie e nazionali', in Clementi, A., Dematteis, G., and Palermo, P.C. (eds), *Le forme del territorio italiano. Temi e immagini del mutamento*, Laterza, Roma-Bari, vol. 1, pp. 239-258.

Dupuy, G. (1991), *L'urbanisme des réseaux. Théories et méthodes*, A. Colin, Paris.

EC (European Commission) DG XVI (1995), *Europe 2000+. Cooperation for European Territorial Development*, Office for the Official Publications of the European Communities, Brussels-Luxembourg.

Ekistics (1991), *Urban networking in Europe. I. Concepts, intentions and new realities*, vol. 58, n. 350/351.

Ekistics (1992), *Urban networking in Europe. II. Recent initiatives as an input to future policies*, vol. 59, n. 352/353.

Esping-Andersen, G. (1991), 'Strutture di classe post-industriali: un confronto fra Germania, Svezia e Stati Uniti', *Stato e Mercato*, n. 32, pp. 219-247.

Ewers, H.J., Goddard, J. and Matzerath, H. (eds) (1986), *The Future of the Metropolis*, Walter de Gruyter, Berlin.

Fabre, J. (1991), 'Qu'est-ce qu'une ville internationale? Réflexions sur les villes françaises et européennes', *Problèmes économiques*, n. 2224.

Fareri, P. (1995), 'Politiche nel Mediterraneo', in Bellicini, L. (a cura di), *Mediterraneo. Città, territorio, economie alle soglie del XXI secolo*, Cresme-Credito Fondiario, Roma, vol. I, pp. 321-346.

Feagin, J.R. and Smith, M.P. (1987), 'Cities and the New International Division of Labor: An Overview', in Smith, M.P. and Feagin, J.R.

(eds), *The Capitalist City: Global Restructuring and Community Politics*, Basil Blackwell, Oxford.

FERE (Fédération Européenne de Recherches Economiques) Consultants (1991), *The International Development of Intermediary Size Cities in Europe: Strategies and Networks*, CEC DG XVI, Paris.

Fielding, A.J. (1982), 'Counterurbanization in Western Europe', *Progress in Planning*, n. 17 (1), pp. 5-52.

Figueiredo, A. M. (1995), 'Theory and Practice of Interregional Cooperation and Urban Networks in Economically Lagging Regions: The Experience of Galicia and the North of Portugal', in Cappellin, R. and Batey, P.W.J. (eds), *Regional Networks, Border Regions and European Integration*, Pion, London, pp. 96-115.

Fondazione Giovanni Agnelli (1992), *La Padania, una regione italiana in Europa*, Edizioni della Fondazione G. Agnelli, Torino.

Fondazione Giovanni Agnelli (1995), 'Catalogo dei progetti per Torino - 1995', in *Atti del Convegno: Nuova progettualità a Torino: la città fisica, la città culturale*, Torino.

Fox-Przeworski, J., Goddard, J. and De Jong, M. (eds) (1991), *Urban Regeneration in a Changing Economy. An international perspective*, Clarendon Press, Oxford.

Friedmann, J. (1986), 'The World City Hypothesis', *Development and Change*, n. 17, pp. 69-84.

Friedmann, J. and Wolff, G. (1982), 'World City Formation: An Agenda for Research and Action', *International Journal of Urban and Regional Research*, vol. 6, n. 3, pp. 309-344.

Fuà, G. (a cura di) (1991), *Orientamenti per la politica del territorio*, il Mulino, Bologna.

Fubini, A. and Corsico, F. (a cura di) (1994), *Aree metropolitane in Italia*, Angeli, Milano.

Gambi, L. (1972), 'I valori storici dei quadri ambientali', in *Storia d'Italia, I caratteri originali*, vol. I, Einaudi, Torino, pp. 5-60.

Gambino, R. (1994), 'Luoghi e reti: nuove metafore per il piano', *Archivio di Studi Urbani e Regionali*, n. 51, pp. 11-43.

Garofoli, G. (1991), *Modelli locali di sviluppo*, Angeli, Milano.

Gibelli, M.C. (1996), 'Tre famiglie di piani strategici: verso un modello reticolare e visionario', in Curti, F. and Gibelli, M.C. (a cura di), *Pianificazione strategica e gestione dello sviluppo urbano*, Alinea, Firenze, pp. 15-54.

Goglio, S. (1986), *Italia. Centri e periferie*, Angeli, Milano.

Goglio, S. and Sforzi, F. (1992), 'Le differenziazioni regionali in Italia', *Economia e Banca - Annali scientifici*, n. 5-6, pp. 153-175.

Gorla, G. and Vito Colonna, O. (1995), 'L'incerto cammino della nuova politica regionale', in Gorla, G. and Vito Colonna, O. (a cura di),

Regioni e sviluppo: modelli, politiche e riforme, Angeli, Milano, pp. 11-34.

Gottmann, J. (1991), 'The dynamics of city networks in an expanding world', *Ekistics*, vol. 58, n. 350-351, pp. 277-281.

Governa, F. (1997), *Il milieu urbano. L'identità territoriale nei processi di sviluppo*, Angeli, Milano.

Granovetter, M. (1973), 'The strength of weak ties', *American Journal of Sociology*, n. 78, pp. 1360-1380.

Hadjimichalis, C. (1994), 'The fringes of Europe and EU integration', *European Urban and Regional Studies*, vol. 1, n. 1, pp. 19-29.

Hägestrand, T. (1970), 'What about people in Regional Science?', *Papers in Regional Science Association*, n. 24, pp. 7-21.

Hall, P. (1966), *The World Cities*, Mc Graw-Hill, New York.

Hall, P. (1990), *International Urban System*, Working Paper n. 514, University of California Press, Berkeley.

Hall, P. and Hay, D. (1980), *Growth Centres in the European Urban System*, Heinemann, London.

Hannerz, U. (1980), *Exploring the city. Inquiries toward an Urban Anthropology*, Columbia University Press, New York.

Hepworth, M. (1989), *Geography of the information economy*, Belhaven, London.

Hohenberg, P.M. and Lees, L.H. (1985), *The making of urban Europe*, Harvard University Press, Harvard.

Indovina, F. (1990), 'La città possibile', in Indovina, F. (a cura di), *La città di fine millenio*, Angeli, Milano, pp. 11-74.

Indovina, F. et al. (1990), *La città diffusa*, Daest, Venezia.

Insolera, I. (1973), 'L'urbanistica', in *Storia d'Italia, I documenti*, vol. V (1), Einaudi, Torino, pp. 427-486.

INU (Istituto Nazionale di Urbanistica) (1990), 'It. Urb. '80: rapporto sullo stato dell'urbanizzazione in Italia', *Quaderni di Urbanistica Informazioni*, n. 8.

IReR/Progetto Milano-Fondazione Agnelli (1986), *Il sistema metropolitano italiano*, Angeli, Milano.

IRES (1995), *Cento progetti cinque anni dopo*, Rosenberg & Sellier, Torino.

ISTAT (1958-79), *Movimento anagrafico dei comuni*, Roma.

ISTAT (1997), *I sistemi locali del lavoro 1991*, a cura di F. Sforzi, Poligrafico dello Stato, Roma.

ISTAT-IRPET (1986), *I mercati locali del lavoro in Italia*, a cura di F. Sforzi, Angeli, Milano.

Jalabert, G., Idrac, M., Grossetti, M., Laurens, J.P., Laumiére, F. and Zuliani, J.M. (1991), *Reseaux et territoires: l'exemple de la technopole toulousaine*, CIEU-Université de Toulouse-Le-Mirail, Toulouse.

Jalabert, G., Laborie, J.P., Grégoris, M.T., Laumiére, F. and Zuliani, J.M. (1993), *Activités économiques, internationalisation des villes et relations interurbaines*, CIEU-Université de Toulouse-Le-Mirail, Toulouse.

Jeger, J.-F. (1991), *Paris et Londres, premières métropoles européennes*, Insee-Direction régionale d'Île-de-France, Paris.

King, A.D. (1990), *Global Cities. Post-Imperialism and the Internationalization of London*, Routledge, London.

Knight, R. (1993), 'Città globali e locali', in Perulli, P. (a cura di), *Globale/locale. Il contributo delle scienze sociali*, Angeli, Milano, pp. 107-137.

Knight, R. and Gappert, G. (1984), 'Cities and the Challenge of the Global Economy', in Bingham, R.D. and Blair, J.D. (eds), *Urban Economic Development*, Sage Publications, Beverly Hills.

Kresl, P.K. (1991), 'Gateway cities: a comparison of North America with the European Community', *Ekistics*, vol. 58, n. 350-351, pp. 351-356.

Kunzmann, K.R. and Wegener, M. (1990), *The Pattern of Urbanization in Western Europe 1960-1990*, Institut fur Raumplanung Universitat, Dortmund.

Labasse, J. (1981), 'Profils des villes européennes à vocation internationale', *Cahiers de géographie du Quebec*, n. 66, pp. 403-412.

Landini, P. and Salvatori, F. (a cura di) (1989), 'I sistemi locali delle regioni italiane (1970-1985)', *Memorie della Società Geografica Italiana*, vol. XLIII, Roma.

Lanzani, A. (1991), *Il territorio al plurale. Interpretazioni geografiche e temi di progettazione territoriale in alcuni contesti locali*, Angeli, Milano.

Laumière F. (1993), 'Processus d'internationalisation des villes: des indicateurs aux acteurs (le cas de Toulouse)', in Carreras, C., Jalabert, G. and Thouzellier, C. (eds), *Restructurations Urbaines*, Presses Universitaire du Mirail, Toulouse.

Levy, J. (1997), *Europe. Une geographie*, Hachette, Paris.

Macry, P. (1994), 'Alla ricerca della normalità', *Micromega*, n. 3, pp. 153-161.

Marchese, U. (a cura di) (1989), *Aree metropolitane in Italia. Anni '80*, Cedam, Padova.

Marselli, G.A. (1987), 'I valori della società napoletana', in Stampacchia, P. (a cura di), *Sviluppo industriale e fattori ambientali. Il caso di Napoli*, Guida Editore, Napoli, pp. 207-253.

Martinotti, G. (1993), *Metropoli. La nuova morfologia sociale della città*, il Mulino, Bologna.

Masser, I., Sviden, O. and Wegener, M. (1992), *The geography of Europe's futures*, Belhaven Press, London and New York.

Mercandino, A. and Mercandino, C. (1976), *Storia del territorio e delle città d'Italia*, Mazziotta, Milano.

Ministero del Bilancio e della Programmazione Economica (1969), *Progetto '80. Rapporto preliminare al programma economico nazionale 1971-75*, Feltrinelli, Milano.

Ministero dell'Industria, del Commercio e dell'Artigianto (1993), *Determinazione degli indirizzi e dei parametri di riferimento, da parte delle regioni, dei distretti industriali*, D.M. 21 Aprile.

Misiti, M. and Gesano, G. (1994), 'Insediamento della popolazione e assetto del territorio', in Golini, A. (a cura di), *Tendenze demografiche e politiche per la popolazione*, 3° Rapporto IRP (Istituto di Ricerche sulla Popolazione), il Mulino, Bologna, pp. 191-226.

Moss, M.L. (1987), 'Telecommunications, world cities and urban policy', *Urban Studies*, vol. 24, n. 6, pp. 534-546.

Muscarà, C. (1967), *La geografia dello sviluppo. Sviluppo industriale e politica geografica nell'Italia del secondo dopoguerra*, Edizioni Comunità, Milano.

Muscarà, C. (1992), 'Dal decentramento urbano alla ripolarizzazione dello spazio geografico italiano', *Memorie della Società Geografica Italiana*, vol. XLVIII, Roma.

Nigris, E. (1996), 'La costruzione del territorio senza pianificazione: l'uso dei Fondi strutturali Cee', in Clementi, A., Dematteis G., and Palermo, P.C. (a cura di), *Le forme del territorio italiano. Temi e immagini del mutamento*, Laterza, Roma-Bari, vol. 1, pp. 258-269.

Palermo, P.C. (1992), *Interpretazioni dell'analisi urbanistica*, Angeli, Milano.

Pavia, R. and Palazzo, A.L. (1995), 'Il medio e basso Adriatico. L'Albania e la 'direttrice adriatica' dello sviluppo', in Bellicini, L. (a cura di), *Mediterraneo. Città, territorio, economie alle soglie del XXI secolo*, Cresme-Credito Fondiario, Roma, vol. II, pp. 643-716.

Piselli, F. (a cura di) (1995), *Reti. L'analisi di network nelle scienze sociali*, Donzelli, Roma.

Proulx, P.P. (1990), 'Éléments d'une théorie globale du développement des villes internationales. Le contexte, le milieu, les réseaux, le couplage local-régional-international et les politiques', *Notes de Recherche du Centre d'Économie Régionale*, n. 111.

Pugliese, C. and Schettino, C. (1988), 'Le trasformazioni del terziario: un'analisi funzionale e territoriale nel Mezzogiorno degli anni '80', *Nord e Sud*, n. 1-2, pp. 101-121.

Pumain, D. and Saint-Julien, Th. (eds) (1996), *Urban Networks in Europe*, John Libbey-INED, Paris.

Pyke, F., Becattini, G. and Sengenberger, W. (eds) (1991), *Industrial Districts and Inter-Firm Co-operation in Italy*, International Institute for Labour Studies, Geneva.

Pyrgiotis, Y.N. (ed.) (1991), 'Urban networking in Europe I: Concepts, intentions, and new realities', *Ekistics*, vol. 58, n. 350-351.

Pyrgiotis, Y.N. (ed.) (1992), 'Urban networking in Europe II: Recent initiatives as an input to future policies', *Ekistics*, vol. 59, n. 352-353.

Rodriguez, N.P. and Feagin, J.R. (1986), 'Urban Specialization in the World System', *Urban Affairs Quarterly*, n. 22, pp. 187-220.

Rossi, P. (1970), 'Storia universale e geografia in Hegel', in Tessitore, F. (a cura di), *Incidenza di Hegel*, Ist. Filosofia Univ. Salerno, Morano, Napoli.

Rossignolo, C. (1998), *L'Europa delle città. Partecipazione alle reti urbane e strategie di sviluppo locale*, Tesi di Dottorato di Ricerca, Dipartimento Interateneo Territorio, Politecnico di Torino.

Rozenblat, C. (1992), *Le réseau des entreprises multinationales dans le réseau des villes européennes*, Thèse de Doctorat, Paris, Université de Paris I.

Saraceno, E. (1991), 'Vecchi e nuovi problemi della montagna', in Fuà, G. (a cura di), *Orientamenti per la politica del territorio*, il Mulino, Bologna, pp. 433-482.

Sassen, S. (1991), *The Global City. New York, London, Tokyo*, Princeton University Press, Princeton.

Schmitt, C. (1974), *Der Nomos der Erde*, Dunker & Humbolt, Berlin.

Secchi, C. and Alessandrini, S. (1992), *Milano vista dagli Europei. Immagine e promozione della metropoli milanese nel contesto della comunità internazionale*, Quaderno Aim n. 13, Milano.

Sengenberger, W., Loveman, G.W. and Piore, M.J. (1990), *The Re-emergence of Small Enterprises: Industrial Restructuring in Industrialised Countries*, International Institute for Labour Studies, Geneva.

Sforzi, F. (1989a), 'The geography of industrial districts in Italy', in Goodma, E. and Bamford, J. with Saynor, P. (eds), *Small Firms and Industrial Districts in Italy*, Routledge, London, pp. 153-173.

Sforzi, F. (1989b), 'L'Italia marginale: una valutazione geografica', in Becchi Collidà, A., Ciciotti, E. and Mela, A. (a cura di), *Aree interne, tutela del territorio e valorizzazione delle risorse*, Angeli, Milano, pp. 203-231.

Sforzi, F. (1990), 'The quantitative importance of Marshallian industrial districts in the Italian economy', in Pyke, F., Becattini, G. and Sengenberger, W. (eds) (1991), *Industrial Districts and Inter-Firm Co-operation in Italy*, International Institute for Labour Studies, Geneva, pp. 75-107.

Sforzi, F. (1991), 'La delimitazione dei sistemi urbani: concetti, definizioni e metodi', in Bertuglia, C. and La Bella, A. (a cura di), *I sistemi urbani*, vol. II, Angeli, Milano, pp. 443-485.

Sforzi, F. (1994), 'The Tuscan model: an interpretation in light of recent trends', in Leonardi, R, and Nanetti, R.Y. (eds), *Regional Development in a Modern European Economy. The Case of Tuscany*, Pinter, London, pp. 86-115.

Sforzi, F. (1995), *Criteri di classificazione dei servizi per l'analisi del cambiamento dell'industria italiana negli anni Ottanta*, IRPET, Firenze.

Sforzi, F., Openshaw, S. and Wymer, C. (1982), 'La delimitazione di sistemi spaziali sub-regionali: scopi, algoritmi, applicazioni', paper presented at the 2nd Italian RSA Conference, Venezia.

Soldatos, P. (1990), 'L'espansione internazionale delle città europee: elementi di una strategia', in Conti, S. and Spriano, G. (a cura di), *Effetto città. Sistemi urbani e innovazione: prospettive per l'Europa degli anni Novanta*, Edizioni della Fondazione G. Agnelli, Torino, pp. 3-25.

Soldatos, P. (1991), *Les nouvelles villes internationales: profils et stratégies*, Serdeco, Aix-en-Provence.

SVIMEZ (1993), *Rapporto 1993 sull'economia del Mezzogiorno*, il Mulino, Bologna.

Tarrius, A. (1989), *Les espaces circulatoires des élites europeénnes: vers de nouvelles morphologies urbaines et sociales*, Inrets.

Tassinari, G. (1983), *Le trasformazioni dell'industria italiana negli anni '70. Analisi dei risultati censuari*, Editrice Clueb, Bologna.

Timberlake, M. (ed.) (1985), *Urbanization in the World Economy*, Academic Press, Orlando.

United Nations Centre for Human Settlements (Habitat) (1996), *An Urbanising World: Global Report on Human Settlements 1996*, Oxford University Press, Oxford.

Vaccà, S. (1993), 'Grande impresa e concorrenza: tra passato e futuro', *Economia e Politica industriale*, n. 80.

Van den Berg L, Drewett, R., Klaassen, L., Rossi, A. and Vijverberg, C. (1982), *Urban Europe. A Study of Growth and Decline*, Pergamon Press, Oxford.

Velardi, C. (a cura di) (1992), *La città porosa. Conversazioni su Napoli*, Cronopio, Napoli.
Veltz, P. (1996), *Mondialisation, villes et territoires. L'économie d'archipel*, Puf, Paris.
Viganoni, L. (a cura di) (1991), *Città e metropoli nell'evoluzione del Mezzogiorno*, Angeli, Milano.
Wellman, B. and Berkowitz, S.D. (eds) (1988), *Social structure: a network approach*, Cambridge University Press, Cambridge.